THE ENLIGHTENMENT AS SOCIAL CRITICISM

PRINCETON MODERN GREEK STUDIES

This series is sponsored by the Princeton University Program
in Hellenic Studies under the auspices of the
Stanley J. Seeger Hellenic Fund.

*Firewalking and Religious Healing: The Anastenaria of Greece and
the American Firewalking Movement* by Loring M. Danforth

Kazantzakis: Politics of the Spirit by Peter Bien

George Seferis: Complete Poems translated by Edmund Keeley and
Philip Sherrard

Dance and the Body Politic in Northern Greece by Jane K. Cowan

Yannis Ritsos: Repetitions, Testimonies, Parentheses translated by
Edmund Keeley

Contested Identities: Gender and Kinship in Modern Greece edited
by Peter Loizos and Evthymios Papataxiarchis

A Place in History: Social and Monumental Time in a Cretan Town
by Michael Herzfeld

Demons and the Devil: Moral Imagination in Modern Greek Culture
by Charles Stewart

*The Enlightenment as Social Criticism: Iosipos Moisiodax and Greek
Culture in the Eighteenth Century* by Paschalis M. Kitromilides

THE ENLIGHTENMENT AS SOCIAL CRITICISM

IOSIPOS MOISIODAX AND GREEK CULTURE IN THE EIGHTEENTH CENTURY

Paschalis M. Kitromilides

PRINCETON UNIVERSITY PRESS

PRINCETON, NEW JERSEY

COPYRIGHT © 1992 BY PRINCETON UNIVERSITY PRESS
PUBLISHED BY PRINCETON UNIVERSITY PRESS, 41 WILLIAM STREET,
PRINCETON, NEW JERSEY 08540
IN THE UNITED KINGDOM: PRINCETON UNIVERSITY PRESS, OXFORD
ALL RIGHTS RESERVED

LIBRARY OF CONGRESS CATALOGING-IN-PUBLICATION DATA
KITROMILIDES, PASCHALIS
THE ENLIGHTENMENT AS SOCIAL CRITICISM : IOSIPOS MOISIODAX AND GREEK
CULTURE IN THE EIGHTEENTH CENTURY / PASCHALIS M. KITROMILIDES.
P. CM — (PRINCETON MODERN GREEK STUDIES)
INCLUDES BIBLIOGRAPHICAL REFERENCES AND INDEX.
ISBN 0-691-07383-X
1. IŌSĒPOS, HO MOISIODAX, FL. 18TH CENT. 2. EDUCATORS—GREECE—
BIOGRAPHY. 3. GREECE—INTELLECTUAL LIFE—1453–1821. I. TITLE. II. SERIES
LA2375.G82I573 1992 306'.09495—dc20 91-23998 CIP

PUBLICATION OF THIS BOOK HAS BEEN AIDED BY
THE PRINCETON UNIVERSITY PROGRAM IN HELLENIC STUDIES UNDER THE
AUSPICES OF THE STANLEY J. SEEGER HELLENIC FUND

THIS BOOK HAS BEEN COMPOSED IN LINOTRON CALEDONIA

PRINCETON UNIVERSITY PRESS BOOKS ARE PRINTED
ON ACID-FREE PAPER, AND MEET THE GUIDELINES FOR
PERMANENCE AND DURABILITY OF THE COMMITTEE ON
PRODUCTION GUIDELINES FOR BOOK LONGEVITY
OF THE COUNCIL ON LIBRARY RESOURCES

PRINTED IN THE UNITED STATES OF AMERICA

1 3 5 7 9 10 8 6 4 2

CONTENTS

List of Illustrations vii

Preface ix

Acknowledgments xv

Note on Transliteration xvii

INTRODUCTION 3
Biography and the Social Sciences 3

PART ONE: ITINERARIES OF A LIFE 15

ONE
The Unknown Years 17

TWO
Challenges 29

THREE
Endeavors 51

FOUR
The Crisis 69

FIVE
Perseverance 95

SIX
The Later Years 111

PART TWO: THE COHERENCE OF A VISION 131

SEVEN
Ancients and Moderns 133

EIGHT
Science as a Vocation 143

NINE
Pedagogy as Social Criticism 153

TEN
Images of the Polity   167

EPILOGUE   183
BIBLIOGRAPHY   193
INDEX   199

LIST OF ILLUSTRATIONS

(*Following p. 129*)

1. Moisiodax's signature in Italian and in Greek
2. Moisiodax's patron, Prince Gregorios Ghikas of Moldavia
3. Moisiodax's patron, Prince Alexandros Ypsilandis of Wallachia
4-9. Title pages of Moisiodax's books
10-12. Mathematical plates from Moisiodax's *Theory of Geography*

PREFACE

IN INVITING the reader to embark upon the present peregrination in the intellectual history of Balkan society in the eighteenth century, I should first clarify for her or him the meaning with which my major conceptual category is to be used and second acquaint them with the protagonist of my story. The "Enlightenment" as used in the following pages is more of a shorthand symbolic expression than a rigidly defined concept. For the informed reader the range of definitions and disagreements over how the term Enlightenment ought to be understood represents a well-known debate in cultural and intellectual history. I should add, however, that despite the breadth and multiplicity of meanings of the concept, the debate over precise definition could be seen as ultimately immaterial: conventional usage has firmly established the main lines of the signification of the Enlightenment as a cultural movement and an intellectual configuration. Meaningful disagreement has now to contend with questions of periodization, geographical extent, and levels of analysis and determination of the margins rather than the core of the phenomenon.

This does not mean that the core content of such a diverse and ever expanding intellectual configuration is unproblematic. No one will disagree that Immanuel Kant captured the philosophical essence of the issue when he framed the answer to the question, What is Enlightenment? with the injunction *"sapere aude."* This essentially denotes the secular, humanist, universalist, rationalist outlook that developed in European culture after the Renaissance and culminated in the critical spirit that we associate with the Enlightenment. This was the spirit expressed in rationalist philosophy, empiricist epistemology, and its practical application in modern science. The secularization of the past and the critical examination of the present of human society and its political and cultural institutions constituted integral components of this outlook. This meaning is commonly ascribed to the Enlightenment. In this sense—admittedly broad and open-ended—this study refers to the Enlightenment. If one must be more specific in pointing to those components of the Enlightenment that were particularly important in defining its Greek or more broadly its Southeastern European version, one could refer to Cartesian and Wolffian philosophy, within certain bounds to Lockean empiricism, to Newtonian natural science, and to the social theory of Voltaire and the Encyclopedists. Influences such as these shaped the intellectual presuppositions of the Enlightenment in Southeastern Europe.

The major questions that motivate the following explorations concern the ways in which the ideas of the Enlightenment were transfused into Balkan society and how they were received. By looking at the reactions—positive and negative—they elicited, I hope to recover the meaning of these quintessential expressions of Western intellectual and moral values in the new context into which they were transferred. This particular instance of intellectual transmission represented the first case of a phenomenon that was to develop on a world scale, as Western ideas began to expand from the context of their original germination and elaboration to non-Western environments beyond the geographical space of Northwestern Europe. Seen in this perspective the present project is a study in the comparative history of modern Western ideas in non-Western contexts.

In this process of intellectual transmission Iosipos Moisiodax, the protagonist of the present study, had a pioneering and critical part. Moisiodax, although building on the foundations of the intellectual and cultural traditions of the Greek East, was the first intellectual personality to accept unconditionally and to voice publicly without qualifications or reservations the ideas of the Enlightenment in Southeastern Europe. His vision of the Enlightenment represented a genuine project of intellectual reconstruction that essentially inaugurated the tradition of modern thought and secular politics in the Balkans. A controversial and tragic figure in his own lifetime because of his ideas and his critical attitude, Iosipos Moisiodax remained an elusive presence in Greek intellectual history throughout the nineteenth and the twentieth centuries. Not only did his biography come down to us in a fragmentary form, in contrast to the broad range of details available about many of his contemporaries, especially scholars more closely associated with the traditions of the Church. But also his six books have survived in very few copies; some are extremely rare, including the most important, the *Apology* of 1780, which represents the culmination of his critical thought.

Even more than this, throughout the nineteenth century and until mid-twentieth century, his presence was engulfed by an extraordinary silence. The early historians and bibliographers of Modern Greek literature in the nineteenth century are either silent or quite uncertain about his life and work. Thus, in the earliest comprehensive historical account of the Greek Enlightenment, published in 1830 by Constantinos Koumas, Moisodax is hastily dismissed in one sentence. When later on Constantinos Sathas compiled his biographical survey of Greek intellectual life in the centuries of Ottoman rule (1453–1821), he drew on the manuscripts of Georgios Zaviras in sketching Moisiodax's life. Though sympathetic to Moisodax, Sathas's accounts, in his surveys of both Modern Greek literature (1868) and the language question (1870), are imprecise about his life and contain a number of inaccuracies, as Archimandrite

Andronikos Dimitrakopoulos pointed out in his 1871 critique of Sathas's work. With the publication in 1872 of Zaviras's pioneering intellectual history of Modern Greece—an important source that had remained unpublished for almost seventy years—the nineteenth-century literature on Moisiodax essentially comes full circle.

In 1887 Manuel Gedeon, the great historian of the Orthodox Church and education under the Ottomans, spoke briefly of the "ferocious antagonism" in which Moisiodax found himself vis-à-vis contemporary traditionalist scholars and of the wisdom of the Church in not condemning his "unheard of" views. After Zaviras, Sathas, and Dimitrakopoulos, Moisiodax in a way recedes into the darkness of oblivion. Apparently his unconventional views and daring critical perspective on Greek culture and society discouraged writing about him in an age when archaism in language and education and the incorporation of Orthodoxy as a primary component of Greek identity made his social and cultural theory sound not simply heretical but odd—and to some probably demented as well. Thus, the most plausible explanation for the marginalization and eventual disappearance of Moisiodax from the history of Greek thought and literature until mid-twentieth century was the triumph of archaism in the language question, which imposed the purist version of Modern Greek—the artificial "katharevousa"—as the language of culture, church, and state. Moisiodax's early and articulate stand against archaism at the dawn of the language question in the eighteenth century would certainly have been anathema to the purists of the nineteenth and the early twentieth centuries. This can explain the persistent silence about him until the sustained attempts of the middle of the twentieth century to break the grip of pedantism on understanding Modern Greek intellectual life.

Important contributions in the 1940s by Emmanuel Kriaras on the character of Moisiodax's pedagogical views and by C. Th. Dimaras on the wider significance of Moisiodax in the history of Greek letters have done much for recognizing the embattled pioneer's historical importance. Soon thereafter the nature of Moisiodax's philosophical ideas was appropriately judged as a genuine expression of the Enlightenment by E. P. Papanoutsos in his 1953 anthology of Modern Greek philosophy. Two contributions in English, by Raphael Demos (*Journal of the History of Ideas* 19 [1958]: 535–536) and even more substantively by G. P. Henderson in his valuable survey of the reawakening of Greek philosophy in the period of Ottoman rule (*The Revival of Greek Thought 1620–1830* [Edinburgh, 1970], pp. 87–98) have established Papanoutsos's contention on a firmer foundation. The biographical record, however, remained remarkably shaky and imprecise as indicated, for instance, by Papanoutsos's sketch of Moisiodax's life and by the pertinent references in such general works, often consulted by foreign students of Greek cultural history, such as Börge Knös (*L'histoire de la littérature néo-grecque. La période jusqu'en 1821* [Stockholm-Uppsala, 1962], pp. 544–546) and E. Turczynski (*Die deutschgriechischen Kulturbeziehungen bis zur Berufung König Ottos* [Munich, 1959], p. 206). The basic biographical profile was not essentially settled until the appearance of the specialized study by the Greco-Romanian scholar Ariadna Camariano-Cioran in 1966 (*Balkan Studies* 7 [1966]: 297–332) and her truly invaluable history of the princely academies of Bucharest and Jassy in 1974. The latter work draws extensively on archival and manuscript sources in Romania; its value for my own work is indicated by the frequent references throughout this book.

Interest in Moisiodax's thought has expanded in many directions ever since, leading to the reappearance, almost two centuries after the original publications, of a second edition of his *Apology* in 1976 and a Romanian translation of his *Pedagogy* in 1974. This revival of studies on Moisiodax, however, has been almost entirely confined within the field of literary history. The focus of attention has been, predictably, on his views on language and education, his lively style, and his liberal outlook on cultural issues, which has been connected, especially by writers on the left, with the origins of "progressive" thinking in the Greek intellectual tradition. Such a perspective was adopted by Yiannis Kordatos as early as 1927. All these, to be sure, are important aspects of Moisiodax's intellectual personality, but much more could be done with his life and thought. The purpose of this book is to break some of this hitherto unexplored ground by bringing the interdisciplinary perspective of the history of ideas to bear on the interpretation of Moisiodax's story.

Because so much of my interpretation focuses on the recovery of Moisiodax's intentions, it might be appropriate to make plain at the outset my own objectives as well. In this study I attempt to reexamine the evidence of Moisiodax's texts and reconstruct his life in a social science perspective, as opposed to the traditional approach of literary history, which has not only dominated the study of this particular case but has determined the very understanding of the Greek Enlightenment as a whole. In attempting to develop this new perspective I have had to resort selectively, depending on the needs and stage of the analysis, to conceptual approaches drawn from such fields as comparative ethnology, social history, and political theory. I make no claim that this is the only possible approach to the subject or that it exhausts all its aspects. On the contrary, I am fully aware of both the limitations of my approach and the additional research that could be done in a number of directions. As the story unfolds, the reader will encounter many allusions to what still needs to be done. I have tried nevertheless to apply throughout the historian's yardstick of good sense, which calls for the strict adherence to the limits upon our understanding set by the available evidence. Seeking a substantive and perhaps deeper understanding by means of this kind of interpretation has been my goal. The reader will judge how far short of it I have fallen.

ACKNOWLEDGMENTS

THE FINAL VERSION of this book has been written in the congenial environment of Clare Hall, Cambridge. I am grateful to the president and fellows of Clare Hall for electing me to a visiting fellowship in 1989–1990, which enabled me to finish this and other projects in the stimulating atmosphere of Cambridge and literally in the shadow of the University Library. I am also thankful to the University of Athens for sabbatical leave and for supporting my research over the years through successive faculty research grants.

I am profoundly grateful to His All-Holiness the Ecumenical Patriarch Dimitrios I for permission to visit the monasteries of Mount Athos to consult their archives in the summer of 1984. I maintain a warm recollection of the late Prior Constantinos, librarian of Vatopedi Monastery, thanks to whose help on July 25, 1984, I had the privilege to become the first researcher to have access to the codices of ancient correspondence of the monastery (1645–1799), several years before this valuable material was photographed by the National Hellenic Research Foundation.

In an earlier and different incarnation this book first appeared in Greek in 1985 in the series "Modern Greek Prosopography" sponsored by the Cultural Foundation of the National Bank of Greece. The English translation has been made possible by a grant from the A. G. Levendis Foundation. I am greatly obliged to the board of the foundation and especially to its President Constantine C. Levendis for their generosity and moral encouragement that has heartened my scholarly efforts over the years. The burden of the translation has been borne by David Hardy. I do not think that I can adequately express my appreciation for our collaboration during the long period of the book's gestation and production. I am particularly obliged to him for the patience and good cheer with which he processed and reprocessed my countless revisions, additions, and rewritings and for his advice and encouragement throughout.

This is a substantially revised and considerably expanded version of the text that appeared in Greek five years ago. Extensive further research has added much new material, and the reconsideration of several issues and the rethinking of the whole subject have made this a quite different and, I hope, more mature book. I should like here to record my appreciation to two of the many reviewers of the original Greek edition, who first suggested in the *American Historical Review* (92 [February 1987]: 168) and in the *Journal of Modern Greek Studies* (5 [October 1987]: 280) the desirability of an English language edition of the work. The constructive criticisms and suggestions, which I did my best to follow, of two anonymous readers for Princeton University Press have been invaluable, and I am most grateful.

In writing this book I profited considerably from membership of the international republic of letters. Former teachers, friends, and colleagues have helped in a number of constructive ways in making this a better work. I am grateful to them all for sharing their knowledge and judgment with me. I should like in particular to thank my two former teachers in America, Fred Greenstein and Michael Walzer, for reading and commenting on sections of the manuscript. My Clare Hall colleague Bruce Hunt of the University of Texas has read the chapter dealing with the history of science and made useful suggestions. A special debt is owed to Quentin Skinner, who found the time amidst a busy summer in Cambridge to read the chapter on Moisiodax's political thought and to share with me his expertise and sensitivity as a historian of republicanism; his concurrence with my appraisal of the significance of Moisiodax's case has been a source of great reassurance and inspiration.

The greatest debt I incurred over the years of the preparation of this book is to George L. Huxley. His unfailing interest in my work, his sound advice, and his intellectual integrity have sustained me in more ways than I could acknowledge.

Finally, I should like to record my indebtedness to two Greek research institutions, the Greek Institute in Venice and the Centre for Asia Minor Studies in Athens for facilitating my work in substantial ways over a long period of time.

More personal debts, always enduring and constantly renewed, are better left unmentioned.

P.M.K.
25 August 1990

NOTE ON TRANSLITERATION

THE ONLY standard system for the transliteration of the Greek alphabet into languages written in Latin characters is that used for the transliteration of classical Greek. The transliteration of ancient Greek, however, is quite inappropriate for rendering the spelling and especially the phonetics of Modern Greek. Accordingly I have used it here with the following modifications to make it conform more to the modern morphology and sound of the language. Diphthongs have been generally retained, except in those cases where the modern pronunciation of Greek requires a consonant to be adequately rendered (e.g., "aftou," not "autou"). The Greek vowels η and ι have been uniformly rendered with "i," and similarly ο and ω have been rendered with "o." The Greek υ has been rendered with "y," except when it forms part of a diphthong; then it is rendered by "u" (e.g., "tou"). The rough breathing has been dropped.

Consonants have generally been rendered phonetically. Thus the Greek β has been rendered by the Latin "v" rather than "b." The Greek consonant φ is rendered by "ph" in all words with an ancient Greek root. Conversely Greek names with Latin roots (e.g., Constantinos) have been transliterated as closely as possible to their original form.

The names of modern Greek authors appear in the form used by the authors themselves if they have published work in a foreign language.

THE ENLIGHTENMENT AS SOCIAL CRITICISM

INTRODUCTION
BIOGRAPHY AND THE SOCIAL SCIENCES

THE IDEA of social science as a comprehensive theory of society and its deeper dynamic developed from the eighteenth century onward in a conscious reaction against the "biographical" approach to the historical process and collective life. The biographical method had its roots in the humanist tradition and more specifically in a conception of history and political action modeled on Plutarchian moral prosopography. According to the humanist view, history is the foundation of moral education and a means of meting out justice for human actions. It is consequently "a spiritual anatomy of human action" and a source of political wisdom.[1] Counter to the certainty of this view, there evolved historical Pyrrhonism, which lay at the root of the Enlightenment. In the bosom of the Enlightenment were formed the alternative theoretical approaches to social reality; these drew attention to the significance of historical factors and deeper, impersonal forces in the determination of forms of political existence, in contrast to Plutarch's biographical approach.[2] The theorist mainly responsible for this was Montesquieu, who was properly, therefore, associated with the roots of sociological thought, first by Emile Durkheim and more recently by Raymond Aron.[3]

Although the rejection of the biographical approach formed *ab initio* a critical element in the self-definition of the science of society, the study of the personality and the actions of outstanding individuals continued throughout the entire nineteenth century to form the main axis of historical research and the fundamental method of historiography. In this, the nineteenth century followed the historiographical model advanced by David Hume in the eighteenth. The mere mention of the work of two representative historians of last century, Ranke and Carlyle, is enough to confirm the validity of this observation. Despite the continuing adherence of scholarly historiography to the biographical method, however, the progress made by social theory tended increasingly to result in the

[1] Paul Hazard, *The European Mind, 1685–1715* (New York, 1963), p. 31; Quentin Skinner, *The Foundations of Modern Political Thought* (Cambridge, 1978), vol. 1, pp. 169–170, 220–221, and vol. 2, pp. 99–100, 269–275, 290–293, 310–319.

[2] For Plutarch's historical method, see Frank J. Frost, *Plutarch's Themistocles: A Historical Commentary* (Princeton, 1980), pp. 40–59. On the place of biography in ancient historiography in general, cf. Arnaldo Momigliano, *The Development of Greek Biography* (Cambridge, Mass., 1971).

[3] Emile Durkheim, *Montesquieu et Rousseau: précurseurs de la sociologie* (Paris, 1953), and Raymond Aron, *Les étapes de la pensée sociologique* (Paris, 1967), pp. 43–53.

disappearance of the individual personality as an analytical category in the study of the social process. By the early twentieth century, the two main trends in social theory, Marxism and Freud's psychoanalysis, were already firmly established; despite the apparent antinomy between them, they shared a common denominator in their rejection of the optimistic images of man as the possessor of an independent will and as a rational being respectively. Both Marxist theory and Freudian analysis demonstrated the impact of impersonal forces, over and above the human will, in shaping human destiny; as a result, despite their humanist presuppositions, they contributed to the elimination of anthropocentric social analysis.[4] Even the leading critics of Marxism, such as Max Weber, applied to social theory the same fundamental method of seeking to identify deeper forces that set the parameters of human action. In the interwar period immediately following, the last bastion of the anthropocentric approach, historiography, capitulated to the siege by the new social sciences.[5] The study of the past ceased to be the history of outstanding personalities and exceptional deeds and began to inquire into the regularities of collective existence. Instead of the pinnacles and the unique, history now began to take an interest in long-term processes and redirected its focus upon the faceless coefficients of inertia and change. The new concept of historiography, fertilized by adapting the theoretical preoccupations of Marxist, Freudian, and Weberian social theory, evaluated the economic components alongside unconscious and irrational elements and cultural factors in the study of social entities.

A natural consequence of this reorientation was the rejection of biography, as established by earlier historiography, as an appropriate method for the study of society. Biography never became a part of the new social science and ultimately even failed to preserve its earlier supremacy in the field of historiography. It was therefore essentially excluded from the legitimate preoccupations of the "scientific" study of society and became merely a literary form, continuing the tradition of political or literary biography of the eighteenth and nineteenth centuries.[6] The question whether biography belonged to artistic forms of discourse or to social science was of serious concern only to practitioners of the former; it was a matter of indifference to those professionally involved with the latter. In her essay on the art of biography Virginia Woolf offered one of the most

---

[4] Cf. H. Stuart Hughes, *Consciousness and Society: The Reorientation of European Social Thought 1890–1930* (New York, 1958), pp. 4–6, 33–66.

[5] See, for example, H. Stuart Hughes, *The Obstructed Path: French Social Thought in the Years of Desperation, 1930–1960* (New York, 1966), pp. 19–64.

[6] For a comprehensive survey, see *Biography in the Eighteenth Century*, ed. J. D. Browning (New York, 1980). The introduction by Clarence Tracy, pp. 1–7, is particularly interesting.

felicitous statements of the question; she draws attention to the peculiarity of biography as a form of artistic creation, limited by the biographer's vision of reality and the evidence through which it is expressed. According to this view, the biographer's task is faithfully to reconstruct this reality by reassembling its historical components. Woolf's art of biography, lies precisely in the ability of the biographer to transform reality, with its given restrictions and limitations, into an artistic experience: "By telling us the true facts, by sifting the little from the big, and shaping the whole so that we perceive the outline, the biographer does more to stimulate the imagination than any poet or novelist save the very greatest."[7]

This observation on the art of biography is not inappropriate to the requirements of the genre as a form of systematic discourse. As part of the organization of the biographical material, the proper selection and evaluation of information can successfully transform the narrative of an individual life-history into a prism through which to understand the dynamic of both social situations and more general phenomena.

Social scientists and historians came to appreciate the potential of this aspect of the biographical method much later. First, there was a "reinstatement" of interest in biographical detail as suitable material on which to base rigorous analysis within the field of the social sciences, followed by the rehabilitation of biography as a "scientifically" legitimate approach. I should note that the rekindling of interest in biographical material did not derive from any "idealistic" retraction with regard to the consequences of the general trends in social theory we have noted above. One main representative of idealism in the debate on the nature of history, R. G. Collingwood, insists that biography is by definition foreign to the purpose of history, however much historical material it may contain. He justified the separation of the two on the grounds that biography is determined by the biological events of human life; consequently, it is the study of a biological process, whereas history can only be the history of the mind.[8]

The revival of interest in the use of biographical data for analytical purposes was to a significant extent a consequence of the recognition in political science and history that psychoanalytic theory was useful in interpreting certain social phenomena and types of behavior.[9] A discussion of

---

[7] See Virginia Woolf, "The Art of Biography," in *The Death of the Moth and Other Essays* (London, 1945), pp. 119–126; the passage cited occurs on p. 126.

[8] R. G. Collingwood, *The Idea of History* (Oxford, 1956), p. 304.

[9] The pioneer in this area has been Eric H. Erikson, with *Young Man Luther: A Study in Psychoanalysis and History* (New York, 1958), and later with *Ghandi's Truth: On the Origins of Militant Nonviolence* (New York, 1969). Among more recent contributions, note the study by Elizabeth Wirth Marvick, *The Young Richelieu: A Psychoanalytic Approach*

the epistemological problems and the ideological preconditions of these new fields of research is beyond the scope of this introductory survey. But I should emphasize, however, that the primary concern in these areas of political and historical research, which to a large degree still retain an experimental character, is to ascertain and evaluate biographical details and place them within broader interpretative frameworks.

Another source of stimuli, of a very general nature, that contributed to the rehabilitation of interest in biography, could be considered to derive from the steadily increasing awareness over the past two decades of analytical and epistemological impasses in contemporary social science. It has been symptomatic that the debates which sprang from this sense of impasse were conducted mainly in those areas in which the individual and his or her personality had been systematically eliminated as legitimate analytical categories in social theory. Gradually, in one field after another, students became aware of a fundamental gap between theory and research. The divorce between the two could result in sterile, often nebulous generalization at the theoretical level. But at the level of research, the impasse was illustrated by the mechanical collection of empirical data and the exhaustion of the scholarly imagination in the transcription of this material into quantitative terms, without ever confronting the need to introduce some theoretical concern into this cognitive exercise. Thus, empirical research was occasionally reduced to giving "scientific" status to measuring trivialities, or, as critical thinkers like C. Wright Mills and Alvin Gouldner warned, to masking true social problems.[10]

From all this emerged an increasing awareness that if the impasses in the social sciences were to be overcome, a closer link between theory and research was required, a true dialogue between analysis and synthesis and the elaboration of theoretical propositions in conjunction with verifying empirical data. Against the background of this critique some European social scientists discovered the value of the biographical method, which was gradually recognized as a vital tool in this task. The arguments marshaled on this issue stressed that the rehabilitation of the biographical approach as an autonomous method of social analysis makes it feasible to exploit biography as a research technique and to adopt an approach "from below" to the phenomena of collective life and the historical process,

---

to *Leadership* (Chicago, 1983). On the methodological problems, see James William Anderson, "The Methodology of Psychological Biography," *Journal of Interdisciplinary History* 11 (Winter 1981): 455–475. For a political science perspective, see F. I. Greenstein, "Personality and Politics," in *Micropolitical Theory*, vol. 2 of *Handbook of Political Science*, ed. F. I. Greenstein and N. W. Polsby (Reading, Mass., 1975), pp. 1–92.

[10] See C. Wright Mills, *The Sociological Imagination* (New York, 1959), and Alvin W. Gouldner, *The Coming Crisis of Western Sociology* (New York, 1970).

while at the same time demonstrating empirically the social side of individual existence.[11] Some time before methodological interest turned to biography, however, three major currents in the field of empirical sociology did use biographical analytical tools: the "Chicago School," with its by now classic, naturalistic analyses of urban subcultures;[12] the school of "symbolic interaction," with its studies of deviant behavior; and the "phenomenological school," with its descriptions of the intersubjective constitutions of social reality. Biographical data formed the central focus of the theoretical analysis of these currents in their descriptions of cultural adaptation, deviant individuals, and states of consciousness, respectively.

The discovery of the value of the biographical method brought the sociologists up to date, to some extent, with the research practice of a cognate field, social anthropology, which for decades had used biography as a fundamental tool for collecting empirical data. The subject of study and method of the anthropologist's work dictated adopting the inductive approach to research and using the analytical method in working up the data. In the attempt to construct a comprehensive picture of the social world, a primary element in anthropological method was collecting biographical details, usually through the technique of oral history. Consequently, the statement that "all anthropology is biography" is not entirely wide of the mark.[13]

The tendency of anthropological analysis to incorporate the biographical method and to use biography as a prism through which to present the findings of anthropological research marked the departure of certain currents of contemporary anthropology from functionalism, in the direction of "ethnobiography." A fundamental demand of contemporary anthropology, therefore, has been for biographical and other raw material to be handled in such a way that the final presentation is not confined to the level of an empirical ethnographic record, but goes beyond this to a comprehensive presentation of the phenomenology of the so-called social construction of reality.

We must end this necessarily brief and incomplete review with a final, but I believe revealing, point. Recognizing the value of the biographical method signals the end of a process, the beginning of which was marked

[11] See Franco Ferrarotti, "Biography and the Social Sciences," *Social Research* 50 (Spring 1983): 57–80. For further discussion, see Ferrarotti, *Histoire et histoires de vie. La méthode biographique dans les sciences sociales* (Paris, 1983). See also Yves Chevallier, "La biographie et son usage en sociologie," *Revue Française de Science Politique* 29 (February 1979): 83–101.

[12] W. I. Thomas and Florian Znaniecki, *The Polish Peasant in Europe and America* (1918–1920; reprint New York, 1958), is especially valuable as an example of using biographical data in sociological analyses.

[13] See L. L. Langness, *The Life History in Anthropological Science* (New York, 1965), p. 4.

by the diminishing significance of positivism in the social sciences. The biographical method was also a suitable means of overcoming the dismantling of the human person by "structural functionalism" and "structuralism," which in the postwar period dominated liberal and Marxist social theory as a result of the influence of the views of Talcott Parsons and Louis Althusser, respectively.[14] The rejection of structuralism's elimination of human experience from social theory was voiced most effectively by one creator of modern social history, E. P. Thompson. His critique, of course, was part of his attack upon the "poverty" of Marxist social theory in its procrustean Althusserian guise,[15] but it may also be regarded as supplementing C. Wright Mills's criticism, two decades earlier, of "bourgeois sociology." Thompson stressed that the fundamental reason for the failure of Marxist structuralism to function as scientific analysis free of ideological dogmatism, especially its transformation into what amounted essentially to a "theology," had been its insistence on ignoring human experience. Mediated through the channels of consciousness and its cultural expression, human experience is an integral factor in the social process that social theory and social history can ignore only at their peril.[16] This criticism constituted an appeal for rehabilitating the emotional and moral awareness of the human person as an element of the social collectivity, the interpretation of which has been the purpose of social theory.[17]

A rather formal but telling indication of the recognition of the value of biography as a tool of social science is provided by its eclipse and reemergence in an authoritative work of reference in the field. When published in 1968, at the height of postwar research in social science, the *International Encyclopedia of the Social Sciences* did not include an entry on biography.[18] One might assume that, in the judgment of its editors and distinguished editorial advisory board, biography was either superfluous or irrelevant to the social sciences; it was accordingly omitted from

[14] See Paul Thompson, "Life Histories and the Analysis of Social Change," in *Biography and Society: The Life History Approach in the Social Sciences*, ed. Daniel Bertaux (Beverley Hills, Calif., 1981), pp. 289–306, esp. 303–304.

[15] E. P. Thompson, *The Poverty of Theory and Other Essays* (London, 1978).

[16] Ibid., pp. 356–357.

[17] Ibid., pp. 363–364. E. P. Thompson's own experience as a biographer (cf. his *William Morris: Romantic to Revolutionary* [London, 1955]) cannot be unrelated to the elaboration of these views.

[18] The only treatment of biography in the seventeen volumes of the *International Encyclopedia of the Social Sciences* comes in vol. 7, p. 323, and this mention is only in connection with the inadequacies of biographical dictionaries as sources of information in the social sciences. Otherwise biography surfaces only incidentally in the surveys of Chinese and Islamic historiography (vol. 6, pp. 402, 404, 409) and in a passing reference to judicial biography (vol. 13, p. 177).

the compendium, which sought to codify basic knowledge in a very broad area of scholarly endeavor. A decade later, when the growth of knowledge required a supplement to the *Encyclopedia*, biography was selected as the most appropriate and effective method of achieving this end, and the *IESS* was brought up to date with the issue of a *Biographical Supplement* in 1979. The biographical approach was explicitly selected for this task because of its value to intellectual history and to the history and sociology of science—the best means of linking new ideas to the social and historical contexts in which they emerged.[19] This acknowledgment of the value of biography may be regarded as the formal certificate of its new legitimacy in social science research.

The rehabilitation of biography as a method of social analysis has at the same time contributed to the emergence of fruitful speculation concerning the nature, the potential, the preconditions and the limitations of "scientific biography."[20] A detailed presentation of the relevant views would take us too far afield. Contemporary biography, as one perspicacious scholar has observed, lies between the social phenomenology of the novel and ethnographic realism.[21] Its aim, that is to say, is the accurate reconstruction of the values and events of a specific life-cycle, but at the same time it seeks to impose on it an acceptable interpretative framework that will give unity to the empirical material. The attainment of this goal is aided by adopting the interpretative insights of other social sciences such as psychoanalysis, anthropology, and social history. Contemporary biography is thus capable of studying in depth the internal dynamic of the personality and tracing the workings of the unconscious element in human behavior; at the same time, however, it may seek to identify and evaluate the external factors of the cultural environment, the social structure, and the forms of symbolic expression that define the world of its

---

[19] See David L. Sills "On the Uses of Biography," *International Encyclopedia of the Social Sciences*, vol. 18: *Biographical Supplement* (New York, 1978), p. x.

[20] See, for example, Daniel Aaron, *Studies in Biography* (Cambridge, Mass., 1978); Marc Pachter, *Telling Lives: The Biographer's Art* (Washington, D.C., 1979); and Anthony M. Friedson, *New Directions in Biography* (Honolulu, 1981). See also comprehensive studies of the genre by Alan Shelston, *Biography* (London, 1977); Robert Gittings, *The Nature of Biography* (Seattle, 1978); and Daniel Madelénat, *La biographie* (Paris, 1984). For the reflections of a leading literary biographer on the nature of his craft, see Leon Edel, *Writing Lives: Principia Biographica* (New York, 1984). On the use of biography in particular branches of scholarship, see A. F. Davies, "The Tasks of Biography," in his *Essays in Political Sociology* (Melbourne, 1972), pp. 109–117; Leon Edel, "The Biographer and Psychoanalysis," *International Journal of Psychoanalysis* 42 (1961): 458–466; and Lewis J. Edinger, "Political Science and Political Biography, I and II," *Journal of Politics* 26 (1964): pp. 423–439, 648–676.

[21] James Clifford, "Hanging Up Looking Glasses at Odd Corners: Ethnobiographical Prospects," in *Studies in Biography*, ed. Daniel Aaron, p. 53.

subject.[22] Without striving to "dismantle" the individual personality, it attempts to elucidate it and detect the shades of light and dark, bringing as close as possible the different contexts and varied stimuli of its subject's behavior. This is the content of "ethnobiography," which seeks to study the particular individual in the context of his or her place and time. How else can it achieve this if it does not suspend mirrors in odd corners to capture the human personality from all sides?[23]

Despite the emphasis on the psychoanalytic approach, which has genuinely maximized our knowledge of the complexity of human motivation, and its possible interpretations, it could nevertheless be claimed that the influence of Marx on biography has been greater than that of Freud:[24] the evaluation of socioeconomic conditions and their effects on human attitudes and behavior has been a more decisive element in writing modern biography than the analysis of psychological factors. This methodological hierarchy of interpretative priorities also accounts for the increased interest in biography as a historiographical genre. Its usefulness to the historian resides in the fact that it condenses the universal in the particular. The individual case and the narrative of the particular individual's experience may illustrate an entire period. Consequently, the writing of biography demands the exercise of historical judgment and the application of criteria for selection so as to distinguish and throw into relief events of historical importance. An acquaintance with the individual case will be more effective if the interweaving of what is exceptional with the social regularity is fully grasped. In this way, biography becomes a prism of history. The "return" of biography in the social sciences in general and in historiography in particular represents not a resurrection of nineteenth-century "great men" approaches, but a rebirth that differs qualitatively in both its conceptual presuppositions and in its intent.[25]

These assumptions underly the biography of Iosipos Moisiodax in the pages that follow. The reader will no doubt discern that the interdisciplinary structure of the biographical method, as applied here, inclines more toward certain analytical approaches than others. Clearly the effects of social cleavages and the ethnological ferment in Balkan society are analyzed more systematically than the psychological factors. This is owing to not only the subjective limitations and preferences of the author but also the decisive fact that there is almost no information on the family back-

---

[22] See Gittings, *The Nature of Biography*, pp. 47–60. Gittings notes the following disciplines that might come to the assistance of biography: psychoanalysis, medicine, economics, sociology, political history, and geography.

[23] Cf. Clifford, "Hanging Up Looking Glasses at Odd Corners," pp. 41–57.

[24] Gittings, *The Nature of Biography*, p. 54.

[25] Cf. Barbara W. Tuchman, "Biography as a Prism of History," in the collection, *Telling Lives: The Biographer's Art*, ed. Marc Pachter, pp. 132–147.

ground, childhood, early youth of Moisiodax. The lack of evidence of this kind makes any psychoanalytic hypothesis hazardous because all psychological interpretations depend on tracing the roots of human behavior in this early stage of life.[26] In Moisiodax's case, moreover, we also lack spontaneous evidence relating to states of mind and feelings such as private correspondence, which might offer material for psychoanalytical interpretation.[27] We do, of course, have his writings, which are pregnant with elements of personal expression and indications of his psychological states. This aspect of the evidence makes it legitimate to speculate about Iosipos's personality and its interconnection with his intellectual outlook. I do not believe, however, that the nature of the sources can meet the technical requirements of a psychological biography.

To the writer of the present study, the material for the biography of Moisiodax presented a different possibility. Biography has been selected as a method of analytical historical inquiry, which can afford the opportunity to deal from an inductive point of view with the broad subject of cultural change and the ideological expression of social and political cleavages. Whereas synthesis presents the challenge of solving the problem of fitting together the pieces of the puzzle and devising the architecture that will balance and include all the dimensions of the subject, analysis possesses its own charm, especially that of wrestling with details, and occasionally it can even approximate the certainty that one has exhausted the sources. The analytical approach enables us to listen to the internal rhythm of phenomena and demystifies the dynamic of the historical process by following its translation into concrete human experience. Analysis turns its lens onto the mechanisms of the historical process and presents them as elements of daily life. By turning its attention to the concrete and the specific, the analytical method gives tangible content to the dialogue between theory and research.

The concrete biographical approach makes it possible empirically to check hypotheses concerning the general phenomena of concern to historical synthesis; simultaneously this treatment provides the opportunity for formulating new hypotheses by taking its substantive clues from the rhythm of daily collective life. At this point we can locate the most important contribution of biography to the study of the history of ideas and mentalities. Its focus on the components of an individual case enables us to ascertain the social standing and meaning of ideologies and forms of symbolic expression on the basis of particular events and sub-

[26] Cf. F. I. Greenstein, *Personality and Politics* (Chicago, 1969), pp. 111–113, and especially Eric H. Erikson, *Identity, Youth and Crisis* (New York, 1968), pp. 91–141.

[27] I cite, by way of example, Erikson's psychological biography of Luther, which is based essentially on evidence drawn from the correspondence of the leader of the Religious Reformation. See note 9 above.

stantive data. Thus, we may avoid the tendency to schematic generalizations to which more general and abstract treatises are often prone. After coming to grips with the material and weighing the details of the biography of Moisiodax, I feel that I have gained a deeper insight into the nature of the Enlightenment as both a movement of intellectual and political change and a catalyst to articulating social cleavages in Balkan society. I hope to guide the reader in such a way as to bring her or him to share this understanding.

For the purposes of this study, therefore, biography has supplied a method for recovering the past and an approach to historical interpretation. In the first part of the book Moisiodax's life story is reconstructed as a case study in cultural and intellectual change in Southeastern Europe, an illustration of social conflict in the feudal society of the Danubian principalities. The ethnobiographical aspects of the evidence discussed below not only form the context within which to make sense of the particular episodes of the life-cycle but also, by defining the life-cycle itself, allow the interpreter to appraise the extent to which it represents and epitomizes broader patterns and regularities. To this extent we have a case study that, by typifying the broader context in the particular, makes it methodologically possible and legitimate to attempt to fill in the stretches of darkness left by documentary lacunae concerning Moisiodax through contextual conjectures and comparisons.[28] Beyond the typical and the representative, however, the uniqueness and individuality marking Moisiodax's experiences make his biography one of those "limiting cases," often at the margins of the social space and ideological legitimacy, which announce the dynamics of social change.[29] The first part of the book attempts to weave such a tapestry by narrating Iosipos's early years and educational ventures, his travels and publication projects in Italy and Central Europe, his teaching career and ideological conflicts, his relations with the contrasting worlds of princes and merchants, his influence upon his younger contemporaries, and his final defeat and capitulation.

The second part of the book attempts to recapture the coherence of Moisiodax's vision of Enlightenment as an ideology of reform and criticism. On the evidence of his surviving texts four salient dimensions of this vision are discussed in detail. His position in the quarrel of the Ancients and Moderns, his views on natural philosophy, his educational the-

---

[28] Cf. Giovanni Levi, "Les usages de la biographie," *Annales. Économies Sociétés Civilisations* 44 (November–December 1989), pp. 1325–1336, esp. 1330–1331.

[29] Michel Vovelle, "De la biographie à l'étude de cas," in *Problèmes et méthodes de la biographie* (Paris, 1985), pp. 191–198. Such "limiting cases" of great value as models of biographical analyses have been Carlo Ginzburg's classic *The Cheese and the Worms: The Cosmos of a Sixteenth Century Miller* (London, 1980), and Vovelle's own *Théodore Desorgues ou de la désorganisation* (Paris, 1985).

ory, and his political thought formed interrelated components of an essentially uniform argument for reconstructing Greek culture and its Balkan social and political context. The breadth and commitment marking this social vision single out Moisiodax as an exceptional thinker in the environment to which he addressed his pleas. The special interest of Moisiodax's arguments in the four spheres in which we are going to examine them in the second part of the monograph lies in the way in which he adapted the Western Enlightenment in laying the foundations of an indigenous Balkan Enlightenment. His ideas possessed both particularity and generality in his own environment; he addressed specific and well-defined problems but did so from the remarkably broad vantage point of the Enlightenment tradition that he espoused with great sincerity and full consciousness of its implications. From this perspective, the historical importance of his thought is in a way Janus-faced: he was both the heir to the intellectual traditions of the Greek Orthodox East and the initiator of novel forms of thought and discourse. Thus, in his thought as in his life experiences, Moisiodax represented the rupture introduced into Greek culture by the Enlightenment, and his arguments can be related to the competing orientations that emerge from the break to mark nineteenth- and twentieth-century Greek intellectual and political history. In discussing his social theory in the second part of the book, I attempt to show how he tried to transform internally the tradition he inherited and how he contributed to the inauguration of an alternative Enlightenment tradition in Greek society, which is at the root of these later competing orientations. With these preliminaries in mind, as a map of what follows, it is time to trace Moisiodax's steps on his far-ranging and eventful itineraries.

PART ONE

ITINERARIES OF A LIFE

I have spent time in a great many places in Greece,
and I know of what I speak—when I say Greece, I mean
all the diasporas of the Greeks.
(*Moral Philosophy*, 1761)

ONE

THE UNKNOWN YEARS

IOSIPOS MOISIODAX is the most fascinating enigma in Greek letters. Almost no details that conventionally delineate an individual's biographical coordinates are available to us in his case. His origins, the precise dates of his birth and death, and even his real name are all lost. The evidence for his eventful career is drawn almost exclusively from the testimony he himself provides in his writings, particularly the *Apology* of 1780. It is as though all traces of his passage throughout the length and breadth of the historical space of Hellenism in his time have been erased by some mysterious Nemesis, as he himself would have put it,[1] which has also deprived us of any visual representation of "what was most precious: his form."[2] The external evidence, then, is virtually nonexistent, and the archives and written records remain stubbornly silent about his personality. Is he really so unknown, however? And did the Nemesis that he himself felt so tormentedly was pursuing him really succeed in the task of irrevocably eradicating his presence?

A significant piece of evidence as to his birthplace suggests that his influence was felt in ways not recorded in the external evidence but which nonetheless mark the sensibility of human beings. Rhigas Velestinlis (1757–1798) notes in his *Great Chart* that the village of Cernavoda on the south bank of the Danube in the Dobrudja region in present-day southeast Romania is the "birthplace of Iosipos Moisiodax."[3] This is the only reference by Rhigas in the *Great Chart* to any contemporary man of letters—and the only source we have concerning Moisiodax's birthplace. This simple record suggests the importance attached by Rhigas to Moisiodax's passage through his life, as a teacher and no doubt a champion of the Enlightenment.

Rhigas's sensitivity has preserved this information about Moisiodax's birthplace. The date on which Iosipos was born, however, and the date on which he left Cernavoda behind to begin his endless peregrinations

---

[1] Iosipos Moisiodax, *Apologia* (Vienna, 1780), p. 128.

[2] C. P. Cavafy, "Tomb of Evrion," *Collected Poems*, trans. by Edmund Keeley and Philip Sherrard (Princeton, 1975), p. 48.

[3] L. I. Vranousis, *Rhigas* (Athens, 1953), p. 257. Cf. also Georgios Zaviras, *Nea Ellas i ellinikon theatron*, ed. G. P. Kremos (Athens, 1872), p. 350, and N. Iorga, *Byzance après Byzance* (Bucharest, 1935), p. 219, which emphasizes Moisiodax's Romanian origins and his relation with Rhigas.

into the wider world are not known with any certainty. His date of birth is conventionally set in 1725,[4] but the sources at our disposal are totally silent with regard to his family and his early years at Cernavoda. Iosipos was the name he assumed later, when he was ordained deacon, a step probably intended to procure for him the educational opportunities and the geographical and social mobility that his origins could certainly not proffer. His secular name is said to have been Ioannis.[5] The surname Moisiodax was not his family name, but simply an indication of his ethnic origin. Cernavoda was one settlement of the Vlach-speaking tribes dwelling to the south of the Danube in the area of ancient Moesia; these were distinguished from the local slavophone inhabitants, who spoke Bulgarian, by their dialect which derived from Latin. As a result of this, they were identified with the "Dacians" of the Principalities of Wallachia and Moldavia to the north of the Danube. These Romanian-speaking inhabitants of north Bulgaria were called Moesiodacians by Greek scholars, to distinguish them from the stock-breeding nomads further south in the Balkans who spoke the same language and were known as Koutsovlachs.[6] One major settlement of the Koutsovlachs in the Southern Balkans was the township of Velestino in Thessaly, to which the transhumant shepherds descended during the winter months, from their summer pasturages on the Pindus mountains.[7] Velestino was Rhigas's native village—hence his surname Velestinlis. His relationship with Moisiodax, therefore, can be seen to originate in not only ideological but also possible ethnic affinities. The surname of Ioannis-Iosipos, then, which he himself does not always

---

[4] A. Dimitrakopoulos, *Prosthikai kai diorthoseis eis tin Neollinikin Philologian Constantinou Satha* (Leipzig, 1871), p. 94. According to Dimitrakopoulos, the name of Moisiodax's village, Czerweno Woda, means "red water."

[5] C. Sathas, *Neoelleniki Philologia* (Athens, 1868), p. 563.

[6] William Martin Leake, *Researches in Greece* (London, 1814), p. 81: "*Moisiodakes* is the appellation given by the politer Greeks to the Wallachians, settled in small colonies in various parts of the country South of the Danube. Those of Greece are called *Koutsovlachoi* or *Vlachoi*." M. Kogălniceanu (Kogalnitchan), *Histoire de la Valachie, de la Moldavie et des Valaques Transdanubiens* (Berlin, 1837), vol. 1, 27, records the name of these "transdanubian Vlachs" as "Moesians," deriving it from the ancient name of the country (Moesia). The theory on the historical origins of this group canonized in Romanian nationalist historiography is delineated in ibid., pp. 27–41. For the complex ethnology of the Danubian lands, see Dionysios Photeinos, *Istoria tis palai Dakias, ta nyn Transilvanias, Vlachias kai Moldavias* (Vienna, 1818), vol. 1, 300–311; for a detailed examination of the phenomenon of the Romanian diaspora in the South Balkans, see Daniel Philippidis, *Geographikon tis Roumounias* (Leipzig, 1816), pp. 23–36. The ethnological problem of the region was at the center of the ideological interests of the Romanian national awakening. Cf. Keith Hitchins, *The Rumanian National Movement in Transylvania, 1780–1849* (Cambridge, Mass., 1969), pp. 58–111.

[7] See A. J. B. Wace and M. S. Thompson, *The Nomads of the Balkans* (London, 1914), pp. 1, 176.

write with a capital letter when signing his name, simply indicates his tribal origins. And yet this name, nothing more than a collective definition, has become identified in modern Greek letters with an individuality unique in the intensity of its self-exploration and personal assertion.

Cernavoda, Iosipos's birthplace, did not remain untouched by the incipient social transformations resulting from the growth of trade in Southeastern Europe in the eighteenth century. There is evidence that already at the end of the seventeenth century merchants from Cernavoda had settled in the commercial centers of Transylvania—Braşov and Sibiu— and were members of the important Greek trading associations in these two cities.[8] The majority of the members of these two organizations were Greeks or Hellenized Vlachs, and the common language used was Greek.[9] In their capacity as members of the associations, the merchants of Cernavoda partook in the ethnic and cultural fermentation within the ranks of these organizations.[10] This formed the basis for creating the network of the Greek Orthodox commercial diaspora in Central Europe. For Iosipos, this world was destined to form a place of refuge and a source of support and comfort in his future struggles.

Of the first twenty-seven years of Iosipos's life, nothing is known. The sources remain obstinately silent as to the circumstances and experiences that formed his singular character and forged his highly developed sensitivity. At some stage of this crucial phase of his life, however, the young Moesiodacian must have made his way from Cernavoda to a center of Greek education, perhaps in Wallachia or Thrace, where he learned the Greek language and received an elementary education. He was taught these first letters according to the traditional educational system of the Greek East, under a clergyman, as he himself testifies. His recollections were not particularly favorable: "I recall that when, despite my tender years, the schoolmaster, a man of fierce countenance, with a wild beard, called upon me to recite the lesson to him, I felt that I was being called upon by a savage beast and, out of fear, I would forget the lesson."[11] He himself points out the potential consequences of this first educational experience:

> And let us recall here the anguish that we suffered, those of us who had the misfortune to chance upon cruel, inconsiderate schoolmasters. The fierce countenance, the grating voice, the stinging of the rod, everything that follows upon fearsome practices, all of them things outside the experience of

---

[8] See Olga Cicanci, *Companile greceşti din Transilvania si comertul european in anii 1636–1746* (Bucharest, 1981), pp. 101, 129.
[9] Ibid., p. 202.
[10] Ibid., pp. 159–168.
[11] Iosipos Moisiodax, *Pragmateia peri paidon agogis i Paidagogia* (Venice, 1779), p. 58.

children, incapacitate them entirely: there follows one of two things, either that their spirit is brought low, or that they are imbued with a hatred of learning that occasionally remains impressed upon them for their entire life.[12]

The young Ioannis survived this danger in his early schooling. Fortunately for Greek letters, instead of instilling an aversion to learning and shriveling his intellectual curiosity, the traumatic experiences of early education in his case forged a determined desire to discover a more humane way of learning.

Despite the negative impressions left by his early schooling, the crucial role played by this phase of Moisiodax's life cannot be overstressed. The reason for this is not merely the general psychological significance of this period of an individual's life in the formation of the personality. It lies rather in the adoption by the Moesidacian youth of a specific cultural identity as a result of his educational experience: his entry into the Greek system of education, which was a common patrimony to all the Balkan Orthodox Christians in the eighteenth century, determined the content of his identity. This was the only route to an education accessible to the Orthodox Christians of the Balkan peninsula and constituted a powerful mechanism for inculcating in them the symbols of the Greek tradition, as well as implanting in them a sense of identification with it; it thus acted as a catalyst in assimilating into Greek culture members of the Orthodox but non-Greek-speaking groups of Balkan society, whose symbolic boundaries remained quite fluid in the period before the emergence of nationalism. The Greek intelligentsia of the eighteenth century, particularly the intelligentsia of the Enlightenment, was in this way enriched by human resources drawn from those Balkan ethnic groups whose collective identity had not yet been articulated. Moisiodax was an eminent representative of this group, as were many others, among them Nikolaos Zerzoulis, Dimitrios Darvaris, Nikolaos Piccolos, and Athanasios Vogoridis.[13] The effectiveness of Greek education as a channel of assimilation was demonstrated by the future careers of some members of this group, such as Moisiodax and Piccolos, who devoted themselves wholeheartedly to the cause of the rebirth of Hellenism, the former with his passion for reconstructing modern Greek education and the latter as a fighter for Greek freedom. This aspect of the role of Greek education in eighteenth-century Balkan society formed the background to Rhigas's revolutionary visions as well. Himself an heir precisely of the cultural and political tra-

---

[12] Ibid., pp. 77–78.

[13] Cf. Peter Mackridge, "The Greek Intelligentsia 1780–1830: A Balkan perspective," in *Balkan Society in the Age of Greek Independence*, ed. Richard Clogg (London, 1981), pp. 63–84.

dition that was inaugurated by Moisiodax, Rhigas visualized a common republic of the Balkan peoples, based on the shared symbolic heritage of Greek civilization.

The first autobiographical details provided by Moisiodax refer to his attempts to broaden his Greek education by traveling to the major cultural centers of Hellenism in the middle of the eighteenth century. Thus began his many years of "wandering" that made him completely familiar with the whole expanse of the Greek world and cultivated in him the belief that, on the basis of this knowledge, he was in a position to express an authoritative opinion on its problems: "I have spent time in a great many places in Greece, and I know of what I speak."[14]

In 1752 Moisiodax was in Thessaloniki, where he attended the classes of the scholar Iannakos, whom he describes as "a man who had frittered away all his years in the study of Aristotelianism."[15] He thus came into direct contact with the conventional academic education of the time, in the person, moreover, of a devotee of the neo-Aristotelian tradition introduced into Greek learning in the seventeenth century by the followers of Theophilos Corydaleus (1570–1646). The Iannakos referred to by Moisiodax can safely be identified with the teacher of the same name, who is known in the history of Greek letters from his brawl in 1722 with another scholar named Pachomios for control of the newly founded school in Thessaloniki.[16] Pachomios, whom Iannakos charged with being an "extreme critic of Aristotle,"[17] was probably merely advocating a less rigid philosophical approach. He was tainted, however, by his association with Methodios Anthrakitis (ca. 1660–1736), who in August 1723 was to be condemned for heterodoxy by the Holy Synod of the patriarchate of Constantinople. Anthrakitis was allegedly favorably predisposed toward the philosophy of Descartes and Malebranche and preferred natural philosophy and mathematics to Aristotelian logic and metaphysics. He was charged, however, with a predilection for the teaching of the Spanish mystic Miguel de Molinos (1628–1696), who had been condemned by the Catholic Church in 1687. Eventually he was forced to recant and his writings were burned in the courtyard of the patriarchate. The controversy surrounding Anthrakitis had raged for a few years before his official con-

[14] Iosipos Moisiodax, *Ithiki Philosophia* (Venice, 1761), vol. 1, p. xviii.

[15] *Apologia*, p. 179.

[16] The incident is recorded in two studies by Manuel Gedeon: "Lykavges pnevmatikis kiniseos par'imin 1700–1730," *Praktika tis Akadimias Athinon* 5 (1930): 49–57, reprinted in *I pnevmatiki kinisis tou genous kata ton XVIII kai XIX aiona* (Athens, 1976), esp. pp. 50–52, and "Thessalonikeon palaiai koinotikai dienexeis," *Makedonika* 2 (1941–1952): 19–22.

[17] See N. Tsoulkanakis, "Ioannis o tou Ioannou," *Klironomia* 7 (1975): 383. The characterization was apparently Iannakos's own and was quoted by his correspondent Makarios Kalogeras, renowned teacher at the school of Patmos, in a letter reporting the dispute to the grand provost of the patriarchate of Constantinople.

demnation. The sensitivity over the issues of doctrine involved in this controversy enabled Iannakos to appeal to several high prelates and other church dignitaries and to secure their support in winning his battle against Pachomios. He apparently remained the unchallenged primate of the educational world of Thessaloniki in the subsequent three decades. In September 1752 he is attested as the "teacher of the school in Thessaloniki."[18] Moisiodax encountered him in the same year. Iannakos's ascendancy possibly accounts for the fact that Thessaloniki, despite its cosmopolitan society of merchants, failed to evolve during the eighteenth century into a significant center of Greek education, like other trading cities such as Ioannina and Smyrna.

Moisiodax remained dissatisfied with the intellectual environment he encountered at Thessaloniki, and in 1753 he arrived in Smyrna. The experiences that awaited him there as well were far from rewarding, given his intellectual expectations. At the Evangelical School, which had only recently been founded, the teaching was by Ierotheos Dendrinos (1697–1780), another well-known champion of Orthodox tradition and grammatical education.[19] Adamantios Korais testifies to the quality of his teaching: "The teacher and the school resembled all the teachers and schools elsewhere in Greece at that time—that is, they offered teaching of very poor quality, attended by liberal use of the rod. We were beaten so unsparingly that my brother, not being able to bear it any more, abandoned Hellenic education, and this against the wishes of my parents."[20]

When Thessaloniki and Smyrna, the two largest cities outside Constantinople, proved unable to satisfy his intellectual aspirations, Moisiodax's thoughts and plans began to turn toward the West. The University of Padua, long an established destination for Greek students in quest of higher education in the West, became the focal point of his intellectual desires. To carry out his intention, however, he needed economic support, to which end he addressed himself to the metropolitan of Smyrna, Neophytos (1731–1765). He also sought the assistance of "the other primates" of the community in Smyrna, but his requests fell foul of the bitter opposition of Ierotheos, whose response was openly ideological: "What did he not do, what did he not say, this Ierotheos from Ithaca, the teacher of Smyrna itself, in order to divert from me the support I was seeking, as in the end he did divert it? 'They are atheists,' he cried,

---

[18] K. Mertzios, *Mnimeia tis Makedonikis istorias* (Thessaloniki, 1947), p. 335.

[19] Matthaios Paranikas, *Istoria tis Evangelikis Scholis Smyrnis* (Athens, 1885), pp. 4–19, and S. Solomonidis, *Oi dyo protoi tis Evangelikis Scholis diefthyntai Ierotheos Dendrinos kai Chrysanthos Karavias* (Smyrna, 1879), pp. 12–21.

[20] Adamantios Korais, "Autobiographia," in *O Korais kai i epochi tou*, ed. C. Th. Dimaras (Athens, 1953), p. 241.

twitching convulsively, 'all those that study in the land of the Franks, and upon their return, they convert others to atheism as well.' "[21]

The image of Ierotheos Dendrinos prevalent in the history of Modern Greek culture has been shaped on the basis of the testimonies left by Korais and Moisiodax. It is worth comparing, however, to the account of both teacher and climate of the school in Smyrna by another mature pupil who, like Moisiodax, also came from the heart of the Balkans to taste the fruits of Greek education. Dositej Obradović (1739/1740–1811) left the monastery of Hopovo in the diocese of Karlowitz and traveled as a teacher in Serbia and Croatia for five years (1760–1765), before turning toward the Greek lands with the aim of becoming initiated into the language of the Church Fathers and into Greek letters. From Corfu he crossed to the Peloponnese and from there to Mount Athos. At the Serbian monastery of Chilandar, where he stayed for two months, he heard of the school that flourished in the early eighteenth century on the island of Patmos. On his way to Patmos, in October 1765, he naturally passed through Smyrna, then the center of communications in the Aegean, and there learned of the Greek school in the city and the fame of its teacher Ierotheos. The latter responded to Dositej's request to study at the school with an offer of free tuition and residence: "This school supports thirty pupils, and if five persons like you had come from so distant a land, I should be glad to receive you all."[22] In this way Obradović became acquainted with the "new Greek Socrates,"[23] as he calls Ierotheos Dendrinos, and studied Greek letters under his guidance for the next three years (1765–1768). His recollections of the school at Smyrna and its teacher were very different from those of Korais and Moisiodax. Of Ierotheos, Obradović wrote in his autobiography of 1788:

> He was pious and devout yet free from all superstition: though a simple monk, he was nevertheless a sworn foe and rebuker of monkish abuses, falsehoods, and begging; of fraudulent ikons and relics; and of miracles wrought for money. Whenever anybody told him that such and such an ikon was miraculous, he would inquire: "Does it float in the air all by itself, or is it nailed, or pasted on a wall or hung on a peg?" And when he heard that the first of these things was not true and the second was, he would say, "So you see that it is not miraculous." Owing to this philosophical and genuinely pious love of truth that characterized him, the Lord knows what all the monks of Jerusalem or Mount Athos, or anywhere else, would have done to him if they could. But his innocence and virtue were so well known that not only

[21] *Apologia*, p. 166, n.1.
[22] *The Life and Adventures of Dimitrie Obradović*, trans. [into English] George Rapall Noyes (Berkeley, 1953), p. 241.
[23] Ibid., p. 242.

all the Christian folk of Smyrna, but even the very Turks honored and loved him more than all the monks in the world, and therefore it would have gone hard with anybody who had touched him.[24]

This embellished and idealized picture of the teacher is supplemented by a similar description of life at the school:

> In the school buildings there were supported about thirty students from various places in Greece and the islands. During the three years that I spent there some departed and others arrived; thus I had an opportunity to become acquainted with the qualities of the Greeks on all sides. All the inmates of the school lived together in the greatest harmony, with mutual affection; nobody ever had any reason to get angry at anyone else or to feel spiteful. Since the teacher himself was like an angel from heaven and behaved to us like a loving father, we all strove to satisfy completely so good a man; and we could not satisfy him in any other way than by diligence in our studies and fineness of character. Those charming Greek young men are fonder of learning and have more talent for it than any other nation on earth. They are naturally quick and sharp; and when from their early years they are guided in the right direction, then there is no goodness and virtue superior to theirs; but for the same reason, if they incline toward evil, then one must be exceedingly careful, for great alertness of mind, if it is converted into craft, is a great evil. But with Hierotheos an evil, wicked and crafty man found no lodging or refuge.[25]

Why did Iosipos see the school at Smyrna and Ierotheos Dendrinos so differently? What is the source of this profound divergence of assessment between the two young men from the Balkan heartlands, who sought to satisfy their thirst for knowledge in the bosom of Greek education? The cultural experiences of Moisiodax and Obradović in Smyrna attested to a number of common points, indicative of the role of Greek education in eighteenth-century Balkan society; their conflicting evaluations of it, though naturally springing in part from differences in psychological makeup, were also owed to their fundamentally different attitudes toward Greek education. Obradović's work reveals in other passages, too, the tendency of a kind nature to show unusual generosity in its praises and expressions of gratitude. Moreover, when he wrote, in 1788, Obradović had every reason to nurture sentiments of magnanimity toward those who had until then helped him in his career, which had led to the fulfilment of many of his aspirations. By contrast, when Iosipos presented his testimony in the *Apology* in 1780, he had been bitterly persecuted

---

[24] Ibid., p. 243. Characteristically, the translator includes Moisiodax's testimony on Dendrinos in his comment on this passage to balance the idealized picture given by Obradović.
[25] Ibid., p. 245.

and reviled, with many of his dreams and ambitions for the good of the Greek nation and education distorted and broken. As presented in the *Apology*, his clash with Ierotheos in 1753 was his first confrontation with tradition and the conventional mentality. This clash had presaged the future persecution that reached its climax in the crisis of 1777–1780. These divergent positions explain in part the two authors' contradictory pictures of Ierotheos and their differing conceptions of his role in Greek culture.

Over and above the questions of subjective attitude and psychological traumas, however, one must consider the "objective" position of the two authors in relation to the Greek culture of their time. Obradović, who possessed a well-developed Serbian consciousness and championed the Serbian national revival, was already beginning to view Greek culture as an outsider. With the beginning of the process of the cultural and national awakening of the Balkan peoples during the eighteenth century, what had for centuries been the common intellectual heritage of the Orthodox peoples of Southeastern Europe came progressively to appear in the eyes of the other ethnic communities to be the particular intellectual patrimony of the culturally dominant group. The attitude of Obradović toward Greek education represents precisely this moment of transition and gives historical substance to the fundamental reorientation taking shape in the cultural tradition of Southeastern Europe.

By contrast, coming as he did from an ethnic background into which the Greek cultural identity had been organically assimilated, Moisiodax viewed Greek education as an insider and was inevitably entangled in its internal brawls. For Obradović, Greek education contributed as an external factor to the advancement of the cause for which he was toiling, and its fruits were therefore welcomed without reservation as a beneficence and a blessing. A stranger to and with no part to play in the internal Greek ideological quarrels, Dositej sought to set an example for his fellow Serbs by projecting an idealized image of the achievements of Greek education. In so doing he assumed the educational posture of the "Korais of the Serbs."[26] But Moisiodax's personal experience of the tensions of a different process of cultural change led him to an alternative assessment, whereby he appraised the obstacles and identified the opponents facing the reform project he wanted to promote. In the final analysis, it was only natural that Moisiodax and Obradović should reach different evaluations of the historical conjuncture and the roles of particular individuals and institutions. The same appraisal of the situation as that reached by Moisiodax naturally also determined the position of Korais. For precisely this

---

[26] The comparison between the endeavors of Korais and those of Obradović was first astutely made by Nikolaos Politis. See "Dositheos Obradović o themeliotis tis servikis philologias," *Estia* 20 (November 17, 1885): 771–774.

reason a comparison of Obradović's testimony with that of Moisiodax is of such great value because it illustrates the alternative ways in which the dynamic of cultural change in the eighteenth-century Balkan world could be perceived and appraised.

POSTSCRIPT TO CHAPTER 1: ETHNIC ASSIMILATION IN EIGHTEENTH-CENTURY BALKAN SOCIETY

The work by Daniel of Moschopolis, *Eisagogiki Didaskalia* (Introductory Instruction), originally published at Moschopolis in 1762 and reissued in an expanded version in 1802 probably in Constantinople,* supplies characteristic evidence on the process of absorption into Greek society of individuals from diverse ethnic backgrounds through cultural hellenization. The evidence of the source in question is particularly pertinent to the argument developed in chapter 1 because it specifically refers to the case of Moesiodacians: "This four-language Lexicon has been compiled solely for the children of the Moesiodacians to accustom themselves to the Romaic language" (p. viii). The glossary was the work of Daniel, Oikonomos of Moschopolis, a city that was a vital point of intersection of the internal ethnic boundaries of Balkan society. The work was designed to teach the Greek language to the Vlach-, Bulgarian-, and Albanian-speaking Orthodox Christians of the central Balkan lands. Its wider purpose is indicated in the "political" verses of the introduction:

> Albanians, Wallachians, Bulgarians, speakers of other tongues, rejoice,
> And ready yourselves all to become Greeks.
> Abandoning your barbaric tongue, speech and customs,
> So that to your descendants they may appear as myths.
> Honor your nations, together with your motherlands,
> Making the Albanian and Bulgarian motherlands Greek.
> It is no longer difficult to learn Greek,
> And to avoid barbarisms with five or ten words.
> Take in your hands and study it often,
> This newly printed book wherever you go.
> You will find whatever answers you need,
> To learn the Greek language well.
> It was most necessary to be published in print,
> Your nations to be honored with this, as I said.
> Take great care, then, in its reading
> Not burdened in cost with its acquisition.
> Acquire ideas of different things

* The original edition of 1762, of which no copy has survived, is reported by M. Nystazopoulou-Pelekidou, "Xenoglossa keimena me elleniki graphi," *O Eranistis* 10 (1972): 80–81. The importance was noted by William Martin Leake who reproduced the glossary in *Researches in Greece* (London, 1814), pp. 383–402.

Making your minds prolific and fruitful.
All bringing renown to yourselves,
In the midst of other nations, and of your fellow countrymen.
People that before spoke alien tongues, but devout in holy matters.
Acquire the tongue and speech of the Greeks.
Greatly benefited in your professions,
And in all your commercial undertakings.
Rejoice young Bulgarians, Albanians, and Wallachians,
Deacons, priests, and monks.
Wake from the deep sleep of ignorance,
Learn the Greek language, the mother of wisdom.
The Moesiodacian Daniel, and honored *oikonomos*,
Being lawfully a priest, produced the book.
The good shepherd and hierarch of Pelagonia
Published it, as a holy prelate of the flock
Wanting to teach the Greek language to all,
And to change the customs of the Bulgarians and Albanians
Decorating your villages and founding schools,
And exercising your children with Greek letters.

The translation, slightly amended, is taken from Richard Clogg, ed., *The Movement for Greek Independence 1770–1821* (London, 1976), pp. 91–92. The opening four lines were first rendered into English by Wace and Thompson, *The Nomads of the Balkans*, p. 6. On the cultural and linguistic Hellenization of the Vlachs of the Greek lands, see C. Koumas, *Istoriai ton anthropinon praxeon* (Vienna, 1832), 12: 530–531. The Greek consciousness of Iosipos was the product of such a process. Cf. the comment by S. Koumanoudis, *Synagogi neon lexeon* (Athens, 1900), p. 665, s.v. *Moisiodax*: "This was the surname used during the last century by a scholar, who perhaps originated from Bulgaria, Iosipos, who was a pupil of Evgenios at the time when the Bulgarians were entwined like ivy around the Greek oak, rising to the height of humanism through letters and never even dreamed of enmity against us." Koumanoudis also notes Moisiodax's contribution to the coining of neologisms in Modern Greek.

TWO

CHALLENGES

IN SEARCH OF what he had been unable to find at the schools of Thessaloniki and Smyrna, Moisiodax turned to the recently reorganized school on Mount Athos. In July 1753, Evgenios Voulgaris, who was noted for his innovative teaching, on account of which he was involved in serious intellectual disputes at Ioannina and Kozani, was invited by a sigilium from the patriarch Cyril V (1748–1751, 1752–1757) to assume the position of director of the Athonite Academy, made vacant by the premature and tragic loss of its head, Agapios Ayiotaphitis.[1] Voulgaris's arrival on Mount Athos ushered in the most brilliant phase in the history of the Athonite Academy, though it lasted for less than a decade, and marked a sanguine moment in the process of Greek intellectual reconstruction during the eighteenth century.

In the intellectual climate of renewal and hope created by the advent of Voulgaris on Mount Athos Moisiodax, who was now approaching thirty, sought to satisfy his thirst for learning. From 1754 to 1755 he was at the Athonite Academy and may possibly have arrived as early as the autumn of 1753, when Voulgaris began his lectures.[2] At any rate, he informs us that he was a student at the Academy "for a period of two years in all."[3]

The living conditions at the Academy were quite difficult and the program of study most exhausting, according to Iosipos's own testimony;[4] he must nevertheless have encountered, in the philosophy courses given by Voulgaris to the advanced classes in the school, a climate of studies entirely different from the Aristotelianism of Iannakos at Thessaloniki and the grammatical drills of Ierotheos at Smyrna. Though Voulgaris was still quite young and not far removed in age from Iosipos himself,[5] he was

---

[1] See G. Smyrnakis, *To Agion Oros* (Athens, 1903), pp. 142–150. The text of the sigillium setting forth the objectives of the academy, on pp. 143–147.

[2] This is deduced from his statement that he was one of the first pupils of Voulgaris at the Athonite Academy.

[3] *Apologia*, p. 16.

[4] Ibid., pp. 16–18.

[5] Evgenios Voulgaris was born in 1716. For the biographical details of this leading figure of the Modern Greek Enlightenment, see A. Papadopoulos-Vretos, *Biographie de l'Archevêque Eugenios Voulgaris* (Athens, 1868). It is rather surprising that despite the explosion of research into the Modern Greek Enlightenment in recent decades we still have to rely for the biography of Voulgaris on nineteenth-century sources such as Papadopoulos-Vretos

nonetheless at his maturity as a scholar. His earlier teaching career at Ioannina and Kozani had supplied him with considerable experience in the presentation of the multiple contents of modern philosophy in the context of Greek education. The weight of the heritage of sacred and classical learning that ecclesiastical education had to transmit made the whole attempt to introduce secular subjects a highly delicate undertaking, with critical symbolic significance.

In his advanced courses, Voulgaris taught philosophy and mathematics. The lectures on philosophy encompassed logic, introduction to philosophy, and metaphysics, while the branches of mathematics taught were arithmetic, geometry, physics, and cosmography. The content of these lessons may be determined with some certainty on the basis of Voulgaris's surviving written works, both published and unpublished. In the area of philosophy, Voulgaris had replaced the neo-Aristotelian commentaries of Theophilos Corydaleus, which Iosipos had encountered at Thessaloniki, with the message of Christian rationalism. This amounted to introducing gleams of the early Enlightenment into the Greek curriculum. His teaching was based on translations of handbooks and abridged versions of philosophical works, which gave his listeners a taste of the new direction taken by philosophical speculation, as it was moving away from the scholastic and the neo-Aristotelian heritage. Through the teaching of Voulgaris, the pupils at the Athonite Academy became acquainted with the philosophical textbooks of Jean Baptiste Duhamel and Edme Pourchot, the *Metaphysics* of Antonio Genovesi and the *Introduction to Philosophy* of G. I. Graavesand, which was essentially a treatise on the basic concepts of physics.[6] Other works taught were the *Elements of Arithmetic* of Christian Wolff, the *Elements of Geometry* of André Tacquet, and the *Physics* of J. F. Wückerer. All these manuals of basic philosophical and scientific notions cultivated the intellectual ground for the eventual transition to the culture of the Enlightenment.

Through these very general and inoffensive works the intelligentsia of Europe in the early and middle eighteenth century were prepared to

---

or Constantinos Sathas, *Neoelliniki Philologia* (Athens, 1868), pp. 566–571. The recent study by Stephen Batalden, *Catherine II's Greek Prelate: Evgenios Voulgaris in Russia, 1771–1806* (Boulder, 1982), is revealing for the last phase of Voulgaris's life, but only partially fills the gap.

[6] That Voulgaris used these texts as instruction manuals at the Athonite Academy, and even earlier at Ioannina and Kozani, is explicitly stated in the printed version of the works themselves. See, for instance, the title pages of *Genouisiou Stoicheia tis Metaphysikis*, trans. E. Voulgaris (Vienna, 1806), and *Eisagogi eis tin Philosophian, J. S. Graavesandou*, trans. E. Voulgaris (Moscow, 1805). On the content of Voulgaris's teaching on Athos, see F. W. Hasluck, *Athos and its Monasteries* (London, 1924), pp. 44–45, and A. Aggelou, "To chroniko tis Athoniadas. Dokimio istorias tis scholis me vasi anekdota keimena," *Nea Estia* 74 (Christmas 1963), pp. 93–100.

receive the message of the Enlightenment. The philosophical texts, in particular, selected by Voulgaris to be translated and taught to his Greek pupils, were the work of moderate compilers, who typified the average intellectual level and the restrained mainstream attitude of the early Enlightenment. Their compilations codified a tendency toward balance in the transition from conventional academic ideas and practices to the quest for the new. Jean Baptiste Duhamel, for example, was a distinguished seventeenth-century astronomer and member of the French Academy, honored for his breadth of knowledge, virtue, and piety; at the end of his career, he wrote a number of important theological works. From his general review of philosophy, *Philosophia vetus et nova ad usum scholae accommodata*, published in 1678, Voulgaris selected the section on logic for the purposes of his own teaching. Antonio Genovesi, too, the best-known representative of the "enlightened Catholicism" of the eighteenth century, supported a rationalized Christianity and at the same time opposed authority and superstition. A Cartesian in his philosophy, he also accepted some of Locke's views.[7] The publication of his *Elementa Metaphysicae* in 1743 was an epoch-making event, and the book established itself as a classic teaching text of its kind. The position represented by Duhamel and Genovesi indicated Voulgaris's philosophical inclinations and strategy for promoting his version of the Enlightenment: the espousal of rationalism and some basic principles of modern science, in conjunction with an unswerving respect for the doctrines of the faith. The result was the philosophical eclecticism of his *Logic*.[8]

In his attempts to break the bonds of Aristotelianism and liberate Greek thought from authority, however, Voulgaris did not hesitate to introduce the scholars of the Athonite Academy to John Locke's *Essay Concerning Human Understanding*. From the first French translation, by Pierre Coste, in 1700, through successive editions and abridgements, Locke's *Essay* acted as a catalyst to disseminate the Enlightenment in continental Europe. By delineating the boundaries of the cognitive power of the human mind and insisting that human judgment was the only acceptable means to knowledge, Locke established the basic preconditions of liberal thought. Greek thought had become acquainted with or at least aware of the *Essay* and its philosophical importance at a relatively early date.[9] The decisive step for the transmission of Locke's ideas into Greek culture was taken by Voulgaris, through the first translation of the

[7] Paul Hazard, *European Thought in the Eighteenth Century* (Gloucester, Mass., 1973), pp. 89–91.

[8] Evgenios Voulgaris, *I Logiki* (Leipzig, 1766), p. 44.

[9] In his correspondence of the early 1720s Nikolaos Mavrokordatos expresses interest in the work of John Locke. See Jacques Bouchard, "Les relations épistolaires de Nicolas Mavrocordatos avec Jean Le Clerc et William Wake," *O Eranistis* 11 (1974): 77.

Essay into Greek and its introduction into the curriculum of the Athonite Academy.[10] Locke's ideas were undoubtedly the most advanced and unconventional part of the philosophy curriculum at the Academy. In this climate Iosipos at last made his initial contact with the spirit of the Enlightenment.

It is worth observing that Voulgaris emphasized the teaching of philosophical method. Through logic and metaphysics he sought to introduce his pupils to methodical thought and a systematic approach to the basic questions of intellectual life. This was also the aim of the second component of his teaching, mathematics. This emphasis on the mathematical sciences was a significant innovation, given the traditional curriculum of higher education in the Greek East, which was dominated by commentaries on Aristotle, especially on the *Organon*, and by theology. To the extent that natural philosophy was taught, it was limited to commentaries on Aristotle's *Physics*. Voulgaris's aim in introducing broad instruction in the different branches of mathematics was presumably to forge a new analytical way of thinking that would eventually lead from merely accepting authority to practicing rational thought. During his two years at the Athonite Academy, Iosipos, already dissatisfied and traumatized by his exposure to the conventional curriculum and its teaching, became acquainted at first hand with the conflict between two alternative forms of intellectual existence and made his own definitive choices.

Perhaps the intensity of the experience involved in making these choices, heightened by Iosipos's sharp sensitivity, determined his future proclivity toward the analytical manner of thinking and sharpened his preference for the mathematical and physical sciences in his work as a teacher and writer. Indeed, in his subsequent critique of Voulgaris's pedagogical methods, Iosipos apparently believes that his teacher should have stressed even more the teaching of mathematics.[11]

Despite the admiration he felt for the man and his intellectual stature and the almost existential response to his message, which can be seen from a certain euphoria in the intellectual climate of those early years in the life of the renewed academy, Iosipos seems to have had serious reservations about the pedagogical methods of his teacher:

[10] That Voulgaris attempted the first Greek translation of Locke's *Essay*, but "only through chapter 9 of Book III," is stated by Philipp Strahl, *Das gelehrte Russland* (Leipzig, 1828), p. 456; his statement has been confirmed by the publication of the autograph list of Voulgaris's works. See Stephen K. Batalden, "Notes from a Leningrad Manuscript: Eugenios Voulgaris' Autograph List of His Own Works," *O Eranistis* 13 (1976): 7–8 (item 9). On the teaching of Locke, along with Leibniz and Wolff, in the Athonite Academy see Ph. Meyer, *Die Haupturkunden für die Geschichte der Athosklöster* (Leipzig, 1894), p. 76.

[11] *Apologia*, pp. 17–18.

When we were being taught, for two years in all, at the school on Athos, where the illustrious Evgenios exercised, with great acclaim, the duties of gymnasiarch, we underwent for the whole of this period indescribable toils, copying, studying, and not coming up for air for even five hours, almost the whole day and night, what fruit did we gather in the end from our unabating toils? An imperfect conception of Logic, and in part of Metaphysics, a confused and superficial conception of Arithmetic, and, finally, knowledge of only a single book of the *Elements* of Euclid, and this not even in full. . . . The illustrious man, then, organized his wise teaching according to the desire of his pupils, and according to the prevailing opinion, with which he was always careful not to come into conflict, or at least not to come into serious conflict. Would that he had been above common opinion, and that he had not given way to the demands of us, his pupils! In this way, while he would have wearied himself less, we, too, his first pupils, and similarly others, who studied with him afterward, would have received first a full idea of the synthetical and analytical method of Mathematics (be it understood, what is absolutely necessary) and second an adequate idea of Physics (be it understood again, what is absolutely necessary) so that, being guided by these in our private studies, we would have been led on from them to all the other matters relating to Physics proper. The intense application and the minds of the pupils were always at such a pitch that all these things could have been acquired by them in a single two-year period. How much dedication to Philosophy would not have been evinced among us if that illustrious man, having weighed accurately the indigence of the situation and the shortness of the time of his associates, and also the most pressing need of Hellas, had taught and proclaimed lessons mainly to be heard, and mainly given over to Mathematics and Physics?[12]

"The most pressing need of Hellas"—with this comment at the conclusion of his pedagogical critique, Moisiodax links the problem of education with a broader concept of social utilitarianism. Education in his judgment should be delivered from the isolation inherent in its traditional unresponsiveness to social needs and priorities, an isolation that Voulgaris's philosophical elitism had certainly failed to overcome, and become part of the theoretical preoccupation with the real needs of collective existence. One indication of the radical reorientation of educational thought brought about by Moisiodax was his belief that a more effective contribution to the diagnosis of these needs could be based on positive knowledge, such as that provided by natural philosophy and mathematics. Initiation into the new knowledge of nature accordingly provided the

---

[12] Ibid., pp. 16–18. Cf. however ibid., p. 36 n.1, for a clarification concerning the spirit in which these criticisms of Voulgaris were voiced.

foundation of the social utilitarianism of his own theory of education. In his experience at the Athonite Academy and in his critique of Voulgaris's pedagogical method, the stimuli can already be discerned that later led to composing Moisiodax's pedagogical and scientific writings.

The circle of his fellow-students at the Athonite Academy was undoubtedly another source of intellectual stimulation. During the period of Voulgaris's directorship, and indeed in the very years that Moisiodax was a student, the student body of the Athonite Academy included a number of scholars who made their mark on Greek intellectual life in the second half of the eighteenth century. Iosipos was one of them. His fellow students included Christodoulos Pamblekis, Sergios Makraios, Athanasios Parios, and Kosmas the Aetolian, the future evangelist and neomartyr, who was later canonized by the Church. Theophilos, bishop of Campania, and Theoklitos Polyeidis were also connected with the school during Voulgaris's time. Moisiodax's path must have crossed with those of at least some of these strong, contradictory personalities during his residence on Athos. The simple recitation of the names of all these future sages, who were to adopt such divergent ideological positions, from Pamblekis's atheism and materialism to the militant Orthodox fundamentalism of Parios and the traditionalism of Makraios, hints at the intellectual ferment and tensions provoked by their association at the same institution. All this cannot have failed to influence Iosipos's own intellectual choices.

Despite his reservations and objections about Voulgaris's educational method, in Moisiodax's judgment, the standards set by the Athonite Academy served as an example of what could be achieved in Greek education if trust and disinterested good will prevailed in determining how best to promote the common good. But the failure of Voulgaris's endeavors highlighted the social constraints lurking in the way of an educational renaissance: "all of them the abominable works of our discord which, like another Fury dwelling amongst us, everywhere throws us into confusion and deprives us of the benefits of salutary concord."[13] This observation flowed from the very lively feelings aroused by his recollection of the Academy ten years after he had left Mount Athos:

> A melancholy glance at that renowned school on Athos, the misfortune, the desolation of which, so to speak, even now hangs like a vapor before us. Where is the illustrious Evgenios? Where the throng of students, which, to

---

[13] Ibid., p. 128. What precisely these "odious works" were is reported by another alumnus of the Athonite Academy, Christodoulos Pamblekis, in his pamphlet *Apantisis Anonymou pros tous aftou aphronas katigorous eponomastheisa peri theokratias* (Leipzig, 1793), pp. 74–80. The relevant extracts of the text are cited by G. Ladas and A. D. Chatzidimos, *Elliniki Vivliographia, 1791–1795* (Athens, 1970), pp. 216–217.

the joy of the whole of Hellas, formed a new Helicon of Muses and their votaries? He has been banished; they too have been banished. The thunder of Nemesis has fallen upon them and scattered teachers and taught alike, and that building, of which there was so much talk in the Capital and the rest of Greece, is reduced (alack!) to an abode, a nest for crows.[14]

After his two years as a student at the Athonite Academy, Moisiodax tells us that he spent the year 1756 on the Aegean islands of Siphnos and Mykonos.[15] His biographer, A. Camariano Cioran, suggests that he visited these islands on professional assignments in the local schools, as part of his attempts to amass the funds needed for the journey to the West of which he still dreamed.[16] This hypothesis is probably correct, though it has proved impossible to locate any external evidence to confirm it. No positive evidence in the educational history of the two islands suggests that Moisiodax passed through their schools. On Mykonos, the school of Saint Luke functioned from 1743 to 1809 in the monastery of the same name. The list of teachers at the school, however, which is preserved in its entirety in the registers of the island, leaves no room for the theory that Moisiodax practiced his profession as a teacher on Mykonos in 1756. The sources unambiguously state the name of the teacher on the island from 1754 to 1790: Grigorios.[17] In the case of Siphnos, the ambiguity of the sources, coupled with bits of available evidence, permits the hypothesis that Moisiodax spent some time there. The departure of the teacher Stephanos of Cyprus in 1753 to take up missionary work in Ethiopia created a serious problem in the local school, which had functioned since 1687 in the Metochion of the Holy Sepulchre under the name *Koinon Paideftirion tou Archipelagous* (Common School of the Archipelago). It may be conjectured from a piece of evidence in a manuscript of the Great Lavra on Mount Athos that at some point after 1753, the Siphnian teacher Apostolos taught at the *Koinon Paideftirion*, following a number

---

[14] *Apologia*, p. 128. Cf. the corresponding quote in the *Pedagogy*, p. 127: "All the learned men who were taught grammar at the Athonite school, at that school, I say, that once rejoiced in the vast numbers and in the achievements of pupils and classes, [but] is now, alas, bereft of both teachers and taught." Voulgaris himself gave his own account of the episode at the Athonite Academy in his *Apology* to the Patriarch Kyrillos V. See E. Voulgaris, *Syllogi anekdoton syggrammaton*, ed. G. Ainian (Athens, 1838), vol. 1, pp. 54–64, and in his letter to deacon Kyprianos published in *Parallilon Philosophias kai Christianismou* (Constantinople, 1830), pp. 80–91.

[15] *Apologia*, p. 188, n.1.

[16] A. Camariano Cioran, *Les académies princières de Bucarest et de Jassy et leurs professeurs* (Thessaloniki, 1974), p. 571.

[17] Tryphon Evangelidis, *I Mykonos, itoi istoria tis nisou apo archaiotaton chronon mechri ton kath'imas* (Athens, 1912), p. 234. See also P. G. Zerlendis, "Peri tou en Mykono scholeiou tou Agiou Louka," *Epetiris Philologikou Syllogou "Parnassos"* (Athens, 1917), pp. 176–179.

of unsuccessful attempts to attract teachers to the island from Smyrna and Athens. The next teacher, Daniel Kerameus, is not mentioned until thirty years later, in 1785.[18] This evidence allows the hypothesis that the gap in the teaching created by the departure of Stephanos was filled for one year by Moisiodax who took advantage of his stay on Siphnos to visit the neighboring island of Mykonos, an important center of Cycladic society at this period. In any case, all that Moisiodax retained from his sojourn on the islands was the memory of the "monstrous" ignorance of the islanders with regard to natural phenomena.

Amongst the autobiographical statements in Moisiodax's *Apology* is a reference to a stay in Athens. The statement in the text is explicit: "I heard this while residing in Athens."[19] In contrast to other autobiographical statements, which are accompanied by a reference to a precise date, Moisiodax assigns no date to his stay in Athens. It would be a reasonable assumption, however, that his visit there followed his teaching appointment in the neighboring Cyclades. It may therefore be assigned to the gap in his biography between his sojourn on Siphnos in 1756 and his arrival in Venice in 1759. Athens was a natural intermediate stopover en route for the ports of Western Greece, especially Patras, the departure point for the sea journey to Venice.

It is worth noting the memories Iosipos retained of Athens. He neither alludes to its classical history, nor does he appear enthralled by the monuments of the past that made Athens a center of attraction for European travelers on the Grand Tour. He does recall, however, the story he heard there of a scholarly discussion "concerning the antipodes" that took place in the presence of the local Turkish magistrate, in which the Athenian teacher Bessarion took a leading part. He also mentions the school, recently (1750) founded in the city by Ioannis Dekas which he describes in some detail: "A fine building, for that place, systematically arranged and capable of holding two teachers and twenty-four pupils, with all the space they need. A fixed income for the school, an adequate library, a sound board of trustees, as far as possible in that place, nothing has been overlooked by Ioannis, of blessed memory."[20] His detailed description and other information leave no doubt that Iosipos had visited the school and was well acquainted with both its working and its history. It is tempting to add yet another hypothesis to fill the lacuna in his biography and suggest that, after Siphnos and before Venice, he may have taught in Athens,

[18] S. M. Symeonidis, *Ta grammata sto nisi tis Siphnou, 1650–1833* (Piraeus, 1962), pp. 14–18, esp. 15–16. Moisiodax's testimony might have been used partially to cover the gap between 1753 and 1785.

[19] *Apologia*, p. 29. The reference to the popular uprising against Sarrhis Mousellimis establishes July 1754 as a *terminus post quem* for Moisiodax's visit to Athens.

[20] Ibid., p. 30, n.1.

but history cannot be written on the basis of conjectures. With respect to Iosipos's passage through Athens, then, we may note one item of great significance: his lively interest in works of contemporary culture, particularly those that sustained the intellectual revival for which he yearned. This explains why, in his recollections of Athens, Dekas's school, not the Acropolis, left the stronger impression.

Soon after his experiences in the Aegean, Moisiodax realized the great dream of his youth, the journey to the West. Here again, it is impossible to establish the chronological framework with any accuracy. His presence in Venice is attested from 1759 to 1762 and the details he himself gives us in the *Apology*,[21] taken together with the history of the University of Padua at this period, suggest that his long-desired studies at the institution should be placed before 1761.

In the spring of 1759, Deacon Iosipos Moisiodax, a new arrival in Venice from the Orthodox East, was invited to preach from the pulpit of Saint George of the Greeks on the Sundays in Lent of that year. For this service he was paid the sum of fifty ducats by the Greek Confraternity of Venice. This is perhaps the best documented biographical detail that we possess about Moisiodax. The information, preserved in the account book for the year 1759 kept by Nikolaos Tsoukalas,[22] the grand warden of the Confraternity of Saint Nicholas and the church of Saint George of the Greeks, was subsequently entered into the trustees' account book for 1755–1763,[23] and noted in the official ledger of the church and the confraternity for 1752–1773.[24] In Nikolaos Tsoukalas's receipt book for 1759, the signed receipt for Iosipos's pay is preserved, with the date 5th May: "I, hierodeacon Iosipos the Moesiodacian, confirm."[25]

As a biographical document, this evidence is of enormous value, though it does not, of course, answer all our questions. It merely furnishes a *terminus ante quem* for Moisiodax's first visit to Italy and his entry into the ranks of the clergy. Both these were common features of the experience of young men who aspired to an education in Greek, and, more generally speaking, in Balkan society under Ottoman rule. Ordi-

---

[21] Ibid., p. 23.

[22] Greek Institute of Venice (hereafter GIV), Old Archive of the Greek Community, Busta 34 (1759–1760), Quaderno 1759: *Cassa tenuta dal Clarissimo signor Nicolò Zuccalà, Guardian Grande della Veneranda Scola di San Nicolò e chiesa di San Giorgio de'Greci*, third unnumbered folio, recto, May 5, 1759.

[23] GIV, Old Archive, Registro 209: *Libro Casse de'Guardiani 1755–1763*, fol. 64ʳ (new numbering), May 5, 1759.

[24] GIV, Old Archive, Registro 26: *Giornale della Chiesa e Scola 1751–1773*, fol. 99ʳ (new numbering), May 5, 1759.

[25] GIV, Old Archive, Busta 34 (1759–1760), Quaderno 1759: *Riceveri tenuto dal Clarissimo Signor Nicolò Zuccalà, Guardian Grande della Veneranda Scola di San Nicolò e chiesa di San Giorgio de'Greci*, second unnumbered folio, verso, May 5, 1759.

nation and entry into the ranks of the celibate clergy provided the sons of the Orthodox peasantry in the Balkans with an outlet of geographical and social mobility and could eventually secure professional status through access to higher education, in a society where the Church and the monasteries, in the absence of a Christian state, controlled enduring mechanisms of social reproduction. A case in point, the ordination of the young Ioannis as a deacon of the Church sealed his cultural Hellenization. Upon his ordination, which must undoubtedly have taken place before his journey to Italy, he assumed the Hellenized version of the biblical name Joseph. For the student of the history of culture, Moisiodax's ecclesiastical appellation Iosipos (Josephus) suggests an evocative parallel with the cultural Hellenization of the first century Jewish historian of that name.

Entry into the celibate clergy automatically gave a young man access to the repository of sacred literature preserved by the Orthodox Church for the intellectual preparation of the priesthood. To share in this tradition, the young eighteenth-century cleric with a proclivity for learning would resort to the hearths of ecclesiastical education at the major monastic centers: chiefly to Mount Athos and Patmos, but also to other, peripheral monastic foundations scattered throughout the Greek East, from the monasteries of Moldavia to those on the rocks of Meteora in Thessaly, and from those on the Agrafa mountains in Central Greece, from Mega Spilaion in the Peloponnese, to Soumela and Vazelon in Pontos, the monasteries of Kykkos and Macheras on Cyprus, and the *lavras* of Palestine and the great imperial foundation at Sinai. The circuit of these centers of faith and learning, even in the form of a pilgrimage, was an indispensable feature of preparing for a career in the church. The first stage in such a career consisted of attaining distinction in learning, as a promise of effective future service in carrying on and reproducing the cultural heritage of Orthodoxy; the second, accession to the episcopate; and the final stage, perhaps even appointment to one of the four patriarchal thrones. We may recall the parallel paths followed by Dositej Obradović and Iosipos Moisiodax to Patmos and Mount Athos, respectively. They both reproduced faithfully the traditional pattern in pursuing their educational aspirations. This was the typical structure of the educational experience of Orthodox intellectuals during the centuries of Ottoman rule.

The eighteenth century, however, witnessed the first signs of internal change in this pattern. The point of departure still retained the outward features of the traditional structure: schooling in a monastic center, education under the aegis of the Church, entry into the clergy. The movements of the "itinerant" Orthodox monks of the Ottoman Empire,[26] how-

---

[26] Dositheos Notaras, "Istoria peri tis episkopis tou orous Sina," in *Symvolai eis tin istorian tis archiepiskopis tou orous Sina*, ed. A. Papadopoulos-Kerameus (Petrograd, 1908), p. 70.

ever, were gradually transformed, in some cases at least, into a factor for cultural change with long-term consequences for the collective destiny of the Balkan peoples.[27] Unconsciously at first, consciously later, the wanderings of the traveling monks ceased to be a matter of mendicancy, pilgrimages to holy places, and the acquisition of sacred learning; instead, this became a window on the world and therefore a factor in ideological change. For some, their subjective experience at a certain point deviated from the traditional curve. Their appetite for learning clashed with the norms of traditional education, and the resulting psychological resistance led to the sacrifice of their predestined careers. A gradual discovery of the inadequacies in traditional schooling and the search for alternative educational choices contained within them the dynamic that led to converting this initial psychological resistance into ideological confrontation, which naturally gave rise to suspicions of heterodoxy. In this way the preconditions were set for the transition from traditional to modern learning that brought the Enlightenment to Balkan society. The phenomenon was reflected in the personal careers of a number of scholars who set out from conventional points of departure, among them the remarkable series of deacons of the neo-Hellenic Enlightenment: Evgenios Voulgaris, as long as he remained in Greek lands, Iosipos Moisiodax, Grigorios Constantas, Neophytos Vamvas. All these sacrificed the certainty of elevation to the church hierarchy in favor of a broader cultural and educational ideal. The transvaluation implicit in this phenomenon recalls the emergence of the radical *abbés* in the broader movement of the European Enlightenment.

The path from the schools of higher education in the Greek East, whose possibilities Iosipos had exhausted, to the University of Padua for a university education formed another regularity in the experience of the Greek intelligentsia in the Ottoman Empire. Venice, with its possessions and wide variety of interests in the Eastern Mediterranean, was for Europe the threshold of the Levant; for Hellenism, however, it had been the gateway to the West ever since the late Byzantine period. The University of Padua, since 1405 the official institution of higher education of the Venetian republic,[28] became the main center of university education for Greeks from those Greek lands occupied by Venice. The Cypriotes, in the fifteenth and especially the sixteenth centuries, naturally the Cretans during the long centuries of Venetian rule of their island (1210–1669), the Chiotes and the Heptanesians, all created a tradition of a con-

[27] Cf. Carole Rogel, "The Wandering Monk and the Balkan National Awakening," *Études Balkaniques* (1976) 1: 114–127.
[28] Frederick Lane, *Venice: A Maritime Republic* (Baltimore, 1973), pp. 215–216. See also Hastings Rashdall, *The Universities of Europe in the Middle Ages*, ed. E. M. Powicke and A. B. Emden (Oxford, 1936), vol. 2, pp. 9–21.

tinuous Greek presence in the student body of Padua. Special institutional arrangements gradually emerged to cater to their needs. Two colleges were founded especially for Greeks—the College of Saint John, or Palaiokapa, in 1583, and later, in 1653, the more famous Cottunian College, both of which made it significantly easier for Greeks to study in Padua. Many Greek students distinguished themselves as teachers at the University of Padua, while those who did not pursue a career in the West became intellectual leaders in the Greek East upon their return.[29] These conditions not only explain why Greek students attended the University of Padua in such large numbers in the seventeenth and eighteenth centuries, but they also account for the reputation and prestige enjoyed by the university in the East, even in periods of crisis and decline, such as the eighteenth century. Undoubtedly this reputation evoked in Moisiodax the desire to complete his education at Padua.

Moisiodax certainly attended courses at the School of Arts and Sciences of the Università degli Artisti in Padua in 1759–1760 and 1760–1761 and possibly also in 1762, and he was probably there for a period of uncertain length prior to his service as a preacher in Venice. His appearance in the pulpit of Saint George in Lent of 1759 could conceivably have been soon after his arrival in Italy; a newly arrived scholar and clergyman would naturally have begun to acquaint himself with his new surroundings from a base within the familiar environment of the Orthodox community and its Church. Equally, however, he could have been invited to Venice as a result of either a certain repute that he might have gained from his performance at the university or acquaintances he had made with leading figures in the Church and the confraternity during the first phase of his stay in Padua. If the former of these alternatives is considered the more probable, Moisiodax cannot have started his studies at Padua before the middle of 1759, while, if we accept the latter, the beginning of his studies may be placed at least one year earlier.

When Moisiodax arrived in Padua, the famous university had just completed a cycle of decline lasting for several decades in the first half of the eighteenth century. The Università degli Artisti, and especially the medical school had lost its preeminence among the medical centers of Europe and had been surpassed by Leyden in Holland.[30] The problem had become a matter of serious concern to the Venetian republic, and there were many attempts at reform in the second half of the century. As early as the late 1740s, a variety of reforms had been introduced into the ad-

---

[29] Steven Runciman, *The Great Church in Captivity* (Cambridge, 1968), pp. 212–219. See also A. Stergellis, *Ta dimosievmata ton Ellinon spoudaston tou Panepistimiou tis Padovas ton 17o kai 18o aiona* (Athens, 1970), pp. 45–53.

[30] M. S. Anderson, *Europe in the Eighteenth Century, 1713–1783* (London, 1961), p. 288.

ministrative organization of the university, while at the same time there had been an endeavor, attended by full debate, to modernize the curriculum and the teaching material so that the content of the courses would match the advances in knowledge brought about by the scientific revolution of the seventeenth century.

Moisiodax's arrival in Padua at the end of the 1750s coincided with the beginning of the period of reform at the university that lasted from 1757 to 1787. The university's problems and the necessity for the reforms were stressed in the report submitted to the Doge, on April 24, 1761, by the university *Riformatori*, who bore the distinguished Venetian patrician names A. Contarini, B. Nani, and F. Morosini.[31] Against this background of demands for and discussion of the modernization of education according to the needs of the times,[32] Moisiodax studied in Padua. Important steps toward renewal had already been taken in the two faculties of the university. In 1761, the teaching of natural law was introduced in the law school, which up to then had stubbornly clung to the medieval curriculum of canon and civil law, faithfully following the Roman law tradition.[33] This development indicated the repercussions of the spirit of the Enlightenment that finally began to be felt in the universities.

The changes were even more noticeable in the faculty of Arts and Sciences, of which Moisiodax was a student.[34] This stronghold of Aristotelian philosophy and science, from which neo-Aristotelianism had emanated to the Greek East during the seventeenth century, following the lead of Theophilos Corydaleus,[35] found itself under close siege from the advance of modern science and philosophy, and its defences were growing steadily weaker. Already, in 1738, one chair of Aristotelian philosophy had been designated a chair of "experimental philosophy," meaning

---

[31] Stergellis, *Ta dimosievmata*, p. 17. Two of these, Angelo Contarini and Francesco Morosini, acting as *Riformatori* of the University of Padua responsible for censorship in Venetian territories, signed, on 6 August 1761, the permit to publish the first of Moisiodax's works, the *Moral Philosophy*, which was published in Venice in the same year. On the creation of this institution in the 16th century, see Paul Grendler, *The Roman Inquisition and the Venetian Press, 1540–1605* (Princeton, 1977), pp. 151–152, 274.

[32] Cf. F. Venturi, *Settecento riformatore*, vol. 2: *La chiesa e la repubblica dentro i loro limiti 1758–1774* (Turin, 1976), p. 155.

[33] Stergellis, *Ta dimosievmata*, p. 30.

[34] Moisiodax's name nowhere appears in the enrollment lists of Greek students at Padua. The relevant enquiries have produced negative results. Cf. G. Ploumidis, "Ai praxeis eggraphis ton ellinon spoudaston tou Panepistimiou tis Padouis. Meros A. Artisti, 1634–1782," *Epetiris Etaireias Vyzantinon Spoudon* 37 (1969–1970): pp. 260–336. Pp. 319–320 contain the details of the registers for the years 1760, 1761, 1762, but have no reference to the enrollment of Moisiodax.

[35] Cléobule Tsourkas, *Les débuts de l'enseignment philosophique et de la libre pensée dans les Balkans. La vie et l'oeuvre de Théophile Corydalée (1570–1646)* (Thessaloniki, 1967), pp. 35–38, 179–195.

natural science. This was the chair to which Moisiodax was attached, and in this way he came into direct contact with the scientific spirit of the time. In this way many of his intellectual concerns and his scientific curiosity, which had hitherto gone unsatisfied, now received an answer. Twenty years later he vividly recorded his recollections in the *Apology*:

> I recall that during my time at the Patavion, whenever experiments were being conducted, almost the entire theater was filled with artisans who, even though the distinguished teachers, first Poleni and then Colombo, spoke in Latin, and concluded their lessons with geometrical demonstrations, nevertheless gladly stayed to the end and praised the speakers either for their knowledge of Latin, or for their grasp of experimental philosophy. Men have an innate desire to learn, and consequently love to learn about things that are outside their experience, though these things must be accessible to understanding and have some point of reference to them; and if they do not understand all the notions, if they do not grasp ideas perfectly, nevertheless, being informed, albeit mechanically, they respect these things, and also respect those who know about them. The subjects of Mathematics and Physical science are mainly things of this sort.[36]

The "distinguished teachers" of Padua, of whom Moisiodax speaks with such admiration, were Giovanni Poleni (1683–1761) and Giovanni Alberto Colombo (early 18th cent.–1770). Both were distinguished scholars of the period, and both had played decisive roles in changing the orientation of the University of Padua from neo-Aristotelianism to modern science. Poleni, long-time professor at Padua, initially taught astronomy (1709–1715) and later experimental philosophy; in connection with this course Moisiodax heard him lecture shortly before his death. Giovanni Alberto Colombo was a clergyman who nevertheless made a significant contribution to the abandonment of Aristotelian cosmology during his tenure of the chair of astronomy, geography, and meteorology (1746–1764). During Moisiodax's studies at Padua, Colombo founded the astronomical observatory of the university (1761). Apparently the influence of these two teachers instilled in Moisiodax his life-long interest in the natural sciences. Although there is no direct evidence, it is a reasonable hypothesis that Moisiodax was also influenced by the teaching of the then young fellow of the Cottunian College, Simon Stratigos, in 1758–1760.[37]

---

[36] *Apologia*, p. 23. On Poleni's experimental laboratory, which so impressed Moisiodax, and his place in the history of science, see Maria Pancino and Gian Antonio Salandin, *Il Teatro di Filosofia sperimentale di Giovanni Poleni (1682–1761)* (Padua, n.d.), which includes a descriptive catalogue of the instruments of the laboratory. For a survey and appraisal of his scientific work at Padua, see Marialaura Soppelsa, *Genesi del metodo Galileiano e tramonto dell'Aristotelismo nella Scuola di Padova* (Padua, 1974), pp. 141–154.

[37] C. Mertzios, *Mnimeia Makedonikis Istorias* (Thessaloniki, 1947), p. 495, and Stergellis, *Ta dimosievmata*, pp. 40–41.

Stratigos, a Cretan by descent, was a man of many talents, which he exercised in several different branches of mathematics and its technical applications, and we may suppose that he was for Moisiodax a living example of the utilitarian view of knowledge so closely bound up with the movement of the Enlightenment.

In addition to his education in natural philosophy, which presumably formed the main content of his studies at Padua, Moisiodax cannot have failed to come into contact with other intellectual currents of the period. His time in Venice and Padua coincided with the penetration into Venetian territories of the spirit of the Enlightenment. The climate of encyclopedism was strong at precisely this period in Venice,[38] and the academic circles at Padua were animated by the continuing debate that had been instigated by the reception of the philosophy of Descartes and the epistemological and pedagogical views of Locke. At the same time, the impassioned intellectual conflicts associated with the quarrel of the Ancients and Moderns, in which the Greek students in Padua had taken an active part, still conjured up vivid images.[39] These features of the cultural climate of the University of Padua in the middle decades of the eighteenth century shaped Moisiodax's mental outlook and are graphically reflected in his work.

The broadening of his horizons was without doubt a source of exhilaration; the satisfaction of his many curiosities merely aroused a desire for further learning, and he received lively stimulation from all sides. Iosipos felt the need to express himself and give his first testimony on the problems of Greek culture and society as he had both experienced them and seen them through the prism of his new intellectual experiences. Moisiodax apparently had a natural propensity to express himself through the written word. He himself was intensely aware of this as an element in his individuality and a distinctive feature of his character: he felt himself "by birth destined, without doubt, for writing."[40]

Despite the academic interest in natural philosophy awakened in him by his education at the University of Padua, his first published work was a treatise on neither mathematics nor physics. He judged it to be more useful for the needs of Greek society—of Hellas, as he put it—to translate a text on *Moral Philosophy*. His choice of both general subject and the particular work hinted at the philosophical concerns that were forming in his thought with regard to the needs of Greek education and society. In his view, the prerequisite for any reconstruction, whether narrowly educational or more broadly cultural, was a new ethic in the wider sense, which would determine the attitude of his fellows in Balkan society to life

---

[38] F. Venturi, *Settecento riformatore*, vol. 2, pp. 109–110.
[39] For the evidence on this, cf. Stergellis, *Ta dimosievmata*, pp. 68–72.
[40] Iosipos Moisiodax, *Theoria tis Geographias* (Vienna, 1781), p. x.

and knowledge. Only moral reform and the adoption of new values, attitudes, and behavior could set in motion those processes of change that might eventually cure the ills of culture and reverse the desperate backwardness of Greek society. His own first-hand experience of the many-sided resistance to progress, when he was seeking to satisfy his yearning for knowledge and learning in the bosom of Greek education, and the contrast with the achievements of contemporary Western civilization with which he had become acquainted at Padua, convinced him of the scale of the problems and the nature of the priorities ahead. Forty years later, Korais was to speak of a fully-fledged "moral revolution" in the Greek world.[41] Moisiodax was the first to grasp the need for this, to proclaim it, and to attempt to set it in motion.

His choice of the particular text to translate was an eloquent indication of the direction given to Moisiodax's thought by his studies at Padua. To convey his message to his compatriots he turned to the work of an Italian antiquary and humanist who had impressed his contemporaries as a reflective supporter of the cause of reform in Italian society. Ludovico Antonio Muratori (1672–1750) owes his place in the history of ideas mainly to the part he played in the revival of Italian historiography; he is also remembered as one of the pioneers of the new moral history, who through their philological and historical researches reconstituted a shared medieval past for the divided Italian people and thus contributed to awakening Italian national conscience.[42] In his own time, however, Muratori was better known as a reforming spirit, admired well beyond the Italian lands. The esteem in which he was held by Montesquieu is revealing of his renown.[43] Thanks to his moderation however, Muratori did not arouse any fears or reactions and this enabled him to argue convincingly for reform in the fields of scholarship, natural philosophy, and moral behavior. It is recorded that about 1726 Muratori was one of the first Italians to study Locke's *Essay Concerning Human Understanding*. He was aware, that is, of the requirements and implications of the new philosophy. To restrain some excesses of the new philosophical positions, however, Muratori was equally determined in his defence of the moral principles of Christianity.[44] In short, Muratori was among the foremost exponents of "enlightened Catholicism."

This was the philosophical standpoint reflected in his *La filosofia mo-*

---

[41] Adamantios Korais, *Mémoire sur l'état actuel de la civilisation dans la Grèce* (Paris, 1803), pp. 52, 54, 60.

[42] Felix Gilbert, "The Historian as Guardian of National Consciousness: Italy between Guicciardini and Muratori," in his *History: Choice and Commitment* (Cambridge, Mass., 1977), pp. 387–409.

[43] Robert Shackleton, *Montesquieu: A Critical Biography* (Oxford, 1961), p. 107.

[44] See Gianfranco Torcellan, *Settecento veneto e altri scritti storici* (Turin, 1969), p. 620.

rale esposta e proposta ai giovani, published in Verona in 1735, which Moisiodax selected for translation. In it, epistemological and ethical questions are woven together into a system of philosophical anthropology. His treatment of the interconnected problems is based on the simple proposition of the Enlightenment that a clear and sound knowledge of the functioning of human nature and of human reason is all that is required for the effective regulation of moral behavior. Muratori, however, does not stop at the rationalistic optimism of this position. In the last decade of his life, just before Moisiodax's arrival in Italy, Muratori, then at the height of his efforts for renewing knowledge and reforming research methods, had finally grasped the deeper essence of the question of cultural change; he concluded that the intellectual reform of men was not enough, but that a transformation of things—of social, judicial, political, and economic institutions—was an essential precondition. In this spirit he wrote *Dei difetti della giurisprudenza* (1742) and *Della pubblica felicità* (1748); both deal with the social dimensions of the problem of human behavior and happiness.[45] This turned his attention to the practical knowledge of political economy, which he considered indispensable for planning the reform of social institutions.[46] Through these concerns Muratori helped to spur the reexamination of the conception of politics as "reason of state" and its replacement by the assumption of responsibility for public prosperity.[47] For this he was later greatly admired by the encyclopedists and physiocrats, and his work proved a useful tool for advancing the ideas of the Enlightenment in regions where conditions required that the attempt begin as a simple project of practical reform.

It is no coincidence that Muratori's work, a source of inspiration for later Italian reformers like Beccaria, also proved particularly useful to their German counterparts.[48] Moreover, it was only natural that he should also attract the attention of Moisiodax who, as can be seen from the prolegomena to the translation, was already fully aware of the intricacies involved in any project of cultural change.[49] Thus, within the sphere of his own experiences, Moisiodax's ideas followed a trajectory parallel to the evolution of the thought of Muratori as outlined above. We

---

[45] F. Venturi, *Settecento riformatore*, vol. 1: *Da Muratori a Beccaria* (Turin, 1969), pp. 66–70, 138–142, 151–160, 161–186, and passim. See also Virgilio Titone, *La storiografia dell'illuminismo in Italia* (Milan, 1975), pp. 109–134.

[46] Cf. Franco Venturi, "History and Reform in the Middle of the Eighteenth Century," in *The Diversity of History: Essays in Honour of Sir Herbert Butterfield*, ed. J. H. Elliot and H. G. Koenigsberger (London, 1970), pp. 223–244.

[47] G. Torcellan, *Settecento veneto*, p. 622. On the social and political thought of Muratori, see also the contribution by N. Badaloni in the collective work *Storia d'Italia*, vol. 3: *Dal primo Settecento all'Unità* (Turin, 1973), pp. 773–785.

[48] F. Venturi, "History and Reform," p. 229.

[49] *Ithikí Philosophía*, vol. 1, pp. xi–xxxiv.

shall return to these matters in due course, however. Here, we must take note of another aspect of the ideological function of Muratori's work, as recorded in a text contemporary with Moisiodax's presence in Venice. A Swedish visitor in 1759 was very impressed by the fact that works of bold social criticism, such as Muratori's *Traité de la meilleure devotion*, could freely be published in Venice.[50] In this work Muratori censured the bigotry, superstition, and excessive attention to ritual of his contemporaries in a tone that might easily have provoked a reaction from the Church. It was nevertheless an attitude quite congenial to Iosipos's taste.

Muratori's *Moral Philosophy* in a translation by the "Deacon Iosipos Moisiodax," was published at the Venetian press of Antonio Bortoli in 1761; the second volume appeared in 1762.[51] A number of features connected with the publication help to define the external context of Moisiodax's thought. The dedication of the work consists of a warm greeting addressed to the Metropolitan of Smyrna, Neophytos:

> Thrice blessed, thrice blessed is Smyrna, with the good fortune that has fallen to its lot! Smyrna which, thanks to the spiritual government of your pastoral reverence is today renowned throughout all the systems of the Orthodox. Let Memphis exult in its pyramids; let Babylon take pride in its hanging gardens; let Rhodes boast of its Colossus. . . . But the boast of Smyrna has no part in the allure of deception, does not share in the excesses of art, where deceivers either bewitch the eye, or make a trade of the simplicity of nature. Smyrna's boast is a venerable hero of the ecclesiastical legion, who glitters with all the charms of virtue. A prominent distinguished pastor, elected by grace and adorned by approval. A most reverend scholar, who is an adornment to the eastern hierarchy. A most precise regulator who orders spiritual government. A perfect example of both civil and moral comportment. He is, I say, the protector of the Muses, the comforting host of strangers, the glory of Ionia, the joy of the Cyclades and the Sporades, all of whom eternally enjoy the effects of his benevolent beneficence. This, this is the boast of Smyrna.[52]

Neophytos was the same prelate from whom Moisiodax had anticipated support for his studies at Padua in 1753, before it was forestalled by the hostile intervention of Ierotheos Dendrinos. Iosipos the deacon, despite

---

[50] Jean Georgelin, *Venise au siècle des lumières, 1669–1797* (Paris, 1978), p. 715. The source of this information is the account of the travels of Pierre Jean Grosley, *Nouveaux mémoires ou observations sur l'Italie et sur les Italiens par deux gentilshommes suédois (1758–1759)* (London, 1764), vol. 2, pp. 57–58. What was probably meant by the title recorded in the text was Muratori's *Della regolata devozion de' cristiani* (Venice, 1747).

[51] See Emile Legrand, *Bibiliographie hellénique, XVIIIe siècle* (Paris, 1928), vol. 2, pp. 2–3.

[52] *Ithiki Philosophia*, vol. 1, pp. vi–viii.

the lessons he had learned from his experiences, apparently still hesitated to burn his bridges with the official Church—reasonable and human behavior from a learned clergyman who had just completed his university studies and knew that he would soon be faced with the problem of earning a living.

The recent discovery of the only surviving letter by Iosipos Moisiodax allows us to explain in more precise terms the above exaltation of the metropolitan of Smyrna.[53] After completing his translation of Muratori's work, Moisiodax visited the communities of Orthodox merchants in the Hapsburg Empire in search of funds for its publication. To carry out more effectively this fund-raising tour, the unknown clergyman needed to establish his own credibility as well as the acceptability of his work. To this end he applied to the archbishop of Karlowitz, Paul Nenadović, primate of the Orthodox communities in the Hapsburg domains; Moisiodax requested the archbishop's written permission to tour the companies of Orthodox merchants in Hungary to solicit their support. Alternatively Moisiodax requested the archbishop to issue him a written testimonial to the effect that the book he had translated was "useful and necessary" and that his own rendering of the text was exact and faithful to the original. If issued with the requested documents, Moisiodax assures the archbishop, he will proclaim him in the preface of the book "universal benefactor of Hellas." Moisiodax does not fail, furthermore, in his letter, to assure the archbishop that the Greek Orthodox merchants of Hungary had shown themselves already "greatly willing" to assist him in his project. "Taking into account the necessary rights of civil and ecclesiastical administration," however, the deacon Iosipos the Moesiodacian thought it unfit to proceed to collect funds without informing and securing the approval of "His Eminence." Finally, Moisiodax assures the archbishop that, if granted the requested recommendation, he would make every effort to answer and silence the thoughtless critics among the Greek clergy and laymen in Hungary who were unjustifiably slandering "His Excellency's" reputation. On a broader note Moisiodax expressed his belief that the archbishop's magnanimity would willingly grant his request because with his translation the humble deacon had only attempted to fulfill an obligation prescribed by the Gospel, that is to maximize, for the benefit of his neighbors, the talent he had acquired after attending "various Gymnasia, Academies, and through private study."

The Archbishop of Karlowitz received Moisiodax's entreaty unkindly

---

[53] The letter has been simultaneously published by Miroslav Vukelić, "Ein brief des Josepos Moesiodax aus dem Jahre 1760," *Balkan Studies* 28 (1987): 59–64; Ch. K. Papastathis, "Anekdoti epistoli tou Iosipou Moisiodakos pros ton mitropolitin Karlovikion," *Aphieroma ston Emmanouil Kriara* (Thessaloniki, 1988), pp. 255–260; and Olga Cicanci, "Une lettre inédite de Joseph Moesiodax," *Revue des études Sud-Est européennes* 27 (1989): 65–71.

and refused his request. If we are to judge from the dedication of the *Moral Philosophy* to the metropolitan of Smyrna, we may suppose that the recommendation he needed was eventually granted by that prelate. The episcopal blessing apparently worked: The "system of Orthodox merchants" in the Hapsburg Empire, not only in the cities of Hungary but also in Vienna, financed the publication of the book through subscription. The abortive application to the archbishop of Karlowitz nevertheless remains an important document in Moisiodax's biography. It represents precisely the kind of evidence necessary to fill the many lacunae in his life story. The letter, assigned April 10, 1760, as its most probable date,[54] constitutes an important piece of information. First, it suggests a *terminus ante quem* for the completion of Moisiodax's translation of Muratori. Second, it adds another historic city in Central Europe to the documented places on the map of Moisiodax's wide-ranging travels. We can thus reconstruct with reasonable certainty his route in the year 1760: from his student's room in Padua early in the year Iosipos must have left for Vienna and Budapest and other cities with communities of Orthodox merchants in Hungary (Kecskemet, Tokaj, etc.), where he sounded out his prospective subscribers; then, in late March or early April, he went to Karlowitz in the hope of securing the archbishop's recommendation; after his failure there and the eventual arrival of the recommendation from Smyrna, he went back to Hungary and possibly Transylvania for the actual collection of his peculiar "alms"; later in the year he returned to Venice, probably via Trieste, to arrange for publication. In the years 1761 and 1762 he was in Venice and Padua while the two volumes of his first book were being printed.

It is important to capture the inner change that marked Iosipos's peregrinations: outwardly Deacon Iosipos might have appeared as another "itinerant monk" collecting alms, on a venerable pattern that had sustained the Orthodox patriarchates and monasteries of the Greek East since the fall of Constantinople. The difference in Moisiodax's case consisted in the purpose of his alms collecting: the aim now was no longer restoring a church, maintaining a place of holy pilgrimage, or defraying the debts of the Holy Sepulchre or some other patriarchate, but publishing a secular book. And Iosipos was carrying with him in his cassock not a holy relic or a miracle-working icon, but a manuscript in the vernacular in his own hand-writing. No wonder the Orthodox archbishop of Karlowitz found all that strange and suspicious and refused to have anything to do with it. Absorbed as he was in his own mission of cultural evangelism, Iosipos could obviously not appreciate how peculiar his projects appeared

[54] Papastathis, "Anekdoti epistoli," p. 255.

to those who had to act as guardians of the ancient tradition, with which he was breaking in many if as yet imperceptible ways.

Finally, the document adds another story of disappointment to the long record of failure by the hierarchy of the Orthodox Church to respond to Moisiodax's cultural and educational initiatives. At Karlowitz, while waiting for the audience that Archbishop Paul Nenadović never granted him, Iosipos may have made the acquaintance of Jovan Rajić (1726–1801), director of the local Serbian gymnasium of the archdiocese of Karlowitz and a distinguished Serb scholar and writer. Two years later, in 1762, Jovan Rajić had to leave his position because he came into conflict with Paul Nenadović, whom he criticized as an "enemy of learning" in his *History of the Catechism of Orthodox Serbs in the Imperial Lands*. If Iosipos's experiences at Smyrna appear to diverge so markedly from those of Dositej Obradović, then the bitter taste of his reception at Karlowitz was shared by another leader of the Serbian intellectual movement, Jovan Rajić.

Although the support of the Church remained in doubt, sympathy and understanding was readily and generously forthcoming from another quarter, according to Moisiodax's own testimony. Support for the publication of the first volume of the *Moral Philosophy* came from Greek merchants in Central Europe, most of them with origins in Northern Greece. From the list of subscribers it appears that the single largest group among them came from Moschopolis, the major commercial and cultural center in Northern Epirus, from where at about the same time the Moesiodacian scholar Daniel of Moschopolis would invite the non-Greek-speaking groups of the Balkans to Hellenize themselves. In quest of economic support for the publication, as we saw, Iosipos had visited Vienna and the Greek communities in Hungary. The journey that Moisiodax made early in 1760, despite the initial setback at Karlowitz, bore the expected fruit. Upon his return to Venice he applied for and obtained from the censor permission to publish on August 6, 1761. The response by the merchants, who eagerly enrolled as subscribers, was a true revelation for Moisiodax: "The zeal they have for the good, and the love they nurture for the Nation, astonished me. These men, whether they be rich, or whether they be moderately well-off, have only to hear the name of the common good, and they at once make a contribution."[55] In this way, Moisiodax became acquainted with "the diasporas of the Greeks."[56] This experience

---

[55] *Ithiki Philosophia*, vol. 1, p. xxxvii.

[56] Ibid., p. xiv. Moisiodax's initiative in seeking to finance the publication of his book by advance subscription was an original concept to promote book production. When he adopted the practice in 1761, he was following a quite novel approach to book marketing, initiated just a decade earlier in Greek publishing with the publication of the *Odos Mathematikis* of Methodios Anthrakitis, edited by Balanos Vasilopoulos (Venice, 1749). Moisio-

must have given him a different impression of the prospects and the appropriate social context of the Enlightenment among the Greeks from the one he had formed in Thessaloniki and Smyrna. Enlightened intellectuals could, it seemed, find social support amongst the merchant class. With his hopes rekindled, his curiosity satisfied, and his program now formulated, Moisiodax set out on his return journey.

---

dax's practice made an impression on contemporary scholars and resulted in conscious attempts to follow his example. See, for instance, Michael Georgiou from Siatista, *Alphavitarion Germanikon* (Vienna, 1768), address "to the grateful reader": "And if anyone would like to contribute, whatever he wishes, the honorable name of each one will be inscribed at the beginning of the Book, as they are in the first volume of the Moral [Philosophy] translated by Iosipos Moisiodax, and he will be given as many Books as are in accord with the proportion of the contribution made by him." The text is reproduced in Ph. Iliou, *Prosthikes stin elliniki vivliographia (1515–1799)* (Athens, 1973), pp. 192–193.

THREE

ENDEAVORS

AFTER HIS STUDIES in Padua, his journey in Central Europe, and the publication of the *Moral Philosophy*, all traces of Moisiodax are lost for three years. His return journey took him not to the Aegean, the scene of his initial educational strivings, but to the Danubian lands, whence his long peregrinations had begun. Are we to assume that after his long absence he went back to Cernavoda, clothed in the habit of the clergyman and the prestige of the "man of letters"?

The *Apology* contains many confessions about his emotional fluctuations and movements, all centered around his educational quests. In the final analysis, however, despite their strong impression of a sharpened sensitivity and individuality, they do not satisfy our curiosity about the personal details we need to form a closer acquaintance with this eloquent, but enigmatic stranger. Although he is unstinting in the information he provides about the way in which he internalized his ideological struggles and adventures, he was far less forthcoming about his personal history. The personality that emerges from his writings is contradictory. It is that of the scholar who complains that "he was reduced to being a vagabond in strange lands" because of his efforts on behalf of the enlightenment of his countrymen and his uncompromising insistence on his principles.[1] At the same time the enlightener embodies the tragic fate of the man whose detachment from the corporate structures and constraints of traditional society has reduced him to the condition of a "vagabond" who, however, gives no expression, in either his actions or his interpretation of his emotions, to a craving for return.

Nonetheless, the motives that directed his return trajectory to the Danubian provinces were not primarily emotional. He was undoubtedly attracted by the cultural climate of the Principalities and their proximity to Central Europe, especially Hungary, where Iosipos knew that he had friends and supporters. The receptivity of the Greco-Romanian society in the urban centers of the Principalities to the currents of European ideas,[2]

---

[1] *Apologia*, p. 83.

[2] See the earlier work by Pompiliu Eliade, *De l'influence française sur l'esprit publique en Roumanie* (Paris, 1898), and the valuable collection of evidence in Ariadna Camariano, *Spiritul revoluționar francez și Voltaire în limba Greacă și Română* (Bucharest, 1946), and especially the recent study by Alexandru Duțu, *Romanian Humanists and European Culture* (Bucharest, 1977), pp. 167–190.

the reforming initiatives taken by the Phanariot princes, and the strong local tradition in Greek letters,[3] readily gave an outside observer the impression that the semiautonomous Danubian provinces of the Ottoman Empire offered the most suitable environment within which a man of letters returning to the East from enlightened Europe might express his concerns. Although Moisiodax's experiences did not live up to his expectations, the image and reputation of Bucharest and Jassy as centers of Greek education and culture enjoying the patronage of the Phanariot courts were justification enough for the direction he took upon his return.

In 1765, Iosipos's trail reappears precisely where one would most logically expect to find it. He was pressed into action to participate in the program of educational reform initiated by the new prince of Moldavia, Grigorios Alexandros Ghikas III.[4] The conditions under which Moisiodax became involved in this project are not known with any certainty. His studies in the West and the reputation he had acquired after publishing the *Moral Philosophy*, which was widely read in the Principalities as a guide to intellectual development in accordance with the demands of the times,[5] had probably secured him a certain social recognition. His arguments in favor of educational renewal, developed so outspokenly in the prolegomena to this work, were apparently judged as befitting a collaborator to the prince's undertakings. The educational ideas that had influenced the prince's program were naturally not as far reaching as his own.[6] But an intention to reform education, within the more general climate of a widespread feeling that the Danubian societies were in decline,[7] certainly formed a lowest common ideological denominator to the endeavors of the reforming princes and the critically disposed scholars of this period. The ranks of the Enlightenment had not yet been broken, politically, and the vision of "enlightened despotism" was still considered a viable political project, despite all of Montesquieu's warnings. Remem-

---

[3] For the roots of this tradition in the pre-Phanariot period, see the survey by A. Karathanasis, *Oi Ellines logioi stin Vlachia (1670–1714)* (Thessaloniki, 1982).

[4] For the spirit of the reforms, see Stefan Barsanescu, "La pensée pédagogique du siècle des lumières d'après les parchemins princiers de la seconde moitié du XVIIIe siècle déstinés aux écoles. Sa genèse," in *L'époque phanariote* (Thessaloniki, 1974), pp. 57–60. For the initiatives of Grigorios Ghikas, see A. Camariano Cioran, *Les académies princières de Bucarest et de Jassy et leurs professeurs* (Thessaloniki, 1974), pp. 96–99.

[5] A. Camariano Cioran, *Les académies princières*, pp. 582–583. The esteem in which this work was held in Phanariot circles is indicated by its citation, long after Moisiodax's death and despite the prevailing silence about his more controversial works, in *Parallilon Philosophias kai Christianismou* (Constantinople, 1830), pp. 43–44.

[6] Barsanescu, "La pensée," p. 59.

[7] Cf. Vlad Georgescu, " 'Progres' et 'décadence' dans la pensée politique roumaine au XVIIIe siècle," *L'époque phanariote*, pp. 341–345.

ber that, at this period, Diderot and Voltaire were corresponding with Catherine II of Russia.

These convergences of ideology are not enough to account for Moisiodax's participation in the reform projects of Grigorios Ghikas. Thus far research has failed to pay sufficient attention to a detail contained in a major source for Greek intellectual history since the nineteenth century, a piece of information that perhaps provides a clue to the ties that led Moisiodax to the court of the prince of Moldavia. One of Grigorios Ghikas's close collaborators and advisers in his attempts at reform was his personal physician, the Thessalian man of letters Constantinos Karaioannis. This was a minor figure in the modern Greek Enlightenment, who played a leading role in introducing reforms into the Academy of Jassy. Karaioannis had been one of Voulgaris's students, possibly at the Athonite Academy and certainly in Constantinople between 1761 and 1763; he later studied in Italy at about the same time that Iosipos was there.[8] The overlapping circles in which the two scholars moved make it likely that they were acquainted with each other, and this may have been the reason Moisiodax was invited to Jassy by prince Grigorios Ghikas in 1765. If we accept the validity of this hypothesis, Karaioannis's recommendation is evidence of the respect in which Iosipos was held in the reforming circles of Greek society after he published the *Moral Philosophy*.

In the context of the reforms of Grigorios Ghikas, Moisiodax was appointed "teacher of philosophy" at the new gymnasium in Jassy in 1765, despite serious personal reservations, born of a feeling that he was "unsuited to teaching."[9] The prince had to insist to persuade Moisiodax to accept. Iosipos only accepted the appointment of director of the school after the prince had pressed him "with almost irresistible force."[10] His salary was not agreed upon until a few months later. A 1766 edict from the prince determined the salaries of the Academy's teaching staff; the salary of the "senior teacher of the sciences" was set at the sum of 1500 francs annually.[11] This rather high sum by contemporary standards might be considered an incentive proffered by the prince to induce Moisiodax to stay on in the position. Moisiodax's reservations about accepting a teaching position at the Academy of Jassy should not be taken to indicate any personal quirk of character; to the contrary, they can only be properly interpreted in the light of his conscious existential choices through

---

[8] G. Zaviras, *Nea Ellas i ellinikon theatron*, ed. G. P. Kremos (Athens, 1872), pp. 399, 404–406; C. Sathas, *Neoelliniki Philologia* (Athens, 1868), pp. 556–558 and Camariano Cioran, *Les académies princières*, pp. 95–96.

[9] *Theoria tis Geographias*, p. x.

[10] *Apologia*, p. 85, n.1.

[11] Theodoros Athanasiou, *Peri ton ellinikon scholon en Roumania, 1644–1821* (Athens, 1898), p. 46.

which he sought to formalize his ideological rejection of tradition. This ideological intent also explains why he declared his reservations in the text of the *Apology*. Clearly, if it had simply been a question of a personal idiosyncrasy, Iosipos would have had no reason to advertize it in a book in which he was attempting to save his good name from his detractors. The rejection of traditional ideology implicit in his instinctive inclination to distance himself from teaching indicates his adoption of a new attitude toward organized society as a whole and a new perception of the nature of his work. The teacher who regurgitates knowledge, thereby preserving tradition and ideological orthodoxy, is an organic member of established society and part of the mechanism of its power structure; thus, he actively contributes toward its reproduction. Moisiodax's stance appears to have been precisely the opposite. He could be seen as the man who questions traditional social sanctions and refuses to contribute to their perpetuation by playing the role assigned to him on the basis of the expectations associated with his social position. Moisiodax sought to break free from these constraints to assert his individuality. The examples of teachers that he had before him merely reinforced his reluctance: Iannakos and Ierotheos were models of the traditional educational behavior that he found intellectually repugnant. But the fate of Voulgaris, a man incomparably more influential than Moisiodax, left him in no doubt as to the difficulties in store if he wished to follow in Voulgaris's footsteps. Moisiodax moved according to an idealism firmly rooted in a practical appraisal of reality.

Moisiodax's attitude cannot be allowed to pass without comment for a further reason. From many points of view, his broad experience could be seen as a typical illustration of the social constraints upon the movement of the Enlightenment. One source of Iosipos's hesitation was probably his awareness of the lack of social support on which he could rely in order to complete the task he was undertaking. The two leading figures of the early phase of the Greek Enlightenment, Evgenios Voulgaris and Nikiphoros Theotokis, who belonged to the gentry of the Ionian islands, enjoyed backing and social protection that allowed them far wider margins of toleration within which they could articulate their dissent. Nonetheless, the opposition and pressure from their social environment compelled them to break off their advance along the road of cultural change long before the cleavages in Greek society were sharpened by the disputes that broke out after 1789. Iosipos appears to have perceived this problem quite clearly. He himself had none of those social props that would have guaranteed some toleration of his public expression of criticism. His social and ethnic origins, economic weakness, ideology of dissent, and even mobility acquired through education did not guarantee to him any firm tangible form of social sustenance. Indeed, they tended to push him to the margins of the community. His position in society was particularly fragile in relation to the various hierarchies of the social pyramid and, in the nature of things, he would inevitably have been crushed if he challenged the communal balance and ideological orthodoxy through his attitudes. The examples of Voulgaris and Theotokis, which he later invoked, confirmed his insecurity precisely because of the social gulf separating him from them. This social gulf explains why the intellectual criticism voiced by Voulgaris and Theotokis, and other members of their class, was acceptable up to a point, while in Iosipos's case it was considered intolerable and presaged his ultimate downfall.

At the Princely Academy in Jassy, Iosipos the "scholarch" was at the same time "teacher of philosophy." This meant that his teaching covered the fields of "modern" knowledge, as opposed first to courses on language and religion and second to the conventional Aristotelian program. "Philosophy" differed from these fields primarily in terms of its subject matter: instead of the grammar and rhetoric of ancient Greek, he taught modern mathematics and physics; instead of scholastic logic and ontology, he taught the principles of rationalism and empiricism. There were naturally some attendant divergences of pedagogical approach.

To some extent the new educational program represented a cultural revolution: it cracked the tradition of centuries, overthrew the unchallenged authority of Aristotle, and introduced "suspicious" innovations and ideas from the heretical West. The experiences of Anthrakitis, somewhat earlier, and of Voulgaris in the recent past left no doubt as to the significance of departures of this nature in the education of Orthodox Greeks. Moisiodax, however, having overcome his initial hesitation, committed himself wholeheartedly to the endeavor. His response to the honor conferred upon him by Grigorios Ghikas was a "violent struggle" on the intellectual battlefield. He devoted July and August 1765 to preparing his lectures, in the midst of a fierce heat wave, as he informs us, by translating André Tacquet's *Elements of Geometry*.[12] He already knew this work from Voulgaris's lectures at the Athonite Academy,[13] and now, at the beginning of his career as a teacher, he judged it suitable—in a Greek version—to replace the antiquated sources and methods used for teaching mathematics in the Greek schools;[14] he substituted it for the "incomprehensible" treatise (as he described it) by Segner, which had

---

[12] *Apologia*, p. 85, n.1. The text of this translation is probably that in Codex Ms. Gr. 1513 in the Library of the Romanian Academy. Cf. Camariano Cioran, *Les académies princières*, p. 229, n. 326.

[13] This work was published much later as *A. Takouetiou, Stoicheia Geometrias meta simeioseon tou Ouistonos exellinisthenta men ek tis latinidos phonis ypo tou Panierotatou Archiepiskopou kyriou Evgeniou tou Voulgareos* (Vienna, 1805).

[14] G. Karas, *Oi physikes-thetikes epistimes ston elliniko 18o aiona* (Athens, 1977), p. 70.

been translated and used by Voulgaris.¹⁵ He set out the precise reasons for his own choice:

> Wishing my audience to take the short path, and at the same time to reap the fruit appropriate to their time and their need, I decided in the end to translate some writer on mathematics who, being comprehensive, clear, unembellished and therefore very brief, would answer the precise needs of either this or that part of my goal. I translated at one time the *Elements* of André Tacquet, up to and including Trigonometry itself; and because the great man proceeds in precisely the same way as Euclid, and is for this reason the most accurate of all the modern mathematicians, and because, indeed, physicists are wont to cite geometric propositions invariably according to his order, I wanted for all these reasons to teach him.¹⁶

This explanation of his reasons for preferring Tacquet reveals Moisiodax's methodical approach to teaching. Basing himself on this translation, Moisiodax taught geometry at the Princely Academy at Jassy until the spring of 1766. A note in a manuscript containing treatises on mathematics in the library of the Romanian Academy of Sciences gives the precise date on which his lectures began: "1766, January 19, Thursday, the teacher Master Joseph began to teach Geometry in Moldavia, in the church of the papists."¹⁷

His course of lectures and his tenure of the position of director commenced in the autumn of 1765 with two inaugural public addresses; he delivered, "in imitation of the Europeans," a lecture "on philosophy in general" and another "on mathematics in particular."¹⁸ Before he had even presented the texts of his lectures, Moisiodax made clear his intention to introduce to the Greek East not only the spirit but also the forms and the customs of European academic life.¹⁹ With its more general content and interest, the initial lecture on philosophy was delivered in the prince's court, the "Princely Porte" of Jassy "in the presence of His Highness Grigorios Alexandros Ghikas, and of the entire body of the most eminent aristocracy of Moldavia."²⁰ It was followed by his introductory lecture on mathematics, with which Iosipos began his course in the gymnasium of Jassy. Moisiodax clearly stated the spirit underlying the choice of subject for these two lectures:

---

¹⁵ *Apologia*, pp. 35–36.
¹⁶ Ibid., p. 37.
¹⁷ Z. Mourouti-Genakou, *O Nikiphoros Theotokis (1731–1800) kai i symvoli aftou eis tin paideian tou Genous* (Athens, 1979), p. 119, n.260.
¹⁸ *Apologia*, pp. 85–86.
¹⁹ Ibid., pp. 79–80, n.2.
²⁰ Ibid., p. 95.

Philosophy and Mathematics were at that time acclaimed in Moldavia, but not by that token well known; reason therefore recommended that each lecture should be woven together in the most beneficial manner—that is, part narrative and part argument. Any other, more novel form of lecture was likely to be both unclear, and uncongenial to the audience, because, if exception is made of two or four persons, all the rest were totally unversed in either Philosophy or Mathematics.[21]

His introductory discourse on the science of mathematics was an entirely professional account of the nature of the field. By way of introduction, he identified mathematics as one of the five branches of "philosophy" (ethics, physics, metaphysics, logic, and mathematics) and briefly defined its object as "quantity, abstractly considered."[22] He followed this with a clear historical review of the evolution of the science of mathematics, in which he extolled in particular the contribution of the ancient Greeks and warmly praised the "work of the genius and of the invincible diligence of the Moderns."[23] He proclaimed the usefulness of mathematics, observing that "in truth, no other science sharpens or regulates the mind through the purity of truth, as does this one." After a brief reference to the methods of mathematics, the new director closed his lecture by warning of the difficulty of the course and simultaneously asserting that there were ways of overcoming this, chiefly through the use of effective, modern teaching methods and hard work on the part of the students: "good things are not acquired save by sweat."[24]

His lecture "on philosophy in general" is one of the most genuine manifestos of the spirit of the Enlightenment in Greek intellectual life. Both in its theoretical assumptions and fundamental positions and in its conception and organization of the particular issues, it clearly expresses Moisiodax's unequivocal espousal of the philosophy of the Enlightenment. This fine text condenses in the Greek language all the fundamental tenets of the Enlightenment.[25]

Moisiodax began his lecture by noting the natural human proclivity to knowledge, "because everything implants in a man the desire for learning." He immediately warns, however, of the difficulties surrounding the quest for knowledge and the probing of the true nature of things:

> Nature seems to have wished to tease man; wherefore she gave him no other guide than the deceptive perception of the senses which, because it repre-

[21] Ibid., p. 86.
[22] Ibid., p. 88.
[23] Ibid., p. 92.
[24] Ibid., p. 94; see the complete text, pp. 87–94.
[25] Ibid., pp. 95–131.

sents things to him now in this wise, now in that wise, continuously deceives him. Nor is this enough. As if the deception of the senses were not enough for him, man then takes pains to ensure that he deceives himself. Prejudice, preference, bias, laziness, excessive curiosity, indiscretion, all these are so many other means whereby man deludes himself.[26]

The point of departure for Moisiodax's philosophical concerns can be traced in the epistemology of Locke, which had become the common philosophical heritage of the European Enlightenment. This transpires from his identification of the worst form of self-deception among those that torment mankind: "And patience, if self-deception merely deluded man; but delusion begets superstition, that most destructive of Furies, which maddens nations and at times makes cemeteries of cities."[27] These comments reveal Moisiodax's aims, at the level of his work as both teacher and scholar and at the level of ideological polemic. The desire to dispel the many different manifestations of delusion led to his enlistment in the cause of the Enlightenment. With all the optimism and faith of the committed intellectual, having identified the problem, he immediately pointed to its solution, taking his clue from the foremost case in which the historical experience of the rejection of delusion provided palpable evidence of the consequences: "This indispensable, this undeceiving guide, then, is sound Philosophy, that Philosophy, I say, by the strength of cultivating which Europe has recently been restored, becoming, instead of a land of misfortune, a land of ignorance, a land without charm, as it was not so long ago, the most blessed, the most beautiful, the most learned region in the entire world."[28] The purpose of Moisiodax's lecture, then, was to reveal what "sound philosophy" is,[29] and he sought to establish it as the foundation of contemporary Greek culture, by adducing in its favor the most convincing arguments possible before his "distinguished audience." Consequently, he founded both the definition of sound philosophy and his arguments in support of it on the concepts of human happiness and social utility. Moisiodax and his contemporary Dimitrios Katartzis (c. 1730–1807) may be regarded as the most representative Greek spokesmen for Enlightenment utilitarianism in the Phanariot society of the Danubian principalities.[30] In the final analysis,

[26] Ibid., p. 96.
[27] Ibid., p. 97.
[28] Ibid., p. 98.

[29] On the notion of a sound philosophy (*hygiēs philosophia*) in Moisiodax, cf. G. P. Henderson, *The Revival of Greek Thought, 1620–1830* (Edinburgh and London 1971), pp. 92–95. Cf. P. Kondylis, *Neoellinikos Diaphotismos. Oi philosophikes idees* (Athens, 1988), pp. 27–31.

[30] Cf. P. M. Kitromilides, *Tradition, Enlightenment and Revolution: Ideological Change*

however, the utility of sound philosophy lies in its liberating effects, which release the creative forces of human thought:

> Sound Philosophy, then, is a comprehensive theory, which investigates the nature of things always with an eye to their end, so that it preserves, it promotes the true happiness that mankind, as mankind, can enjoy upon the earth. . . . Itself a lover of what is useful, of what is needful, it shuns all useless talk and, taking into account the needs that encompass our lives on all sides, and also the brevity of this life, pursues only the necessary things, only the useful things of life. . . . A hater of tyranny, having struggled indomitably and steadfastly against prejudice, and having crushed that yoke strangling the work of Philosophy, it proclaimed all its followers free men. Plato, Aristotle, Leibniz, Newton, and all those whose fame resounds in the theater of learning, all these it glorifies and immortalizes, but none of them does it call distinguished merely on the grounds of *ipse dixit*.[31]

Of interest in these views is the secular and this-worldly orientation of Moisiodax's thought and the abandonment of the transcendental values that had been imposed on philosophical thought by its incorporation into Christian metaphysics. Iosipos's break with the prevalent religious tradition was revealed both by the recognition of earthly happiness as an intrinsic value and by the elevation of the brevity of life to the level of a decisive factor in determining the priorities of human action. In both these claims he echoed the secularism of the Enlightenment as reflected in the ideal of human happiness.[32] Furthermore, he unequivocally rejected the authority of tradition by denouncing *ipse dixit* as a source of knowledge and as sound proof in philosophical argument. The resulting philosophical position, that is, "sound philosophy," was nothing other than a secular, practical and utilitarian, liberal intellectual posture.

Moisiodax's lecture on sound philosophy was divided into two parts. In the first, he generally reviewed the five branches of knowledge of which sound philosophy is comprised: "Ethics, Metaphysics, Physics, Mathematics, Logical Criticism are mainly its most comprehensive parts." In his exposition of the basic principles and content of these sciences, Moisiodax adopted the Enlightenment's epistemological conception about their object and methods, as opposed to the neo-Aristotelian

---

in *Eighteenth and Nineteenth Century Greece* (Ph.D. diss., Harvard University, 1978), pp. 206–207, 340–341.

[31] *Apologia*, pp. 98–99.

[32] Cf. the classic study of R. Mauzi, *L'idée du bonheur dans la littérature et la pensée française au dix-huitième siècle* (Paris, 1960), and P. Hazard, *European Thought in the Eighteenth Century* (Gloucester, Mass., 1973), pp. 14–25. The most eloquent echo of this in Greek thought was contained in the work of Athanasios Psalidas, *Alithis evdaimonia itoi vasis pasis thriskeias* (Vienna, 1791).

concept prevailing in contemporary Greek education. After referring to the variety of different applications of mathematics, he added: "And here, one cannot but pity the condition of the schools in the Greece of today. These schools are unheeding of the academic exhortation: *Let no one unversed in geometry enter*, and remain deaf to the young, who cry: nature is incomprehensible without teaching—and yet they exhaust all their zeal in quest for words. And behold one of the most crucial causes of the lack of learning, which prevails, which may prevail for no short time in this wretched, this lamentable climate of ours."[33] His reference to logic, finally, begins with a similar critique of Greek educational practice:

> We come to the last level of Philosophy, Logic. This Logic is new in every way; I do not mean that Peripatetic Logic which even now echoes through the schools of the scholastic philosophers, and upon which the scholastics lavish names such as the key, the hand, the advance guard, the instrument of philosophy, the guide, and many similar praises. That Logic has grown old, has fallen into decay, and in like wise as the weapons used of old, is of no use today, except as an indication of the dialectical quarrels of the ancients. The Logic we are discussing, speaks here and now, is called Logical Criticism* to distinguish it, and is divided in all into five sections, or parts. Logical Criticism investigates, in the first part, what is the mind, what are its illnesses and what its treatments; whence springs ignorance, whence delusion, which, once it has set in, holds back the mind, like a fog, from the brightness of truth. It investigates in the second part what are the origins, what the nature, what the kinds of complex ideas; what and how many are the kinds of propositions. It interprets how sciences are to be approached, how and when particular authors can be read, how the terms by which things are expressed must be capable of being understood. It investigates in the third part what is truth, what is falsehood, how and when the mind inclines toward the truth; what is the correct use of the senses; how are the sacred books to be understood, how to be interpreted. It investigates in the fourth part the nature of reflection, lists all the different kinds of it, interprets the use of it, checks the intricate plots of sophistry, and many other such. Logical Criticism investigates in the fifth place what is the much vaunted method, divides it into analysis and synthesis; it teaches what is the former, what the latter; it teaches, finally, what is the art of dialectic, what are the laws, what the rules according to which debates are conducted and should always be conducted.[34]
>
> * The term Logical Criticism is given to this science because, in a way, as the highest critic, it surveys or judges all the sciences, all the liberal arts,

---

[33] *Apologia*, p. 118.
[34] Ibid., pp. 120–121.

examining either their subjects, or their proper structures or presentations. As regards the other treatises that are known under this name, much is said of the *Logical Criticism* of Antonio Genovesi, whose *Metaphysics*, albeit in the first edition, was translated and taught by the illustrious Evgenios, partly while he was in Ioannina and partly in Kozani. I say in the first edition because the distinguished Genovesi later expanded the *Metaphysics* to four times its size, and if the wise man had written elsewhere, there is certainly no doubt that he would have composed a complete treatise on metaphysics, and of such a kind as required by truth, or by the need for the true enlightenment of mankind. The term Logical Criticism could similarly be applied to the *Logic* of the illustrious Evgenios, at least to most of it. I think that anyone would conclude from this that such treatises should be approached after the completion of the other sciences, and that, whenever they are taught before the other sciences, the order is reversed, and that consequently the benefit derived from them is very little. The reason that Logical Criticism, which alone can properly be called Logic, is mentioned here at the last is simply the reason I note above. But of this, more, perhaps, elsewhere.

The second part of his lecture directly posed the question: How is sound philosophy to be acquired? Returning insistently to its social utility and to the constructive example of the historical experience of the European nations, Iosipos unequivocally identified the greatest obstacle in the way of sound philosophy: this, he stressed, consisted of the prejudices and superstitions of all kinds on which obscurantism and self-deception rest: "How much superfluous piety, finally, how much excess in our way of life predominates among us, which, however, are not even perceived by us, because ignorance does not permit them to be perceived!"[35] The solution to this problem, according to Iosipos, might be a general mobilization in the cause of cultural change and reconstruction so that the foundations of delusion could be removed and the agencies of change—"schools, academies, libraries, and whatever contributes to the cultivation of the intellect"[36]—could be supported so as to bear fruit. Moisiodax did not doubt that the struggle would be hard and that its outcome would not be decided exclusively in the field of education but in the wider context of social alignments and cleavages. He had in mind the example of Voulgaris at the Athonite Academy and referred to it toward the end of the lecture in a dramatic apostrophe. Still at the outset of his own endeavors, he himself, however, seemed determined to fight on by placing his hope in the support of the enlightened princes who had enlisted him in this enterprise.

[35] Ibid., p. 127.
[36] Ibid., p. 128.

Despite its expressions of goodwill to the Phanariot establishment of Moldavia, the inaugural address was, in terms of the cultural realities of the period, a quite radical proclamation. With his ideas and his outspokenness Moisiodax called for a "cultural revolution" that, as far as his own personal involvement was concerned, was to last for almost one and a half decades in the area of the Danubian principalities. From the very beginning there was no shortage of adverse comments, and the immediate occasion for them was his inaugural lecture: "I do not recall what was said then about these two lectures, but idle prattle did not leave them unsullied."[37] Iosipos ignored them all and threw himself into his new teaching vocation. During the academic year 1765–1766 he taught mathematics and more specifically geometry at the Princely Academy at Jassy; he used Tacquet's work that he had translated the previous summer. He also taught philosophy by using his own Greek edition of Muratori. It is worth noting that this was the first time that a modern philosophical text had been introduced into the curriculum of the Princely Academy.[38]

Iosipos, devoting all his energies to the task he had undertaken, seems to have worked very hard that winter. As a result, he seriously damaged his health and the following spring developed the symptoms of tuberculosis, which ultimately compelled him to resign the directorship. He himself comments on this development:

> At the onset of spring I began to feel a slight burning, combined with a dry, though not a violent cough; which burning ran ceaselessly through my body, and when the dog-days were upon us, I began to spit blood. I sought the advice of the doctors who were in Jassy at that time, and they all told me that my complaint was the beginning of consumption, and that if I wanted public esteem, I would have to die a consumptive in the school, and if I wanted life, I would have to resign from the school. Of the two evils in question, I chose the lesser and resigned from the school. This, in the main, was the true cause of my resignation at that time, though society did not fail, as is its wont, to perpetrate other rumours about me on this occasion too.[39]

The pragmatism with which Iosipos dealt with the deterioration of his health is noteworthy. Freed from traditional constraints and compulsions, and with his feet firmly anchored in his secular ideals, he unhesitatingly chose life and the restoration of his health as the greater good. The public affirmation of these values and their philosophical basis and

---

[37] Ibid., p. 86.

[38] Camariano Cioran, *Les académies princières*, pp. 222–223. Cf. Panayiotis Kodrikas, *Meleti tis koinis ellinikis dialektou* (Paris, 1818), p. xxiv: "The first person to attempt to give philosophical lessons in the demotic idiom, from a teacher's chair, was Iosipos Moisiodax, when he was scholarch of the Princely Academy at Jassy."

[39] *Apologia*, pp. 85–86, n.1.

practical applications, so unhesitatingly made by Iosipos, drew him ineluctably into ideological confrontation and social conflict.

During his directorship of the Academy at Jassy, in 1765–1766, Iosipos experienced his first involvement in ideological controversy, with a traditionalist priest.[40] The circumstances are recorded in general terms by Iosipos himself, though he does not supply enough factual details. His views in support of the philosophy of the moderns, which were already known through his pronouncements in the introduction to the *Moral Philosophy*, had apparently rendered him suspect in the eyes of conservative circles, while, at the same time, his own uncompromising attitude had fueled the confrontation. This was the background to his dispute with the anonymous priest—the "most reverend Such-and-such," as he calls him to conceal his opponent's identity. This conflict prompted Iosipos to produce the kernel of the *Apology*. From the details he gives in his account of this episode and its effects on his personal disposition and reactions, one may conclude that the composition of the *Apology* was a long-term, gradually evolving program that lasted, presumably with interruptions, from 1765, when his first polemical pamphlet appeared in manuscript form, until the publication of the first volume of the work in 1780.

At some point during the early phase of his directorship of the Academy in Jassy in 1765, a learned priest came to the city. According to Moisiodax, he was well known among the circles of Greek men of letters,[41] and Iosipos paid him a courtesy visit. The meeting developed into a dispute over the value of modern philosophy. The priest supported the views of Aristotle on natural philosophy, a circumstance that irritated Iosipos and prompted him to refute them; consequently, his interlocutor accused him of holding pro-Catholic religious views. The divergence of philosophical views took a personal turn and culminated in a polemic against Moisiodax, who felt obliged to defend himself: "This bitter slander, which struck at the heart of my reputation, disturbed me greatly, and obliged me to defend both the Philosophy of the Moderns and my own innocence, by means of the present account."[42] As he informs us, he circulated this account of the incident in six copies among the learned circles in Jassy—"to the princely court, to the doctors, and to the noble

---

[40] The episode may be dated with some accuracy because Iosipos, in the *Apology*, gives us both the *terminus post quem*, after he assumed his duties at Jassy for the first time, and the *terminus ante quem*, before the publication of Nikiphoros Theotokis's *Stoicheia Physikis* (Leipzig, 1766). See also *Apologia*, p. 153, n.1.

[41] The biographical details relating to "Such-and-such" given by Iosipos are insufficient for us to attempt an identification with any reliability. The only unequivocal statement refers to the age of "Such-and-such": he was seventy-five years old in 1765. See *Apologia*, p. 135, n.1. Various other hints in the text suggest that "Such-and-such" probably came from Ioannina in Epirus; see pp. 136 and 153.

[42] *Apologia*, p. 134.

households."[43] This gesture could be seen as the starting point of what was described by later historians as "the battle of the pamphlets," which was one means of making public the ideological conflict between the Enlightenment and its critics.

Iosipos's text was composed of two sections: first, a series of specific philosophical and scientific rebuttals confronted the Aristotelian views advanced by the "most reverend Such-and-such" during their discussion; and second, his own counterarguments culminated in a more general proclamation of the principles of the Moderns in the quarrel of the Ancients and Moderns. The Aristotelian positions that Moisiodax was concerned to refute were presented systematically in the form of general premises, followed by Iosipos's own counterpropositions. They are appended here as a specific example of the content of the disputes between eighteenth-century men of letters, against the background of the confrontation between neo-Aristotelianism and modern philosophy and science:

PREMISE:
   That prime matter and form are contemporary with each other.
   First proposition: that the formless, the unshaped, the prime matter of Aristotle, or however else you Aristotelians are wont to call it, is completely impossible.
   Second proposition: that form is completely impossible.

PREMISE:
   That whatever does not have pores is indivisible.
   First proposition: that atoms, considered as atoms, are always possible.
   Second proposition: that of all the natural principles that are referred to by Philosophy, the atoms are the ones that are first, most acceptable, and second, most appropriate to the evolution of things.
   Last proposition: that atoms are set in motion by God, and that I am not dealing in theology, but in physics, in holding that God is the cause of the movement of atoms.

The "demonstrations" and "comments" by means of which Moisiodax refutes the probability of the Aristotelian view on prime matter and form and supports the opinion of the Moderns on atoms illustrate well his views on natural philosophy.[44] For the historian of science they may constitute evidence of the stirrings in Greek culture of a modern conception of nature that resulted from contact with the achievements of European science. Moisiodax, a representative of the natural philosophy of the Enlightenment, was one of the earlier interpreters of the new scientific language in Balkan culture in the middle of the eighteenth century.

After refuting the Aristotelian theses and projecting the ideas of mod-

---

[43] Ibid., p. 137. For the text "I Ekthesis i i Apologia i pros ton Ieromenon," see pp. 135–172.
[44] Ibid., pp. 139–152.

ern science, the text of Moisiodax's *Apology* culminated in an ideological counterattack. This section of the text marked the point at which the argument of the entire work reached a climax and showed Iosipos to be a virtuoso polemicist on behalf of the Enlightenment. In the first part of the pamphlet, Moisiodax had confined himself to the context of the quarrel of the Ancients and Moderns, the formal content of which was precisely the kind of learned dispute that he had fought with Such-and-such. In the second part, however, Iosipos brought out the broader ramifications that represented the real stakes in the quarrel, above and beyond the symbolism of the scientific discussion. Beginning with a defence of the Moderns and indignant at the imputations of the priest, who had described the Moderns as "blockheads,"[45] he extolled the achievements of modern civilization, especially the progress achieved by the Moderns in solving the riddles of nature and improving technological accomplishments. He attributed the hostility of the Aristotelians toward the Moderns to simple ignorance and self-interest, hinted that their motives were political, and alleged that they attempted to exercise ideological control by exploiting religious fears. Finally, having once more drawn attention to their self-deluding ignorance in questions of physics and astronomy, which could be exposed "easily by both reason and experience,"[46] he did not hesitate to repeat the comment with which he had prefaced his translation of the *Moral Philosophy*: "Yes, your Reverence, I do not hesitate to state that Greece does, does need Europe, because whereas Greece is lacking in everything, Europe abounds in everything."[47] The candor of this response represented not only an element in Moisiodax's psychological disposition but also an ideological stance. In combination, they produced a personality radically at variance with the mentality and behavior defined by convention as socially acceptable. This contrast contained within it the dynamic of the future conflict that sealed Moisiodax's personal fate and eventually determined his place in the modern Greek intellectual tradition.

Iosipos provides no clue concerning his movements after his resignation from the Princely Academy and departure from Jassy, nor does he tell us by what means he sought to restore his shattered health. All traces of him are effectively lost for the next ten years. A contributing factor to this was the general confusion in the Principalities created by the Russo-Turkish war of 1768–1774. The Danubian territories were a main theater of war: Russian forces invaded in 1769, and Moldavia and Wallachia were occupied by the Russians until the conclusion of the Treaty of Kutchuk Kainardji in 1774. It may seem peculiar that these major convulsions find

[45] Ibid., pp. 152–154.
[46] Ibid., p. 160.
[47] Ibid., pp. 165–166. *Ithiki Philosophia*, vol. 1, p. xx.

no echo in Moisiodax's work, though at the same time this could indicate his total absorption in his studies, following his retreat from public life.[48]

On the very eve of the outbreak of the war, Iosipos was in Bucharest. No doubt his search for a healthier and warmer climate had led him southward to Wallachia, far away from the "by nature sickly," the unhealthy climate of Jassy. In Bucharest he worked on his lecture notes and composed the first draft of his geographical treatise. The manuscript has survived in an autograph codex in the library of the Monastery of Saint Panteleimon on Mount Athos, and the title page gives the exact date of its composition: *"Theory of Geography composed by Iosipos Moisiodax. In the year 1767, September 15. In Bucharest of Hungary-Wallachia."*[49] This evidence provides the chronological background to his statement in the *Apology* that at some point he had written the *Geography* in Wallachia.[50] In fact, he taught this text when he returned to the Academy in Jassy in 1776, and he quoted a number of passages from it in his *Apology*.[51]

The manuscript of the *Theory of Geography* furnishes another important biographical detail that has hitherto been unnoticed by students of Moisiodax's life. The text of the treatise is prefixed by a brief dedication to an eminent prelate, who is not named, but to whom Iosipos expresses his gratitude for the benevolence he had shown him:[52]

> *Your Beatitude:*
> *Behold, most reverend Lord, a small labor that I have already completed, and which my duty obliges me to offer to your Beatitude. When I consider its extreme simplicity, I do not know the words with which to accompany it to make it seem in any way worthier. The benevolence with which your Beatitude has from the beginning put me in your debt may as well commend to your attention the work proffered.*
>
> > *Your Beatitude's most pious and humble servant*
> > *Iosipos the Moesiodacian*

The title "beatitude" employed by Iosipos in his address to the unnamed prelate makes it clear that the dedication was intended for one of the Orthodox patriarchs of the East. This must presumably have been the learned patriarch of Jerusalem, Ephraim II, the Athenian, who had been

---

[48] See M. S. Anderson, *Europe in the Eighteenth Century* (London, 1961), pp. 188–192. Isabel de Madariaga, *Russia in the Age of Catherine the Great* (London, 1981), pp. 205–214.

[49] See S. Lambros, *Catalogue of the Greek Manuscripts on Mount Athos* (Cambridge, 1900), vol. 2, p. 424, no. 6256. The date is given on p. 1 of the manuscript.

[50] *Apologia*, p. 41. See also *Theoria tis Geographias*, p. 37.

[51] *Apologia*, pp. 61–79.

[52] Ms. *Theoria tis Geographias syggrapheisa par' Iosipou tou Moisiodakos*, pp. 3–4.

elected head of the Church of Sion in 1766 and the following year visited Wallachia on a pastoral tour to collect alms for his church. The connection between Iosipos and the scholar-patriarch revealed by the brief dedication of the first draft of the *Geography* adds another important eighteenth-century figure to the circle of his acquaintances. Iosipos probably rested some hopes of economic assistance for the publication of his work on the goodwill of the patriarch; undoubtedly he remembered the support obtained from Ephraim that same year by Neophytos Kafsokalyvitis (1713–1784), another contemporary Greek scholar active in Wallachia, for the publication of his *Grammar*.[53] Iosipos's hope was not fulfilled, perhaps owing to the departure of the patriarch from Wallachia on account of the outbreak of the war, but more probably owing to the reservations that the modern scientific contents of the book might well have aroused in him. As a result, Iosipos's ambitions for its publication were postponed for more than ten years, and when he did finally publish it, the support came not from patriarchs or princes, but from merchants.

For nine years after his resignation from the position of director of the academy in Jassy, Moisiodax seems to have had the opportunity to devote himself to the independent study of mathematics and physics and to writing. Evidence of this devotion emerges both from the manuscript of 1767 and the works he published in 1779 and from his extensive publication program announced in 1781, when he stated that he had a whole series of scientific treatises ready for the printers.[54] These works could have been written neither after he renewed his educational activities in 1776–1777 nor during the turmoil of ideological dispute, persecution, and wandering of the following three years. One may therefore suppose that, in the interval separating his two periods as director at Jassy, a time he probably spent in Bucharest, the independent intellectual Moisiodax was able to satisfy his deeply felt craving to immerse himself "in mathematics and in physics, always in private and primarily for one's own use."[55] He no doubt earned his living by giving private lessons in "noble households" in Wallachia. Such tutoring was probably made possible as the center of gravity of the Phanariot society had shifted to the Principalities since the early part of the century: not only might a Greek-speaking scholar be in demand as a private tutor in the polished society, but also receptivity to European culture was observable in the area during the years that Moisiodax was there in need of employment. This climate turned the Principalities into the most culturally active region in Southeastern Europe in the decades preceding the French Revolution.

[53] Camariano Cioran, *Les académies princières*, p. 415.
[54] *Theoria tis Geographias*, p. ix.
[55] *Apologia*, p. 41.

FOUR

THE CRISIS

IOSIPOS REAPPEARED on the stage of Greek culture in 1776, when he left Wallachia to seek the protection of the prince of Moldavia, his former patron, Grigorios Alexandros Ghikas, who had returned to the Moldavian throne in 1773. He viewed his obligation to leave Bucharest and the independent life of study and writing as a great misfortune.[1] In Jassy surprises were in store for him. The position of scholarch of the Princely Academy had just fallen vacant, upon the departure of Nikiphoros Theotokis—an event precipitated by scheming and machinations against him, as Iosipos implies.[2] The prince and his court at once offered the post to Moisiodax, who responded by voicing his two reservations with great candor: "First, because I felt in myself an opposition, which was almost insuperable, to the assumption of teaching duties, and second, because I always suspected that I would fall foul of what I eventually did indeed fall foul of."[3] He clearly states the source of these suspicions:

> Recalling the many machinations that were practiced first against the wise Evgenios on the Mountain, and second against the eminent Nikiphoros in this very school at Jassy, whom noble origins, eloquence, erudition and many other good qualities had been unable to protect against the wicked attacks, and reflecting also that I was inferior in every way to these distinguished men, and consequently would of necessity suffer worse things, I

---

[1] *Apologia*, pp. 38–39: "Driven by my most malign fate (how else am I to express it?) from Wallachia, I had recourse to the strong protection of the then ruler of Moldavia, the late Grigorios Alexandros Ghikas, beseeching as a suppliant the favorable influence of his highness."

[2] See Z. Mourouti-Genakou, *O Nikiphoros Theotokis (1731–1800) kai i symvoli aftou eis tin paideian tou Genous* (Athens, 1979), pp. 119–125, and A. Camariano Cioran, *Les académies princières de Bucarest et de Jassy et leurs professeurs* (Thessaloniki, 1974), pp. 561–563. It is remarkable that on both occasions that Moisiodax was invited to assume the directorship of the Princely Academy of Jassy, in 1765 and 1776, he succeeded Nikiphoros Theotokis, who was leaving because of reactions against the modern scientific content of his teaching. Because Moisiodax was clearly not a conciliatory man, nor one to make compromises, his presence exacerbated the situation and resulted in his reaping the fruits of the crisis.

[3] *Apologia*, p. 41.

rose up and requested the eminent rulers to secure the services of another philosopher.[4]

But the pressures brought to bear and the promises held out by the powerful overcame Moisiodax's resistance. In the end he seems to have been persuaded by the intervention of Christodoulos of Kastoria, the third logothete at the court of Moldavia, and of Gabriel Kallimachis, metropolitan of Moldavia. Regarding both these magnates as friends and patrons, Iosipos placed his faith in their "sworn promises" that "at no time, and in no way, shall I come to harm" and accepted the post of scholarch and professor of philosophy—that is, of modern natural science. After the necessary agreements had been transacted with the trustees of the Academy, Moisiodax assumed his new responsibilities. His recent studies had convinced him that Tacquet's book, which he had translated and used as a teaching aid during his first professorship at Jassy, was not, after all, suitable, and he reached an agreement with the governing body of the school that he should spend the first two months of his new term of office translating the *Mathematical Way* by the famous French mathematician and astronomer, Jean André Nicolas Louis de La Caille (1713–1762), a work he judged more appropriate and useful for teaching purposes:

> The author, then, that I tried to render, was Jean André de la Caille, a Frenchman by descent and a professor of Mathematics and Astronomy in Mazarin's Academy in Paris, an eminent man, like no other, in both branches of his profession, and a respected member of all the most prominent academies of Europe. Whoever, out of curiosity, desires to see, in Jassy, the titles in which this philosopher rejoices, all of them according to merit, let him scrutinize the title page or the beginning of his *Mathematical Way*, which is in the possession of the learned Ioannis Kallousios, respected teacher attached to the most reverend metropolitan of Moldavia, Gabriel Kallimachis, and my true, honorable and charming friend. The most illustrious de la Caille deals in two very small volumes with every aspect of mathematical analysis and synthesis, beginning by way of introduction with Arithmetic, and progressing to the subsequent subjects, always applying himself according to the capacity of his listeners to understand. Comparing the quantity of the entire treatise with the time required to teach it, and teach it in an unhurried and complete manner, I considered that it could all be taught in ten and six months at the most, without any burden on either the audience or the teachers.[5]

Moisiodax taught at the Princely Academy of Jassy for four months after completing his translation of de la Caille. His teaching program included

---

[4] Ibid., p. 39.
[5] Ibid., pp. 37–38.

daily lectures dealing on alternate days with topics in mathematics and geography according to the wishes of his audience. He delivered fifty-five lectures: the twenty-seven in geography were based on his treatise on *Geography*, which he had completed Bucharest in 1767, and the twenty-eight in mathematics were based on his translation of de La Caille.[6] Despite his antipathy for ex cathedra teaching, which had engendered in him his belief that he was "by nature unsuited to school teaching," he devoted to his duties all the care and methodicalness inculcated in him by his scientific training:

> The moderate mind that I inherited from nature, the continuous irregularity of my life, and many other factors of which I do not speak, did not permit me to prosper, like others, either in mathematics or in physics. To these should also be added the decision to which I always held, that is, that I would never take upon myself instruction in Philosophy, or the systematic teaching of Philosophy: for what reason? First, because I felt in myself an opposition, which was almost insuperable, for the teaching profession, and second, because I always suspected that I would fall foul of what I eventually did indeed fall foul of. These two reasons, and the ones I have just stated above, made me always involve myself in mathematics and physics only in part, and for my own private use, not for the common use, as I would certainly have had to do if I had made a profession of it, particularly the assumption of public teaching duties. Nevertheless, though my nature was such, I did not despair of being successful in teaching. If I study (so I would tell myself) each lecture carefully and put together the appropriate items in each of them, and do this fully, clearly, and plainly, always employing a teaching style suitable to my listeners' powers of comprehension, why should I not be successful?[7]

This approach to the irksome and difficult task, for which he felt an almost instinctive repugnance, clearly reveals the practical philosophy of the man of the Enlightenment, who was convinced that nothing was inaccessible to the practice of sound method and the application of the rules of reason.

However, neither Iosipos's academic stature, which in the judgment of the prince and the trustees of the school was equal to that of Nikiphoros Theotokis, nor his personal dedication and conscientious efforts to teach the sciences as effectively as possible could mitigate the reactions of the opponents of educational reform. This, indeed, had been his fear from the beginning. The defenders of strict grammatical schooling and the use of the ancient language in modern Greek education had obliged the "em-

---

[6] See the texts of his lectures in ibid., pp. 43–60.
[7] Ibid., p. 41.

inent" Theotokis, whose connections with the social and ecclesiastical hierarchy were solid and impeccable, to depart "by night, like a fugitive from the school at Jassy" because "he was so cast down by this most unworthy behavior."[8] Iosipos—a man without roots, with fewer and more tenuous connections, and furthermore an uncompromising ideologue in favor of modern philosophy—naturally neither expected nor received a better reception: "I had scarcely made a beginning with my teaching, when all kinds of machinations began to be practiced against me."[9]

The polemic against Moisiodax took two forms. From his own account it emerges that the usual ideological charges and personal abuse were unleashed against him, as against other proponents of modern philosophy and science before and after him. Already, in his earlier dispute with the anonymous priest, against whom he had circulated his critical rejoinder, Iosipos had been accused of being pro-Catholic because of his preference for European education. The charge of heterodoxy, the first step in a potential stigmatization for atheism, with the serious personal dangers and the enormous social cost attendant upon it, had been an almost classic method of social control in traditional culture. It had been in evidence in Greek society since the time of Methodios Anthrakitis and even the days of Theophilos Corydaleus. Moisiodax had suitably replied to this accusation in the first version of his *Apology*.[10] In its new form, the indictment against him drew its content more directly from the substantive points at issue in the specific ideological dispute, although it was formulated as a series of personal barbs that betrayed his enemies' considerable ideological insecurity. Iosipos lists the charges against him on the first page of the introduction to the *Apology*:

> The idle prattle, a plague almost inseparable from our schools, and especially from the grammar schools, became public, and becoming public, convinced people: first, that my lessons were of a "grocery-store level"; second, that I write and teach in the simple style because I do not comprehend ancient Greek; and third, that I do not teach the *Logic* of the illustrious Evgenios because, likewise, I do not comprehend it.[11]

The charge that his lessons were of a "grocery-store" level was an expression of the traditionalists' ideological disdain for scientific knowledge and mathematics; these pursuits they regarded as vulgar, fit only for grocers and men concerned with the keeping of accounts, and consequently alien to the proper, normative content of higher education, which could be nothing other than the venerable and dignified Aristotelian philosophy.

---

[8] Ibid., p. 82.
[9] Ibid., p. 39.
[10] Ibid., pp. 164–170.
[11] Ibid., p. iii.

This attitude on the part of the Aristotelians toward scientific knowledge is delightfully described by Moisiodax, who adds the following anecdote:

> Why are you spending your time in vain?—certain scurrilous individuals would ask the audience. Do you want arithmetic? Here are the grocers of the Three Hierarchs,* make them your teachers if you want to learn arithmetic in a short time and accurately. This criticism was also leveled against the distinguished Evgenios when, after his unworthy experience in the Mountain, he became scholarch in Constantinople; here the insolence of certain evil-minded grammarians reached the point where they sent to the wise man a grocer, not in order to learn, but mainly to discuss arithmetic, holding in his hands a filthy copy of Glizounis, and giving off the compound stench of his trade at a distance of at least fifteen or eighteen feet.[12]

* The Three Hierarchs is one of the most famous monasteries in the city of Jassy, both within and without which grocers are always to be found in plenty.

The connection drawn between his own experience and that of his teacher was meant not only to silence his accusers, by showing that Moisiodax and Voulgaris had the same enemies and were therefore aligned on the same side in the ideological conflict, but also directly revealed the sophistry and bad faith involved in the third charge. The second accusation leveled against him, however, questioned his linguistic preferences; it contained a personal innuendo that went beyond the cleavages of the language question. Moisiodax was, of course, one of the first thinkers to endeavor to establish the modern Greek vernacular as the language of Greek education, and he attempted to develop theoretical arguments, mainly of a pedagogical and social content, in support of this view. His specific ideas were never developed as fully as the more advanced views on language voiced by his contemporary, Dimitrios Katartzis. Whereas Katartzis's writings on this subject remained unpublished and accessible only to a narrow circle of followers,[13] Moisiodax was the first to have the courage to proclaim his views officially from his professorial chair, practice them in his teaching, and give them wide publicity by committing his writings to print. Likewise, on the issue of the language he diverged radically from Voulgaris, who had insisted on the use of ancient Greek, despite his leanings toward philosophical rationalism. Moisiodax's ene-

---

[12] Ibid., pp. 81–82. The *Glizounis* referred to in the text was the most widely used popular book of arithmetic during the Tourkokratia and formed a simple introduction to the four mathematical operations. See G. Karas, *Oi physikes-thetikes epistimes ston elliniko 18° aiona* (Athens, 1977), pp. 74–75.

[13] On the personality of Katartzis, the importance of his work, and his eloquent silence, see C. Th. Dimaras, *Neoellinikos Diaphotismos* (Athens, 1977), pp. 177–243, and G. P. Henderson, *The Revival of Greek Thought* (Albany, N.Y., 1970), pp. 78–85.

mies in this matter did not confine themselves to ideological polemic but slid into bigotry by asserting that the reason he sought to simplify the language was that he did not understand ancient Greek. This point contained a clear reference to his non-Greek descent; the hint was repeated four decades later by Panayiotis Kodrikas during the heated debates over the language question at the height of the Greek Enlightenment.

> The man was indeed erudite. He had a knowledge of many foreign languages, and had been excellently educated in the basic sciences in the academies of Western Europe. But he was a foreigner to the nation of Greeks by birth and consequently had not tasted the milk of a Greek upbringing. For him the Greek language was a question of learning and study and not naturally acquired by habit and use since infancy. His sight and mind were trained in the reading of ancient authors. But his hearing was not accustomed to the harmony of the language of the Modern Greeks. It was not easy for him, therefore, either to imitate the accomplished style of writers, or to express himself properly in the simple demotic language. As a result, he had recourse to the familiar resort of semi-educated pedagogues: that the language commonly spoken by the Modern Greeks is corrupted and in need of correction. And he himself attempted to make, in his own opinion, what he imagined to be the correction. He thus wrote in an arbitrary language. It is, of course, easier to correct a living, spoken language according to one's opinion and imagination, than to practice and speak the common idiom of the nation. He assumed as a principle and basis for his linguistic theory that we should speak as we write, and he took as the archetypal model of how we should write his own ill-founded style, which he had arbitrarily invented. As soon as it appeared, however, this arbitrary style was by common consent pronounced vulgar and suitable for grocers, as being illegitimately born, and unsuited to the character of the common dialect. And he himself, having of his own accord resigned from the position of scholarch, took pleasure in publishing his *Apology* in two volumes (in 8º); while his creation was strangled at birth, by common opinion, as a monster.[14]

The student of the formation of Modern Greek consciousness cannot fail to note at this point the distant origins of a strain of intolerance, which would never recognize the right of public criticism and would counter disagreement by stigmatizing the motives of dissenters and seeking their moral ostracism from the community of the true faithful, or later, patriotic Greeks. The fact that Moisiodax's critics attempted to stigmatize his

---

[14] P. Kodrikas, *Meleti tis koinis ellinikis dialektou* (Paris, 1818), pp. xxv–xxvi. Kodrikas's attitude, almost half a century after the crisis of 1776–1777, repeats the condemnation of Moisiodax's teaching and to some extent represents a refutation of the hopes of cultural evangelism, expressed in the *Eisagogiki Didaskalia* in 1802. However, cf. also the criticism of Kodrikas's position in the journal *Ermis o Logios* 9 (1819): 577.

views on the language question by linking them to his ethnic origin was an example of ideological bigotry, which responded to dissent with arguments ad hominem without connection to the substantive questions at issue.

The second form taken by the polemic against Moisiodax at the Princely Academy at Jassy was much baser than the criticism of the content of his courses; it took the simple and vulgar form of the disruption of his teaching: "Whenever the incessant noise in that school, noise invariably maliciously contrived, whenever the continuous commotion, which unceasingly shook my suffering mind, either through calumnies, or through the naive credence that was lightly accorded to these calumnies; whenever, I say, these two causes of difficulty permitted, I attended carefully to my lectures."[15] These attempts to undermine his work formed the background against which Iosipos carried out his duties during his second period as scholarch at Jassy. Apparently foremost among those who sought to undermine him was another member of the teaching staff of the Academy; he does not name this professor of grammar and a supporter of traditional learning, but, in Moisiodax's judgment,[16] he was a mediocre scholar in his own field, who enjoyed considerable support from the powerful. Reluctant from the beginning to become involved in teaching, Moisiodax lost no time in tendering his resignation, on the grounds of his colleague's subversive activities.

It is possible at this point to trace the coordinates of ideological conflict in the society of the Danubian principalities: a teacher of natural philosophy and a teacher of grammar were competing for influence in the field of advanced education, each of them supported by a section of the social hierarchy. In Moisiodax's case, we know that the social support for scientific knowledge and the ideology of reform reached as high as the immediate circle around the prince and the summit of the ecclesiastical hierarchy. Despite their support, however, which certainly prevented his withdrawal on two occasions, the ultimate failure of his endeavors and his personal humiliation could not be averted. On the contrary, it was achieved with impressive swiftness: within the space of six months, Iosipos was obliged to submit his resignation on three occasions. The struggle had proved unequal, and those in the social hierarchy who favored cultural change turned out to be of doubtful effectiveness and commitment. It is true that scientific teaching did not disappear from the Academy: Moisiodax was succeeded as director by Prokopios the Peloponnesian, "a young man, well-trained in Physics and Mathematics," who had

---

[15] *Apologia*, pp. 41–42.
[16] Ibid., p. 40, n.1.

studied in the West.[17] The latter's tenure of the post of scholarch guaranteed some continuity to the program of his predecessor and allowed the reformers of Jassy a certain satisfaction. Nevertheless, immediately after Iosipos's withdrawal, the Academy fell into disrepute. This was, at least, the impression of a contemporary witness, Jean Louis Carra, who spent a year at the court of Grigorios Ghikas as his French secretary and preceptor to his sons, probably during the prince's last year in office (1776–1777). Carra notes that at the school of Jassy, "to which they gave the pompous name Gymnasium, . . . two or three ignorant monks gave lessons in the Latin and Greek languages and in theology."[18] Apparently Carra arrived in Jassy after Moisiodax's departure; in his text there is no evidence that he ever met him, and his description of the teaching staff at the Academy could hardly be compatible with the image that Iosipos created there. With Moisiodax's departure, his pioneering spirit of renewal, his strong commitment to his task, and his vision of a new secular humanism in Southeastern Europe reached their limits. His experience revealed just how constrained these limits were within the social reality of the period.

Moisiodax himself, of course, did not abandon the struggle. His decision to carry on is reflected in his last act before leaving the Academy for ever. He circulated six autograph copies of the texts of his lectures, which he had asked his students to sign and thereby authenticate them as true records of his courses.[19] At the moment of his departure, Iosipos thus secured solemn evidence in writing of the scholarly quality of his teaching. By publicizing these texts and submitting them to the community's judgment, he could counter the deprecatory comparisons leveled against him by his enemies. This last act, however, determined the nature of the struggle in which Moisiodax had become embroiled. The signatures of his pupils were collected as evidence in an endeavor to restore his personal reputation and damaged professional respectability. The struggle did not become collective; rather, it continued as an individual attempt to secure personal rehabilitation. This explains why the *Apology*, the crowning moment of this individual struggle, is a peculiar and idiosyncratic work, infused with an intensely personal tone. By extension, nevertheless, these events reflect some broader social cleavages that were reflected in Moisiodax's case, to which we shall return.

After his adventures in Jassy and the traumatic experience of his triple resignation, Iosipos sought refuge and relaxation in 1777 in Braşov, on the northern slopes of the Transylvanian Alps, which divided Ottoman

---

[17] Ibid., pp. 26, 166, n.2. For Moisiodax's successor, see Camariano Cioran, *Les académies princières*, pp. 610–611.

[18] Jean Louis Carra, *Histoire de la Moldavie et de la Valachie* (Neuchâtel, 1781), p. 186.

[19] *Apologia*, p. 42, n.1.

Wallachia from the Hapsburg territory of Transylvania. In the context of the situation at the time, Moisiodax's move to Braşov has a complex symbolic significance that has not, however, been appreciated by his biographers. Braşov, in its beautiful valley, was noted as a summer resort. Because of its geopolitical position, across the Hapsburg-Ottoman frontier, moreover, the city formed a refuge for all those who had fallen from favor and were being persecuted for challenging the political status quo in the Principalities and seeking to change it in various ways. For example, all the boyars who had sided with the Russians in the Russo-Turkish war of 1768–1774 migrated there in mass.[20] The fact that Moisiodax withdrew here after his experience in Jassy gives rise to the interesting hypothesis that his move was not unconnected with the political change in Moldavia after the fall of Grigorios Ghikas in 1777. There could, however, be a more substantial reason to explain Moisiodax's move to Braşov. The city formed the opening link in the network of the Greek commercial communities in Transylvania and Hungary, where Iosipos had many friends, whom he had invariably found understanding about and supportive of his endeavors. Braşov, in particular, was the headquarters of one of the most important Greek companies in Transylvania. As noted earlier, among its members the Greek company of Braşov counted several merchants from Moisiodax's native Cernavoda.[21] The move to this city was thus for Moisiodax a return to the bosom of a society he could trust after his disappointment at the courts of the princes.

Nonetheless, his stay at Braşov had another minor adventure in store

[20] See Vlad Georgescu, *Political Ideas and the Enlightenment in the Romanian Principalities (1750–1831)* (New York, 1971), pp. 28–29.

[21] The phenomenon of the Greek diaspora in Central Europe was of such historical importance that it attracted the interest of research at quite an early date. The pioneering work was the study by Spyridon Lambros, "Selides ek tis istorias tou en Ouggaria kai Afstria makedonikou ellinismou," *Neos Ellinomnimon* 8 (1911): pp. 257–300. The density of Greek colonization in Hungary may be seen from the evidence assembled by Lambros, and published as "Erevnai en tais vivliothikais kai archeiois Romis, Venetias, Voudapestis kai Viennis," *Neos Ellinomnimon* 17 (1923): 113–139, 368–386, 18 (1924): 276–291, 374–382, and 19 (1925): 225–232. See also Th. N. Natsinas, *Oi Makedones pramateftades eis tas choras Afstrias kai Ouggarias* (Thessaloniki, 1958), and Odon Füves, *Oi Ellines tis Ouggarias* (Thessaloniki, 1965), with Hungarian bibliography. For Transylvania, in particular, see N. Camariano, "L'organisation et l'activité culturelle de la compagnie des marchands grecs de Sibiu," *Balcania* 6 (1943): 201–241; Cornelia Papacostea-Danielopolu, "L'organisation de la compagnie grecque de Braşov (1777–1850)," *Balkan Studies* 14 (1973): 313–323; and Olga Cicanci, *Companile greceşti din Transilvania şi comertul european în anii 1636–1746* (Bucharest, 1981), esp. pp. 101, 137, 155, on the merchants from Cernavoda at Braşov. See also K. Hitchins, *The Rumanian National Movement in Transylvania 1780–1849* (Cambridge, Mass., 1969), pp. 138, 157, on the role of the Greek merchants of Braşov. For the general historical significance of the phenomenon, the best work is still the classic study by Traian Stoianovich, "The Conquering Balkan Orthodox Merchant," *The Journal of Economic History* 20 (June 1960): 234–313.

for him. In 1777 he met there the "legendary"physician, doctor Theodorakis.[22] Although on the basis of the available evidence it is not possible to identify this figure with any precision, Moisiodax's account leaves no doubt that he was an imposing personality in the Principalities. Katartzis also mentions him as a contemporary, an important man of learning, and author of works in the Atticizing style.[23] Iosipos discussed a variety of scientific subjects with him:

> The man was good at mathematics, good at medicine, good at the languages of Europe as well, and had a bombastic manner in his speaking, which he was wont to regulate always in a new and unusual way because Asiatics always like to speak in this manner, which made the man even more imposing. This great man, however, this very great man, was not himself in Physics, Hydraulics, Statics, Mechanics, and other general theories, which are of undoubted relevance to Medicine, and which all those who profess to be theoretical doctors certainly ought to know, all of these things were hidden from him. . . . He greatly wanted to become legendary as the man who knew everything, and, moreover, having a high opinion of his deep wisdom, and being *infatué de son éminent savoir*, as the French say, he deliberately annihilated and shouted down all our prominent scholars. . . . He sought in all things to emulate Phoebus in prophesying, and to be unquestioned, and if anyone ventured to oppose him, the earth was consumed with fire. He shouted, he swore, he cried "rubbish!" He became sarcastic.[24]

To avoid a clash with this awesome man, Moisiodax began tacitly to avoid his company, but this did not avert the dispute. Doctor Theodorakis, offended by Moisiodax's behavior, began to accuse, slander, and threaten him: "There were none, whether they knew me or not, to whom he did not paint me in the most repulsive of colors and insults."[25] Thus, quite unexpectedly, Moisiodax had found another persecutor in the ranks of the powerful and become embroiled unwittingly in yet another scientific dispute, for Doctor Theodorakis accused him of being ignorant with regard to a range of natural phenomena. This gave rise to indignation in Moisiodax's professional conscience. He drew up a synopsis of the discussions and the four points of disagreement between himself and Doctor Theodorakis. Invoking right reason and continuous empirical observation,[26] he defended his own views and refuted the unscientific theories of his accuser. In Moisiodax's judgment, Theodorakis's views bore no relation to scientific fact and consisted of nothing more than monstrous con-

[22] *Apologia*, p. 85.
[23] D. Katartzis, *Ta Evriskomena*, ed. C. Th. Dimaras (Athens, 1970), p. 8.
[24] *Apologia*, pp. 173–174.
[25] Ibid., p. 174.
[26] Ibid., p. 190.

jectures and astrological beliefs, with which "His Excellency" the "wise doctor," having "felt the pulse of his naive associates and seeing that they relish monstrous conjectures, always intones to them monstrous conjectures."[27] Finally, he decided to send his "essay" to his new adversary on the eve of his departure from Braşov, certain of the doctor's reaction but confident, too, that science would prevail against the pseudoscience of conceited sages:

> I am certain that your excellency, with the unanimous agreement, of course, of those fine gentlemen, your excellency's admirable companions, will deploy against this essay all that your genius is capable of devising and deploying. But your excellency may be sure that the day will in the end come when those who pass judgment on our difference will not be so-and-so and such-and-such, whose worth is all cubits and rupees, or pigs and sheep, but men of wisdom, men of integrity, whose votes, even if they are not held in respect by your self-esteem, will nevertheless be held in respect by all who respect the truth.[28]

Precisely to these judges Iosipos was addressing himself, when he invited them to judge his essay and decide "which one of us, I or the late Theodorakis, is the more credible, and whether the late man spoke justly against me."[29]

Iosipos's judgment of Theodorakis should be viewed against the evidence of another contemporary, Jean Louis Carra. The French secretary's assessment of the society of the Principalities did not lack anything in its harshness when compared to that of Moisiodax, and he was especially severe in condemning what he judged the corrupting presence of the Greeks in the area.[30] Yet amidst the general malaise brought upon the Danubian lands by "oriental despotism," Carra could distinguish four men, "privileged by nature," who stood out among the "barbaric and idiotic multitude of monks, people and boyars."[31] Three of these persons Carra had met in Jassy and the fourth in Bucharest. Foremost among them was Jassy's "celebrated physician called Theodorati," whom Carra describes: "Theodorati speaks, writes, and translates perfectly the French, Latin, Greek, and Turkish languages; but his greatest talent consists in being singularly versed in geometry and algebra; his least talent consists in being probably the most skillful physician in the Ottoman Empire. Boerhaave and Astruc are equally familiar to him as Homer; nothing is more

---

[27] Ibid., p. 176.
[28] Ibid., p. 190.
[29] Ibid., p. 174.
[30] Carra, *Histoire de la Moldavie*, pp. 171, 190–191.
[31] Ibid., pp. 162, 188–189. The rendering of the name as "Theodorati" in Carra's text was probably a misprinting.

foreign to him than the absurdities of superstition and scholasticism."[32] When this testimony is set alongside that of Moisiodax, little doubt is left that he and Carra are describing the same man: both acknowledge his social prominence as well as his competence in mathematics and medicine and his linguistic prodigy.

But their appraisals appear to diverge over Theodorakis's attitude to the scientific interpretation of natural phenomena. Carra categorically describes him as a proponent of modern scientific knowledge: he not only knew well the work of Boerhaave and Jean Astruc, those lights of eighteenth-century medicine, but he was also unequivocally described as an enemy of scholasticism and superstition. Over these points Moisiodax seems to diverge from Carra's assessment and charges that Theodorakis tended to indulge in astrological and unscientific interpretations of natural phenomena to please the ignorance of his sycophants. Moisiodax, of course, does not claim that Theodorakis was an Aristotelian—as some others of his intellectual rivals had been—but he imputes to him a certain intellectual opportunism, stemming from inadequate knowledge of physics. Thus, the substance of the two testimonies does not differ, but the image of Theodorakis that emerges from their respective narratives does. The difference in image might be attributed to Carra's possible superficiality as a judge of character. Theodorakis, certainly an imposing personality by both accounts, does not appear to have had a kind and appealing character. This, however, should not obscure the fact that Iosipos in his turn, either by psychological predisposition—a certain contentiousness in his character—or through an intellectual inflexibility equal to that of his opponent's, unfailingly tended to be embroiled in quarrels and disputes that eventually earned him the reputation of "disorderliness."

Iosipos's disputes, first with the anonymous priest in 1765, then with the teachers of the school at the monastery of Saint Savvas, at this same period—whose hostility Nikiphoros Theotokis had also experienced—[33] with his conservative colleagues at the Princely Academy in 1776, who ultimately obliged him to resign, and with Theodorakis in 1777, leave us with the impression that the major crisis in his relations with his social environment was primarily ideological in character. Because these disputes have come down to us only through Moisiodax's own accounts, we tend to understand them largely in his own terms as an intellectual contest between the proponents of traditional and modern learning. The sheer power of Iosipos's prose, his sensitivity and commitment, tend not only to win the reader over to his point of view but also to extend a rather attractive invitation for a "whig interpretation" of the whole story of the

[32] Ibid., pp. 188–189.
[33] See Z. Mourouti-Genakou, *O Nikiphoros Theotokis*, p. 119, n.261.

Enlightenment in the Balkans. It is easy and natural to succumb to this temptation because Moisiodax and the other followers of modern scientific and liberal ideas are the harbingers of our own world. They, not their rivals, speak to us more directly and are therefore more persuasive. The task of historical analysis should nevertheless be to rescue the significance of the point of view of Moisiodax's and the Enlightenment's opponents as well. The "Enlightenment" and the "Counter Enlightenment"—or what I have described as the conventional or traditional view—formed essentially alternative approaches to a shared intellectual past and a common future in Greek, and more generally Balkan, society. The novelty, the exceptionality, occasionally the inflexibility of the stands of the proponents of the Enlightenment themselves provoked suspicions and reactions from all those who could not understand what the new ideas meant, and they remained attached to known and familiar ways of thought and practice. Until at least 1789 this often tended to be the case. After that year the impact of the French Revolution changed the picture in significant ways and transformed the earlier alignments of alternative intellectual points of view into political cleavage and conflict.

Moisiodax, therefore, and before him Evgenios Voulgaris and Nikiphoros Theotokis—to mention just two of the best-known representatives of the battles of the Enlightenment in the mid-eighteenth century in Southeastern Europe—contributed through their very intellectual positions to the precipitation of ideological cleavages that brought about their downfall. Difficult as it is for the modern observer to grasp the point of view of their adversaries, retrograde and obscurantist as it might appear to us, it could still have its own inner logic, which often was none other than the pragmatic and empiricist logic of genuine conservative conviction. Captivated by the magic of the new ideas and enthused by the prospect of a new civilization, the followers of the Enlightenment often failed to capture this logic or rejected it as backward-looking or, as Moisiodax did, self-interested and dishonest. This attitude, however, engendered to a considerable degree the rigidity of reaction that undermined the prospects of the Enlightenment.

Yet the cleavage was not always simply ideological. The story with Theodorakis makes this quite plain. Although Iosipos does not appear willing to admit it, his difference with the "legendary doctor," whose fame "resounded throughout Wallachia and Moldavia,"[34] could not have been as radical in scientific terms as he implies. Theodorakis was after all a follower of the Moderns like Moisiodax; only his knowledge of physics was not up to Iosipos's professional standard, and of course the doctor's vanity would not let him admit it. Their quarrel could therefore be seen

---

[34] *Apologia*, p. 173.

as arising from different social attitudes. The fight appeared essentially over their respective positions in society: Theodorakis would not tolerate being challenged by a Moesiodacian whom he considered his social inferior, and Iosipos would not suffer being humiliated by someone—however powerful—whom he considered to have no more than pseudoscientific pretences. To unravel the riddle of Moisiodax's biography we must now attempt to interpret this social aspect of the conflict.

Iosipos's clash with the famous doctor, which in a way marked the climax of the crisis in his relations with the milieu of the Principalities, could be explained as merely a symbolic expression of a deeper cleavage that was gradually opening up between two social worlds. Iosipos's opposition was directed at the mores, attitudes, and mechanisms of social control—which did not exclude violence, as hinted in his description of the doctor's reaction—that defined the character of the society in which his rival was so highly acclaimed. In Doctor Theodorakis, Iosipos perceived a typical representative of a world that he found repugnant: "Character, friendship, age, in short, whatever once restrained the most insolent of men, were all reckoned as secondary to his disdainful, his unrestrained impetuosity. The unwarranted vanity of the man, in short, reached the point of paranoia."[35] Moisiodax apparently considered this ethos typical of the higher echelons of the Greco-Romanian society of the Principalities. In that world, the right to be different was not recognized, the social hierarchy was inviolable and unrelenting, and arrogance and conceit were socially sanctioned standards of conduct for the powerful. This source of authoritarianism formed the essential content of social ideology. In this context, human behavior was regulated on the basis of patron-client relations and networks of dependence on which the social pyramid was erected.[36] The prevailing social expectation was that intellectuals would adjust to the existing clientele networks, solicit the patronage of the powerful, and contribute to the reproduction of the dominant values and norms of behavior. Any deviation from one's predetermined social calling and any expression of dissent provoked reactions like that of Doctor Theodorakis to Moisiodax: "His remorselessness reached the point where he defamed me before the military governor of the place himself, and even threatened me with exile."[37]

During the twenty years of his maturity, Iosipos moved in the Greco-Romanian Phanariot environment, which functioned and reproduced itself through the mechanisms described above. The term "Phanariots" denotes the group of families, mostly of Greek origin, resident in the

---

[35] Ibid., p. 174.

[36] See A. Duțu, *Romanian Humanists and European Culture* (Bucharest, 1977), pp. 120–121, 124–125.

[37] *Apologia*, p. 174.

quarter known as Phanari in Constantinople, where the Ecumenical Patriarchate had been located since 1599. Phanariot society had, over a period of two centuries, firmly rooted itself in the Romanian lands, and the Greek officials and professionals had been integrated with the Romanian landed boyars into a unified society. The Phanariots had risen to political prominence in the Ottoman Empire during the later part of the seventeenth century through service to the Sublime Porte. From among the Phanariot families the Porte, as the sovereign power over the Principalities of Wallachia and Moldavia, appointed hospodars (governors) to the two provinces in the period from 1711 to 1821. This was the era of the political ascendancy of the Phanariots in the Principalities, but their historical presence there extended considerably both before and after those dates.

The psychological insecurity attendant upon the initial settlement of the first Greek families in the sixteenth century had, by the beginning of the eighteenth, been replaced by a feeling of complete adjustment and acclimatization. Thus, in 1578, a Greek lady wrote from Bucharest: "This country is not our heritage; today we are and tomorrow we are not; we are in the appointing of God and the hands of the Turks, and we do not know in the end where we will be."[38] In 1719, also from Bucharest, a Greek man of letters wrote: "All the Phanar is here; I no longer remember the City [Constantinople]."[39] The consolidation of Phanariot society in the Principalities, and the feeling that it had found in the Danubian lands the natural environment in which to develop, were owing to its intermixture with the native landed estate of the boyars. The conjunction was made possible and legitimized by the common ideological heritage of Orthodox Christianity shared by the Greeks and the Romanians. The spiritual patrimony of the Orthodox Church found fertile soil in the Danubian principalities, already under the pre-Phanariot princes in the late seventeenth century, especially during the reign of Constantine Brancoveanu in Wallachia (1688–1714). The greatest flourishing of an integral post-Byzantine culture, so eloquently described by Nicolae Iorga as "Byzance après Byzance," came under the Phanariots.[40]

[38] C. Th. Dimaras, ed., *Neoelliniki epistolographia* (Athens, 1955), p. 10. Cf. E. Stanescu, "Préphanariotes et Phanariotes dans la vision de la société roumaine les XVIIe–XVIIIe siècles," in *L'époque phanariote* (Thessaloniki, 1974), pp. 347–358, where the attitude and disposition underlying this uncertainty are discussed.

[39] Eudoxiu de Hurmuzaki, *Documente privitoare la istoria Românilor*, vol. 14: *Documente Grecești*, ed. N. Iorga (Bucharest, 1917), Part 2, p. 847. For both the quantitative parameters of the phenomenon at the political level and the forms of interpenetration on which the Greco-Romanian Phanariot society was based, cf. Ion Ionascu, "Le degré de l'influence des Grecs des principautés roumaines dans la vie politique de ces pays," in *L'époque phanariote*, pp. 217–228.

[40] N. Iorga, *Byzance après Byzance* (Bucharest, 1935), pp. 126–200. At roughly the same

The social osmosis this produced nonetheless set in motion processes of social change that critically effected Phanariot society: the settlement of the Phanariots in the Principalities and their adoption of forms of social behavior and values akin to those of the local landed gentry transformed the original character of the Phanariot social group, which had been based initially on commerce, finance, and the scientific professions (medicine, diplomacy), and gave it the stamp of the closed society of the Romanian landowners. In its new environment Phanariot society assimilated the attitudes, mentality, and norms of control and reproduction prevailing among the feudal aristocracy of Eastern Europe.[41] The Phanariots, as bearers of the Ottoman administration, brought in turn to this environment the ethics of court dealings and intrigue essential for survival in the shadow of Ottoman despotism during the period of its decline. As a result of a complex process of inner transformation and assimilation, came to be forged the social traits of Phanariotism, which

---

time as Iorga, a young Greek historian was making similar observations on the creation of a unified Greco-Romanian society in the Principalities. See N. G. Svoronos, "O Dionysios Photeinos kai to istorikon ergon aftou," *Ellinika* 10 (1937–1938): 133–136, 168–178. Regarding Moldavia, in particular, see Ekkehard Völkl, "Die griechische Kultur in der Moldau während der Phanariotenzeit (1711–1821)," *Sudöst-Forschungen* 26 (1967): 102–139. This cultural integration is disputed by V. Georgescu, *Political Ideas and the Enlightenment in the Romanian Principalities*, pp. 76–77, who attempts to emphasize the Romanian national color of the culture of the Principalities by both stressing the opposition or the indifference of Romanian intellectuals to Greek influences and playing down the appeal of Greek intellectual currents and movements in the Principalities. These views, however, are contradicted by the evidence itself, for behind the Romanized names and Romanian titles of books in Georgescu's account, anyone who knows the history of Greek letters has no difficulty in detecting the original Greek versions. The most authoritative sources on the extent of Greek cultural influence in Wallachia and Moldavia are the several specialized studies by Cornelia Papacostea-Danielopolu. See especially *Literatura în limba greacă din principatele române* (1774–1830) (Bucharest, 1982), which brings together the findings and conclusions of many years of research. This important cultural configuration is appraised by W. Theodor Elwert, "Zur griechisch-rumänischen Symbiose der Phanariotenzeit," *Beiträge zur Südosteuropa-Forschung* (Munich, 1966), pp. 391–402.

[41] The use of the term feudalism (féodalité) in describing the society of the Principalities belongs to an eighteenth-century French observer with first-hand knowledge of the subject. See Alexandre-Maurice Blanc de Lanautte, Comte d'Hauterive, *Mémoire sur l'état ancien et actuel de la Moldavie, présenté à S. A. S. Prince Alexandre Ipsilandy Hospodar Régnant 1787* (Bucharest, 1902), pp. 78–82, 160–164. Cf. R. Okey, *Eastern Europe, 1740–1980: Feudalism to Communism* (London, 1982), pp. 13–34, and P.F. Sugar, *South Eastern Europe under Ottoman rule, 1354–1804* (Seattle, 1977), pp. 126–141. On the feudal model, see also R. Rosdolsky, "On the Nature of Peasant Serfdom in Central and Eastern Europe," *Journal of Central and East European Affairs* 12 (1952–1953): 128–139. For the nature of the society of the Principalities and the profound contradictions in its social structure, see Radu Florescu, "The Fanariot Regime in the Danubian Principalities," *Balkan Studies* 9 (1968): 301–318.

provided the target of attack or caricature in the nineteenth century, for both Greek and Romanian authors.[42]

Phanariot society, despite its many contradictions and inner cleavages, took the lead in opening the Principalities to Western European culture and moving toward the currents of new ideas. It built upon the foundation of policies in favor of education and culture laid both by Romanian princes such as Brancoveanu and Cantemir and by the Greeks who succeeded them, beginning with Nikolaos Mavrokordatos, who inaugurated the century of Phanariot rule in the Principalities. Nikolaos Mavrokordatos, repeatedly prince of Moldavia and Wallachia between 1709 and 1730, and his son Constantinos, who became prince of Wallachia five times and prince of Moldavia three times between 1730 and 1762, proved great reformers, who introduced the theory and practice of enlightened despotism to the Principalities. The reforming spirit of enlightened absolutism could be seen as continuing the modernizing traits of the Phanariots as a social group, which had marked their seventeenth-century experience. The prestige attendant upon the endeavor to draw close to the European cultural experience and the wind of intellectual change that had brought the ideas of Voltaire to Jassy[43] and turned Bucharest into the most important center of the Enlightenment in Southeastern Europe in the second half of the eighteenth century, attracted the Greek men of letters to the courts and the academies of the princes. Moisiodax was one of them.

How closely integrated into this social world Moisiodax had become and how intimate a knowledge of its inner workings he had acquired would probably transpire more clearly if we consider the following hypothesis concerning the motives of his movements in the decade after his first tenure of the post of scholarch at the Academy of Jassy in 1765–1766. That first professional appointment bestowed upon him by Prince Grigorios Ghikas permanently attached Moisiodax to the retinue of that prince during the succeeding ten years. As a client—albeit an unwilling one according to his own protestations—of the prince, Moisiodax had to share his changing fortunes as well. His movements in the Principalities follow closely the footsteps of the prince's political career: Grigorios Ghikas held the throne of Moldavia in 1764–1767, when he first invited Iosipos to his court. In 1768–1769 the prince was transferred to Wallachia:

[42] For a sensible historical appraisal and a discussion of conflicting views and interpretations, see Cyril Mango, "The Phanariots and the Byzantine Tradition," *Byzantium and its Image* (London, 1984), study no. XVIII. See also the balanced appraisal by Andrei Pippidi, "Phanar, Phanariote, Phanariotisme," in his collection *Hommes et idées du Sud-Est européen à l'aube de l'âge moderne* (Bucharest, 1980), pp. 341–350.

[43] Carra, *Histoire de la Moldavie*, p. 196.

Moisiodax was there with him. During the Russian occupation of the Principalities (1770–1774) Grigorios Ghikas, with the tacit approval of the Sublime Porte, remained in Bucharest as an observer of the Russian military governor. Moisiodax was probably close by, only to be summoned to Jassy when Grigorios Ghikas resumed the office of hospodar of Moldavia (1774–1777). Moisiodax's flight from Jassy to Braşov in 1777 coincided with the disgrace and execution of the prince in that year. It is likely that once the prince was gone, Moisiodax, who had already resigned from the directorship of the Academy found it prudent to leave the city as well. The hospodar and his scholarch were driven from Jassy at the same time—the standard practice in the principalities upon the deposition of a prince.[44] Moisiodax's frustration at the constraints of his social environment, which forced the intellectual to become the client of the powerful in order to survive, thus sealing his personal fate, was passionately voiced in his criticism.

His critique was premised on a picture of the social behavior and ethics of the Phanariot power structure of the Principalities, which ranged from the vanity of outward appearance to the boastful arrogance displayed by members of the aristocracy toward those whom they considered their social inferiors. It is worth examining this picture: "Those parents who have the brilliant fortune to be wealthy consider it a necessary law of their condition that they should attire their children in the latest modes of clothing, and keep them stuffed inside Indian fabrics, *kakoumia* and *samouria*, embellished, moreover, with knives and rings: in short, all the things that ingenuity, that an excess of vanity devises daily to manufacture."[45] Vanity, concern for fashion, and an ostentatious appearance were merely the external dimensions of the social behavior that called forth Iosipos's disapproval. The daily occupations of the "noble" members of Phanariot society—horses, hunting, and card playing—aroused the same revulsion: "If I were a father, a rich father, of course, I would never consent to treat my child with such manner of treatment that I would then see it proud, vain, and, moreover, not knowing how to talk of anything other than carriages, horses, saddles, bridles: that is, that I would see it rustic, unlearned, like the grooms and coachmen who would be working for it."[46] He observed caustically that these occupations lead to both material and moral ruin.

The Phanariot "gentlemen," he insinuates, lack the cold calculation typical of the bourgeois mentality. Their behavior shows that they were the victims of their own unbridled appetites:

---

[44] See d'Hauterive, *Mémoire*, p. 202.
[45] *Paidagogia*, pp. 27–28
[46] Ibid., p. 31.

There are some who neglect their own affairs and the public weal, and spend their nights and days, and frequently the entire day and night, playing cards. There are also some who, tormented by the fire of greed, or turned into animals by fear of loss, no longer observe any bounds of decorum or self-restraint. They swear, they sneer, they use foul language, they grow angry: every kind of blasphemy, of oath: every act of shamelessness, of thoughtlessness is excusable as far as they are concerned.[47]

In addition to playing cards, the "gentlemen" found another way to squander their time: "In the burning heat and the dust of summer, in the ice and the snow of winter, they chase hares every day through the forests, and their financial affairs, or their business deals they hand over to servants, or officials, who mismanage the matters entrusted to them, each in his own way, and for the most part reduce things to complete chaos."[48] In these pursuits the "gentlemen" were surrounded by "the pestilential," by the destructive "parties of wickedness":

These are the parasites, the clowns, the flatterers, the buffoons, and others, with whose names I do not deign to bespatter my papers. The table of almost every famous, wealthy gentleman nourishes some of these scum, and every aristocratic house has, so it is said, for the sake of company, its own evil-livers, whom, moreover, it honors and calls "intimate friends." No dinner party is ever held at which men of this kind are not present, where they are not invited in advance and are considered to be the seasoning, the soul of the feast. No hunt or excursion into the countryside ever takes place without their being included, riding on horses, or in splendid carriages, assuming an air of equal importance to the gentlemen who include them in their party.[49]

Surrounded by flatterers, who cultivate the worst side of his character, the "gentleman" assumes an attitude similar to theirs:

The roughness of some of them, which does not allow them to consider what others like or dislike, the vanity, which persuades them to seek only their own interest, the contemptuous arrogance, which convinces them that everyone is indebted to them, while they owe nothing to others, the contentious, censuring, ironical spirit, which derides and condemns everything, and makes no effort save to be irksome: all these are features of rustic boorishness. . . . Nobility consists of nothing more than a knowledge of the duties demanded by civil behavior, and then the performance of them. How can a young gentleman be reckoned more bearable than a peasant, when the nobleman himself, a mocker, a derider of all formalities and of all reason, and

[47] Ibid., p. 43.
[48] Ibid., p. 46.
[49] Ibid., p. 47.

a despiser of all those with whose honor he considers himself at liberty to toy, proves to be a burden, an object of disgust even, to every gathering, every company? . . . As for myself, I now prefer the company of a rustic who, though his conversation may be heavy, does not offend with his character, rather than have anything to do with a gentleman, even an erudite one, when this same nobleman obliges me to stand with my mind suspended, on guard, and compels me through his wicked rustic boorishness to be careful of my every word, my every movement.[50]

Moisiodax's testimony has been set out at some length because it constitutes a shrewd analysis of the character of the society with which he had clashed. His opposition was openly directed against this semifeudal society, its morals and values, and the nexus of patron-client relations that formed the mechanism by which it was sustained.[51] Iosipos's displeasure and contempt could find no clearer expression than the declaration of his preference for the "rustics"—that is, for the peasant cultivators who formed the productive element of society, the exploitation of whom sustained the Phanariot social order in the Principalities.[52] This social cleavage formed the background to the crisis in the relations between Iosipos and the Phanariot environment. The preference he voiced for the society of rustics over that of "gentlemen" reveals the real essence of his conflict with the Phanariot social structure. The ideological dispute was nothing more than a means of expressing this deeper confrontation.

Iosipos's critical evaluation of the social mechanisms and his rejection of the established forms of social behavior were not allowed to pass unpunished. They resulted in stigmatization and persecution. This obliged him to publish his *Apology* to defend himself and launch a counteroffen-

---

[50] Ibid., pp. 94–95.

[51] In addition to the testimony of Moisiodax, the social image of the world of the boyars he paints is confirmed by other contemporary evidence. Almost concurrently with Moisiodax's disputes, another keen observer with first-hand knowledge of the society of the Principalities, Caisarios Dapontes (1713–1784), published an "Epistle on the Vanity of the World Addressed to the Nobles of Wallachia and Moldavia." See his *Epistolai dia stichon aplon kata tis yperiphaneias kai peri tis mataiotitos kosmou* (Venice, 1776), pp. 89–109; cf. ibid., pp. 16–18, 26–27, 49–51, 112–113, for a broader sense of his social criticism. See also Michael Perdikaris, *Ermilos* (Vienna, 1817), pp. 17–20, referring to the world of the Principalities, with a *terminus ante quem* of 1806, and mentioning many known names of the local intelligentsia, such as Katartzis and Lambros Photiadis; see also p. 57, where there is mention of Daniel Philippidis, Gabriel Kallonas, and probably Panayiotis Kodrikas. The most comprehensive picture is given by d'Hauterive in his 1787 *Mémoire*, pp. 176–206, which is acknowledged by M. Kogălniceanu, *Histoire de la Valachie, de la Moldavie et des Valaques Transdanubiens* (Berlin, 1837), vol. 1, p. ix, as the most trustworthy among foreign sources.

[52] Characteristic evidence from contemporary authors on social cleavages in the Principalities is discussed in "Postscript to Chapter 4: Social Cleavages in the Danubian Principalities—Some Testimonies."

sive. In the *Apology* he sets out the charges brought against him and thereby indirectly informs us of the substantive content of the dispute:

> It is the prevailing custom among our people to hold the common view that all educated men, and especially those who come from the academies of Europe are disorderly. What kind of disorderliness is it, that the educated man does not suffer to be despised without cause? The many hardships he has suffered, the dangers he has endured whether at sea or on land, the sense of his ability, and above all, the end for which he has gone through all that he has gone through, that is, honor and reputation, everything obliges him not to suffer dishonor. Our notables demand that educated men, in addition to all else, should be as enduring as the Apostles, as the Martyrs themselves, and do not refrain from quoting to them examples of the endurance of the Apostles or the Martyrs, while they themselves do not suffer even their hounds to be dishonored. Educated men are of the civil party, and do not profess the endurance of Apostles or Martyrs; consequently, they proceed forward into a place or profession if they are treated and honored according to their status. See how the European nations deal with their educated men, and as a result prosper in terms of civility, wisdom, and all other benefits that attend their intellectual cultivation. How can the philosopher not be disorderly, when he sees pack mules, loaded on one side with five grammatical cases, and on the other with five conjugations, being preferred to himself, or flatterers, buffoons, obsequious homunculi and leeches, who are nevertheless judged better than himself? The nobles love to forgive tailors, shoemakers, and other tradesmen the most serious faults, favoring them, each according to his particular skill, whereas, if an educated man chance to have some peculiar eccentricity, even though it be harmless, they nonetheless heap every slander upon him. Difficult, hypochondriac, disorderly, these are some of the more tolerable of the epithets that are applied to him. But why go on? There is no more difficult, no more essential profession among us than that of learning, and at the same time there is no profession more greatly despised than that of learning. How will young men gird themselves for those boundless, those unending struggles, without which it is impossible to acquire learning among us when they see before their eyes so many discouraging examples, and when they do not anticipate a reward commensurate with the toils ahead of them? All admit that learning is a necessity for us, and at the same time, as if out of general agreement, all emulate one another in despising it. The priest, the nobleman, the merchant, one finding it not to be very consonant with his situation, one finding it superfluous, one useless, all speak of its good (as understood as an extra benefit), and all then act against its good. In this, we resemble the ancient Athenians, all of whom, with one accord, would demand war against Philip, but all of whom, magis-

trates, citizens, demagogues, each for his own reasons, would then prevent war, or wage it ineffectively.[53]

It is worth pausing to examine Iosipos's points in these comments concerning the charges brought against him. The "disorderly man" (*akatastatos*) is the man who has no "order" (*katastasis*), that is, who has no place in the established social hierarchy. "Disorderliness" (*akatastasia*) thus means subversion of the social hierarchy of status—revolution—and the disorderly man is the one who "is unstable, disorderly" (*astatei*) and rises in revolt—the revolutionary. The "disorderly" are those who break free of the limitations and constraints of the closed traditional society and become bearers of social mobility, primarily as a result of studying in Western Europe. This experience contributes to the secularization of their values; that is, it makes them members of the "civil party," as opposed to the "party" espousing the religious values of submission, self-denial, and humility. By contrast, once they have acquired an awareness of secular values, individual endeavor and merit, and personal competence and achievement as factors contributing to social success, they then question the established hierarchy and "become disorderly" (*astatoun*) when faced with the social expectation that they will take their place in the patron-client networks of conventional social relations, which would reduce them to the level of "flatterers, buffoons, homunculi, servile creatures, leeches," the familiar "parties of wickedness," that so repulsed and disgusted Moisiodax. Their questioning of the mechanism by which the semifeudal society functioned drew upon the "educated," the exponents of secular values, the charges that they were "difficult, hypochondriac, disorderly." The escalating intensity in the adjectives by which social critics were stigmatized was no coincidence: they were difficult because they appeared not to be socially compliant elements; they were, moreover, hypochondriac because their criticism was regarded as a form of social pathology, and those who gave expression to it were consequently deemed abnormal persons, misfits; and finally, they are "disorderly," agitators and subverters of the social order of the semifeudal society, to which they held out the challenge of modern liberal rationalism. Iosipos's perspective on the social reality around him was precisely that of secular liberal values: Not only his declaration that as "an educated man" he belonged to the "civil party" but also his concept of education, of learning, of "polymathy," as a vocation from which he expected to receive material rewards proportionate to the effort he had expended to acquire it. Through this professional concept of education, moreover, the educated man was perceived as being involved in a competitive relationship with the members of other professions, including the most traditional.

[53] *Apologia*, pp. 83–85.

These views and values lay at the heart of Moisiodax's opposition to Phanariotism. The Phanariots' behavior, which in Moisiodax's perception was expressed in the ethos of vainglorious boasting, vulgar arrogance, and corruption was judged by him as essentially antisocial—that is, out of tune with the values and requirements of "civil society," as others would have called it. As one groping his way toward these values, Iosipos subjected the society around him to criticism for failing to actualize them. Collision was the inevitable outcome, and unrelenting harassment and stigmatization the price for his challenge.

The outspoken criticism through which Moisiodax attempted to distance himself from the social order of the Principalities could be seen as symptomatic of a broader crisis in the prevailing ideology of enlightened absolutism. The original faith in enlightened absolutism that Iosipos had shared with the mainstream of political thought in the Danubian principalities had been nurtured by the hopes stimulated by the reforms of a number of modernizing Phanariot princes, especially those of Constantinos Mavrokordatos, who had abolished serfdom with his edict of August 5, 1746. Despite the opposition of the landed boyars to the reforms, confidence in the prospects of enlightened absolutism survived in the subsequent decades amongst intellectuals, a section of the higher clergy, and the modernizing boyars. Optimism was occasionally rekindled by new reforming initiatives, such as those of Moisiodax's own patron, Grigorios Ghikas, who drew his inspiration from Frederick the Great in the 1760s and 1770s.[54] After the Russo-Turkish war of 1768–1774, however, the decline of the Ottoman Empire became apparent, and with this trend the vulnerability of the Phanariot regime emerged. The limits of enlightened absolutism as a viable political project in the principalities were thus clearly drawn and opposition grew, this time among former supporters who now thought the reforms were not going far enough.[55] As a consequence, in the 1770s it is possible to detect an ideological crisis that focused on the legitimacy of the Phanariot regime and its ideal of enlightened monarchy. This crisis in political legitimacy could be seen as the

---

[54] On the question of "enlightened despotism" in the Principalities, see N. Iorga, "Le déspotisme éclairé dans les pays roumains au XVIIIᵉ siècle," *Bulletin of the International Committee of Historical Sciences* 9 (1937): 101–115. The difficulties confronting a reforming prince on account of the reactions and obstructions of the boyars were signaled by d'Hauterive in his 1787 *Mémoire*; see pp. 164–170. On the reforms of Constantine Mavrokordatos, see especially Florin Constantiniu, "Constantin Mavrocordato et l'abolition du servage en Valachie et en Moldavie," and Şerban Papacostea, "La Grande Charte de Constantin Mavrocordato (1741) et les réformes en Valachie et en Moldavie," in *L'époque phanariote*, pp. 377–384, 365–376, respectively.

[55] See Al. Duţu, "La Roumanie," in *L'absolutisme éclairé*, ed. B. Kopeczi, A. Soboul, et al. (Paris, 1975), pp. 331–337, esp. pp. 334–335.

background of Moisiodax's gradual abandonment of his faith in absolutism and his unsparing critique of its social order.

Although in his critique he was careful not to attack the prince himself, there can be little doubt that his disappointment stemmed at least partly from the prince's failure, despite his original promises, to afford him effective protection. Personal complaints, however, could not have been a sufficient reason for Iosipos's break with the court and with the society of Jassy. Moisiodax's disenchantment should not be interpreted by reference to personal grudges, like those that determined the attitude and colored the judgment of Jean Louis Carra, his near contemporary at the court of Grigorios Ghikas.[56] Everything that Iosipos wrote in the *Apology* points rather to a perception of his patrons' broader failure; both lay and ecclesiastical they failed to live up to the standards of fairness and justice that in his judgment constituted the necessary preconditions of viable reform. That failure could be connected with the concessions that the landed boyars managed to extract during both his reigns from Prince Ghikas at the peasants' expense. The prince's reform edicts in 1766 and 1777 extended the peasants' obligations to the landed boyars, instead of alleviating their burdens. Ghikas's second reign, which coincided with Moisiodax's second tenure of the directorship of the Academy of Jassy, was punctuated by pressure from the great boyars, led by Iosipos's other patron, Metropolitan Gabriel Kallimachis, for more concessions. In the year of his downfall the prince eventually granted these in the form of five more days of obligatory peasant labor on the boyars' estates, as well as a number of days for repairs to dams and ditches.[57] Instead of making the society freer and more just, enlightened absolutism appeared to be yielding to the unrelenting pressure of the landed estate, whose attitude had apparently hardened in opposition to the reforms of Constantinos Mavrokordatos. In view of Iosipos's courage to express his preference for the society of peasants as against that of their feudal overlords, it might be reasonable to trace the specific origins of his disenchantment with the ideology of enlightened absolutism to this aspect of its policies. His social criticism was to a large measure motivated by this disenchantment that,

---

[56] If we are to lend credence to Carra, *Histoire de la Moldavie*, pp. 160–161, 169, 172–177, 186, the prince was a far cry from the model of the virtuous and magnanimous monarch envisaged by the theory of enlightened absolutism. This testimony, however, was certainly colored by Carra's grudges against the prince. See *Histoire*, p. 177. N. Iorga, although aware of Carra's testimony, does not hesitate to include Grigorios Ghikas III among the foremost enlightened reformers in the principalities. See "Le despotisme éclairé," pp. 112–113.

[57] David Mitrany, *The Land and the Peasant in Rumania* (London, 1930), p. 19.

as we shall see in due course, turned his political thought in more radical directions.

PostScript to Chapter 4: Social Cleavages in the Danubian Principalities—Some Testimonies

The deep cleavage in the agrarian society of the Danubian Principalities is the subject of a lively discussion by Dionysios Photeinos, *Istoria tis palai Dakias*, vol. 3 (Vienna, 1819), p. 174, where he notes that the *tzaranoi* (the peasants of Wallachia) differed radically in their way of life from the rich, who imitated the customs of the Ottomans and behaved like "European Turks" in their daily life. This description of the aristocratic caste of Wallachia by Photeinos offers a social diagnosis similar to that of Moisiodax and at the same time identifies its political cause: "The aristocrats of Wallachia show all the symptoms of despotism and behave autonomously, though severely, in their courts, in their villages, and toward their subjects; I do not say this of all of them, without exception, but the fact that the majority of them are not like this, is to say that the majority do not bring up the young children as they should; these, from their infancy are surrounded by their slaves and gypsies, and fawning, useless servants, and grow accustomed to giving orders before they become accustomed to obey" (p. 175).

"Consequently, the young scions of the aristocracy who have a spirit capable of learning and a mind capable of understanding, as soon as they arrive at the age of fifteen, or a little more, neglect their lessons and cease to attend to them, and have thought for nothing but offices at the Court; and if one reprimands one of them, asking why he is not devoting himself to the study of his lessons, he answers that he will not become a teacher because he is a noble; as though learning is not necessary for nobles who are destined to serve as rulers and judges of the people, and as though teachers are contemptible for possessing knowledge" (pp. 175–176). As for the intellectual interests of this "enlightened" class, Photeinos adds: "Rarely does one find among the nobles any who like to read treatises that contribute to civil government and moral improvement; those who know French perhaps like to read, but romances and the like" (p. 177).

The sharp division between peasants and boyars in the body of Romanian society was also pointed out by the leader of the Wallachian uprising of 1821, Tudor Vladimirescu, who described the peasants as "men whose blood nurtures the boyars." See Georgescu, *Political Ideas and the Enlightenment*, p. 93. Korais saw the problem in a similar light; he noted that the aristocrats of Moldavia and Wallachia "are nurtured by the blood of the wretched Wallachians and Moldavians." See *Lykourgou Logos kata Leokratous*, ed. A. Korais (Paris, 1826), p. xxxvii.

In closing this subject, it is worth adding a few indicative hints gleaned from the personal diary of an experienced observer of the scene at the Phanariot courts in Constantinople and the Principalities. Panayiotakis Kodrikas notes, just before his arrival in Wallachia: "The *tzaranoi* lamented their burdens to me" (1793). Later, in Constantinople, he writes: "After dinner I go to the house of the prince, where, for the most part, I suffer various mortifications as a result of the bad manners and boundless conceit of his sons" (1795). He also hints that there was an explanation for the behavior of the Phanariots: "For the prevailing God of all the inhabitants of Constantinople is financial self-interest, and everything is secondary where this is concerned. These are the depths to which slavery has reduced the nation of the Romans." See P. Kodrikas, *Ephimerides*, ed. A. Aggelou (Athens, 1963), pp. 88, 98, 96, respectively.

FIVE

PERSEVERANCE

MOISIODAX'S DEPARTURE from Braşov in 1777 marked the beginning of four years of wandering in Central Europe that made him complain bitterly that he had been reduced to the situation of "a vagabond in foreign lands, frequently in want of my very daily sustenance, made old before my time by hardships and, the worst of all for a sensitive man, always fighting against dishonor, for what? To restore my impugned reputation. Behold the prize awarded, for the most part, by our Nation to educated men—those who do not have an obsequious mind, or those who do not have the endurance of an Atlas."[1] Despite all the "suffocating ills" that befell him,[2] however, this long "wandering in foreign lands" coincided with his most productive period in terms of publication. For the most part his movements within the domains of the Hapsburg Empire were dictated by the requirements of his publishing program. This, in turn, was determined by two needs, one internal, the other external. The satisfaction of the former need afforded an outlet for his bent for writing. At the same time his publications allowed him to give a substantive response to his persecutors either indirectly, as with his publications of 1779, or directly, as with those of 1780–1781. In these writings his purpose was to counter the intolerance, the academic censure, and the personal slander by setting out a scientific, pedagogical, and political argument at the highest level and dealing with the essence of the questions at issue.

When he left Braşov, Moisiodax traveled to the communities of the Greek diaspora in Central Europe to visit his merchant friends—most of whom came from Moschopolis, Siatista, and Kastoria—who were now resident in Hungary. The renewed contact brought him back to a world very different from that of the Phanariot mandarins and provided him with encouragement in his endeavors. This was the world of the "most honorable" and "experienced" merchants, men of the world who had been taught by the requirements of their commercial activities to appreciate letters, skill at languages and scientific knowledge, and the value of "civil" and courteous behavior. The contrast with what in Iosipos's experience had been the closed society of the grandiose magnates and schem-

[1] *Apologia*, p. 83.
[2] Ibid., p. vii.

ing sycophants at the courts of the princes, the narrow-minded literati, the bigoted priests, and the conceited scholars who formed the Phanariot world of the Principalities could not have been more striking. Whereas the latter had persecuted and demoralized him, the world of the merchants of the diaspora inspired in him confidence in their social values and aspirations. Among them, it seems, he found his natural social environment on which he felt that he could rely and with which he could even enter into cooperative ventures.

Among Moisiodax's close friends and supporters at Pest, in Hungary, of whom he speaks warmly, were two distinguished merchants from Moschopolis, Theodoros Ghikas son of Ioannis and Naum Moschas son of Michael. These two came from the great center of the Moesiodacians in the Balkans. The ethnic affinity that drew Iosipos to them is obvious.[3] Having secured from Theodoros Ghikas financial support for printing his treatise on education, Iosipos left Pest for Venice, a major center of Greek printing, to attend to the publication. En route for Venice he called at Trieste, the last bastion of the Hapsburg Empire on the borders of the Venetian republic and Adriatic port for the Austrian hinterland. Iosipos met with a good reception from members of the Greek trading community there, too, especially from the provost of the local church, the *protosynkellos* Ephraim Kallergis from Chania, in Crete, and the merchant Apostolis Zographos from Mytilini.[4] He warmly commended the virtues of these two notables of the Greek community in Trieste and their socially minded activities: he cites Ephraim Kallergis's exertions as a peacemaker in settling disputes within the community and Zographos's philanthropic work. Moisiodax probably visited Trieste in the year 1778, on his way to Venice, and again in 1779 or early in 1780, on his return journey to Vienna, where he was intending to carry on with his program of publications and engage in scientific research.

Iosipos returned to Venice at the end of 1778 or the beginning of 1779, after an absence of sixteen years. The political climate had changed, as

[3] Ibid., p. viii.

[4] Ibid. Ephraim Kallergis, in Trieste from 1765 to 1805, was active in the life of the Greek community as a private tutor. Apostolos Zographos, a distinguished notable of the Orthodox community of Trieste from the time he settled there in 1748 until his death in 1809, was a merchant and a benefactor of the community. In 1782 he contributed to the establishment of the second Greek community in Trieste by purchasing the land near the quay on which was built the Greek church of Saint Nicholas. See Olga Katsiardi-Hering, *I Elliniki paroikia tis Tergestis (1751–1830)* (Athens, 1986), pp. 133–138, 172, 215–216, 251–254, 89–91, 127–128, 181–183. The disputes to which Iosipos refers are presumably the conflicts of those years between Serbs and Greeks, which led to the break up of the Orthodox community and the establishment of a separate, purely Greek community, which in 1982 celebrated two centuries of life and activity in Trieste. See Giuseppe Stefani, *I Greci a Trieste nel Settecento* (Trieste, 1960), pp. 211–248.

the Most Serene Republic was entering upon the last twenty years of its long independent history. The intellectual climate, however, was livelier than ever before: the effects of the radical Enlightenment were increasingly perceptible, and the mechanisms by which the Venetian oligarchy exercised its iron control were gradually being paralyzed. The local Greek community was indirectly affected by these stimuli and its political sensitivity had been sharpened in response to political upheaval in Eastern Europe, caused by the new aggressive policy of Russia against the Ottoman Empire.[5] Venice, with its printing presses, continued to be the center of the "industry of Greek letters,"[6] and Moisiodax returned there to print two of his works, a pamphlet on political theory and a pedagogical treatise.

In 1779, at the Greek press of Dimitrios Theodosiou in Venice, Moisiodax printed a short political pamphlet under the title *A Paraphrase of the Speech of Isocrates to Nicocles concerning Monarchy, or Chapters on Politics*.[7] The sixty pages of this work are divided into twelve chapters, accompanied by a brief preface and epilogue; in it, Iosipos presents a paraphrase in modern Greek of Isocrates' oration to Nicocles, together with a translation of each chapter in French. The intention of the work was clear. By using Isocrates' treatise on monarchy that together with Plato's dialogue *Politicus* formed the fountain head of the parenetic political literature known as "mirrors for princes" Moisiodax was attempting to reveal to his contemporaries the duties incumbent on the prince. The fact that this is his only writing without a specific dedication to some contemporary magnate could be seen to indicate that Iosipos destined it for the only ones among his contemporaries to whom the princely dignity was accessible, the Phanariot dynastic families of Moldavia and Wallachia. The French version, set along-side the modern Greek paraphrase of the ancient text, is a curious feature of the book and might be interpreted in two ways. It could be seen either as a practical demonstration of an exercise in translation designed for teaching purposes or alternatively—and more ambitiously on Moisiodax's part—as an attempt to express his political ideas in the contemporary *lingua franca* of political discourse. If the second suggestion is accepted as a possible interpretation, Moisiodax's French translation of the Isocratic text could be seen as

[5] An indication of this ferment was the publication, in six volumes, of a Greek translation by Spyridon Papadopoulos of the history of the Russo-Turkish war by the Venetian author Domenico Caminer under the title *Istoria tou parondos polemou anametaxy tis Rousias kai tis Othomanikis Portas* (Venice, 1770–1774).

[6] S. Lambros, "Peri tis paideias en Ioanninois epi Tourkokratias," *Neos Ellinomnimon* 8 (1916): 303.

[7] See the study by Katerina Kinini, "Le discours à Nicoclès par Misiodax," *Ellinika* 29 (1976): 61–115.

an outlet against possible misunderstandings that his attempt to formulate the vocabulary of political theory might have encountered in the modern Greek version.

We do not know whether the work fulfilled the purpose for which the author intended it. There is no evidence as to how it was received at the courts of the Principalities. We do know, however, that Moisiodax presented a copy of the work to the French Hellenist Villoison,[8] who was in Venice from 1778–1782 carrying out the research that led to his monumental two-volume publication *Anecdota graeca* (Venice, 1781). Through the catalogue of Villoison's library, the publication also became known to Korais, who at once expressed an interest in acquiring it.[9] His judgment of it, however, was severe: "The *Nicocles* of Isocrates is a most wretched work, both in Greek and in French."[10]

Iosipos's treatise on education secured a permit from the censor, dated April 22, 1779; it was printed "at [the press of] Nikolaos Glykys of Ioannina," under the title *A Treatise concerning the education of Children, or Pedagogy*, and was in circulation before the year was out.[11] At the specific level of educational practice it had the same purpose as *The Paraphrase of the Speech to Nicocles* at a wider political level. It consisted of an exposition of the principles and methods of sound pedagogical practice—the practice that Moisiodax believed ought to be introduced into the Greek schools if the problem of Greek education was to be dealt with seriously. The educational reform proposed by Moisiodax was based on a critical examination of Greek educational experience in the light of the

---

[8] Ibid., p. 80. The copy in Villoison's library bears the inscription *ex libris d'Ansse de Villoison et ex dono Auctoris*.

[9] Korais declared his interest in a letter of 20th March 1806 to Alexandros Vasileiou: "Add . . . the vernacular translation by Moisiodax of Isocrates' speech *In Nicoclem*, printed in Venice. I learned of this from the catalogue of Villoison's library, no. 1064, but I learned of it too late; and since I am now preparing the edition of Isocrates, it would be no bad thing to have it, though in a wondrously macaronic language, as I believe." Adamantios Korais, *Allilographia*, vol. 2, 1799–1809 (Athens, 1966), p. 314. Cf. *Catalogue des livres de feu M. d'Annse de Villoison* (Paris, 1806), p. 95.

[10] A. Korais, *Allilographia*, p. 337.

[11] A later manuscript copy (about 1800) of an apparently early version of Moisiodax's *Pedagogy* had been noted by Mr. Leandros Vranousis in the manuscript collection at a monastery in the diocese of Roman in Moldavia. During his examination of the manuscript, he noted some important differences from the printed version, mainly of a linguistic and stylistic character. These differences reveal, as Mr. Vranousis noted, that Moisiodax handled the Greek language with less skill in the first version of the *Pedagogy* than in the printed form of the work. This is an extremely interesting observation. The existence of the manuscript opens up the possibility that a systematic study of the text will yield more definitive conclusions on questions such as the extent of Moisiodax's knowledge of Greek and how the texts were copyedited before publication. If this proves possible, some questions left unanswered by the uncertainty and oblique allusions of the sources may perhaps be answered.

pedagogical views of John Locke. It constituted a plea for the renewal of Greek education, inspired by the progressive principles of contemporary educational thought and supported by Iosipos's systematic and direct knowledge of the ills for which he was suggesting a cure. With this pedagogical program Moisiodax intensified the criticism that he had indirectly and mildly initiated in the *Paraphrase*. His diagnosis of the problems of educational practice and the treatment he prescribes were genuine products of his own personal experience and judgment; therefore, they constituted a direct answer to his opponents. The tone of his criticism, which became sharper in the pages of the *Pedagogy*, was merely the prelude to a more far-reaching assessment of Greek culture and mentality and of their social components that was maturing in his thought.

After completing the printing of his works in Venice, Moisiodax repeated a journey of sixteen years earlier and left for Vienna, the home of the most important Greek community in Central Europe. The timing of Iosipos's arrival in Vienna was particularly propitious. He reached the Austrian capital in the first year of the sole rule of Joseph II, after the death in 1780 of his mother Maria Theresa with whom he had ruled jointly since 1765. Freed from the restraining influence of his mother, Joseph in that momentous year initiated his reform program, which aspired not only to make absolutist government more effective but also to respond to some of the ideas of the *Aufklärung*. The reforming spirit of the emperor culminated in the Edict on Toleration of October 13, 1781 and the abolition of censorship that freed political and cultural expression. All this combined to transform Vienna at the beginning of the 1780s into a scene of remarkable ideological fermentation.[12] The public expression of dissent in religious, political, and educational issues created a climate of expectancy and fostered the spirit of inquiry. In this environment, Iosipos completed his program of criticism free from fear or constraint. To the books and pamphlets of political and social criticism issuing in those years from the presses of Vienna, he added his own manifesto. In the Vienna of Josephinism in 1780–1781 he found a suitable milieu in which to give final form and expression to his views. The con-

---

[12] See T. C. W. Blanning, *Joseph II and Enlightened Despotism* (London, 1970), pp. 64–72, and E. Wangermann, *From Joseph II to the Jacobin Trials* (Oxford, 1968), pp. 5–35. The intellectual background to the Edict on Toleration is admirably set out in Charles H. O'Brien, *Ideas of Religious Toleration at the Time of Joseph II. A Study of the Enlightenment among Catholics in Austria* (Philadelphia, 1969) in *Transactions of the American Philosophical Society*, 59, part 7. Paul P. Bernard, *Jesuits and Jacobins: Enlightenment and Enlightened Despotism in Austria* (Urbana, Ill., 1971), provides, in addition to valuable information on the Austrian literary and intellectual scene, a balanced appraisal of "Josephinism."

temporary testimony of the Jesuit classicist and orientalist Franz Karl Alter, whom he met in 1780 in Vienna, expresses well the harmony between Iosipos's position and the atmosphere around him. Moisiodax seemed to him "to have a great knowledge of secular philosophy, but with ecclesiastical learning he was in no way concerned."[13] Alter had been professor of Greek and since 1779 keeper of books at the University Library in Vienna. He probably met Moisiodax during the latter's researches in the libraries of the Austrian capital in 1780–1781 and was apparently impressed by him. It is possible that during his residence in Vienna, Iosipos earned his livelihood through teaching at the school of the local Greek community, in whose library copies of his *Apology* and *Pedagogy* have survived.

Another possible encounter of Moisiodax's Vienna years might have been with his former classmate at the Athonite Academy, Christodoulos Pamblekis (1733–1793). The Hellenist Franz Karl Alter appears to have known both of them.[14] According to G. Zaviras, the pioneer literary historian of the beginning of the nineteenth century, Pamblekis was teaching at Vienna before his departure to Leipzig, where he died in 1793.[15] The precise dates of his movements are not known. In the history of Greek letters, Pamblekis is, if anything, even more elusive than Moisiodax. He must have been at Vienna, however, at least as late as 1786, when he published at the press of Baumeister of that city his book *Of Philosopher, Philosophy, Physical, Metaphysical, Spiritual and Divine Principles*, which was extensively based on translations from D'Alembert's *Encyclopédie*.[16] In April 1781, however, Pamblekis was probably

---

[13] A. Dimitrakopoulos, *Prosthikai kai diorthoseis eis tin Neoellinikin Philologian Constantinou Satha* (Leipzig, 1871), p. 96. Alter's testimony about Moisiodax occurs in a note in *Algemeiner litterarischer Anzeiger*, Vol. 4 (1799), col. 662.

[14] Besides being an authority on the classical, Oriental, and Slavic languages, as well as on textual criticism of the Bible, Franz Karl Alter (1749–1804) was a prolific contributor to periodical publications. From his writings it is clear that he was particularly interested in the intellectual activities of contemporary Greeks, especially those who were active in Vienna, many of whom he knew personally. One source of his information was the Greek scholar and clergyman Anthimos Gazis. Alter was aware of the work of Theodore Kavalliotis, of the publishing activities of the brothers Markides-Pouliou in Vienna, of Rhigas Velestinlis's cartographical projects, as well as of Moisiodax's unconventional intellectual interests and Pamblekis's subversive religious views. He commented upon all these and other Modern Greek and Balkan subjects in a long series of articles, book reviews, and shorter notes in the Leipzig periodical *Algemeiner litterarischer Anzeiger* between 1796 and 1801, and in the *Annalen der Österreichischen Litteratur* from January 1802 to his death in 1804. In addition to these sources, which constitute a mine of information, see Franz Karl Alter, *Philologisch-Kritische Miscellaneen* (Vienna, 1799), pp. 163, 232–234.

[15] G. Zaviras, *Nea Ellas*, ed. G. P. Kremos (Athens, 1872), p. 552. The information is repeated by C. Sathas, *Neoelliniki Philologia* (Athens, 1868), p. 494.

[16] See Christodoulos from Acarnania, trans., *Peri Philosophou, Philosophias, Physikon,*

in Venice, where he obtained the censors' permission for the publication of his first book, *True Politics*, a translation of *La véritable politique des personnes de qualité*.[17] This book was printed at the same press as Moisiodax's *Pedagogy*, the venerable Greek printing house of N. Glykys. Typographically, the two books are remarkably similar: the same type and woodcuts were used in producing both. Thus, Moisiodax and Pamblekis appear around 1780–1781 to move along closely parallel itineraries. The possibility of a meeting between the two cannot be excluded therefore. It is likely that the meeting took place in Vienna in 1780.

The significance of a possible meeting between the two at the time of the production of Iosipos's most radical work is evident. Pamblekis is mostly known as the boldest religious critic in the Greek Enlightenment. He was the only author who went so far as to question openly the very foundations of Christian doctrine and religious faith itself. These views were not stated in print until the publication of his third and last work, *Of Theocracy*, which appeared two weeks after the author's death in August 1793,[18] but his radicalism must have been in the making for many years. Besides the *Encyclopédie*, he knew the political writings of Rousseau and the philosophy of Spinoza. It is interesting therefore to speculate which way the radicalizing influence went between the two. As made plain by the *Apology* he published in the same year as his meeting with Pamblekis, Moisiodax's social and political radicalism was already fully formed. But Pamblekis's views, as stated in a long note on the nature of politics that he appended to the first chapter of his translation of *True Politics*, appear remarkably close to Iosipos's general outlook. The two alumni of the Athonite Academy, therefore, could conceivably have sustained each other in their dissent when they met in the Vienna of Josephinism.

Moisiodax remained in the capital of the Hapsburg Empire for about two years. During this time he did research work in the Imperial Library in Vienna, supervised the publication of his two most important works, and made many new friends among the local Greek merchants, some of whom he embarked upon joint cooperative enterprises with to fund the publication of his books. In the preface to the *Apology* he expresses warm

---

Metaphysikon, Pnevmatikon kai Theion Archon (Vienna, 1786). On the original of Pamblekis's translations, see P. C. Noutsos, *Neoelliniki Philosophia* (Athens, 1981), pp. 55–57.

[17] See *I Alithis Politiki* [trans. from the French] (Venice, 1781). The attribution to Pamblekis is based on Zaviras's authority. See *Nea Ellas*, p. 553. The identification of the original of the translation as *La véritable politique des personnes de qualité*, attributed variously to Nicolas Remond des Cours or to the Sieur de Cherbonnièrre and first published in Paris in 1692, has not, so far as I know, been made before. Pamblekis probably worked from the joint French-Italian edition published in Strasbourg in 1752.

[18] For details on this text and on its significance, see Ph. Iliou, "I siopi yia ton Christodoulo Pambleki," *Ta Istorika*, no. 4 (December 1985): 387–404.

thanks to three notables of the Greek community of Vienna, who were distinguished merchants and also played a prominent role in social life: Nikolaos Kostikas, son of Constantinos, from Moschopolis, a lover of the arts and patron of the "learned" members of the Greek community in Vienna; Pavlos Hadji Michalis from Siatista, "one of the foremost men in the commercial marketplace in Vienna"; and Constantinos Kouskouroulis from Tyrnavos, a philanthropist and "sweet-voiced" chanter at the Orthodox chapel in Vienna, who also underwrote the printing of Moisiodax's *Apology*.[19] The publication finally became economically feasible when Iosipos secured advance subscriptions from twenty-five "nation-loving" Greeks and other Balkan merchants of Vienna;[20] the work was printed at the imperial press of Johann von Trattner, which had been founded in 1748 and became the most important channel for the dissemination of the Enlightenment in the Austrian lands.[21]

The *Apology*, the first part of which was printed in 1780 in Vienna, is a singular book. The second part, announced by Moisiodax,[22] never appeared, and the manuscript, which he may possibly have had ready to make so specific a reference to it and its contents, has never been located. The book is not a unified, continuous text. Apart from the preface and an extensive introductory essay setting out Moisiodax's basic philosophical views and the reasons and events that moved him to publish his work, the book consists of a series of earlier texts dating from between 1765 and 1777. Iosipos describes the introductory essay: "A somewhat exhaustive discourse, in which it is demonstrated that Mathematics and Physics (that is, modern Physics) are more essential and more useful to us than Logic and Metaphysics; in which are included various notes, some on philosophy, some on ethics, all of them relating in one way or another to the subject of the treatise or to the present condition of our nation."[23] This is followed by the texts of the lectures at the Princely Academy—three on arithmetic and three on geography—that he had asked his pupils to sign before he left Jassy in 1777. He added a few pages of comments and polemic, written at the same time as the introductory essay, to identify the reasons that had prompted him to publish the *Apology*. The remaining section of the book consists of a collection of his oc-

---

[19] *Apologia*, p. ix.

[20] Ibid., pp. x–xii.

[21] Robin Okey, *Eastern Europe, 1740–1980: Feudalism to Communism* (London, 1982), p. 39.

[22] *Apologia*, p. v. Iosipos hints that in the second part he will be even more aggressive: "My zeal for Hellas and the proper performance of our schools; this is what made me so bold, and will in the future make me even bolder." The uncertainty of the earlier literary historians concerning the work is striking. See, for example, A. Papadopoulos-Vretos, *Neoelliniki Philologia*, Part 2 (Athens, 1857), p. 72.

[23] *Apologia*, p. 191.

casional writings that are representative of his views or responses to his accusers; these include his two inaugural lectures of 1765 on philosophy and mathematics, the apology of 1765 to the anonymous priest, and his essay addressed to Doctor Theodorakis in 1777. The second part, Iosipos tells us, was intended to include a more comprehensive refutation of the charges against him.

The publication of the *Apology* represents the pinnacle of Moisiodax's critical thought. Through this act he felt he had discharged his duty to himself and the truth:

> I swear by God himself that it is not an excess of pride, nor a desire for revenge that has moved me to venture the present apology, but simply the rehabilitation of my reputation, which has suffered unworthily, for which I spent the whole flower of my maturity, sailing oceans, crossing continents, and depriving myself of the sweet things of life, and by the strength of which alone I hope in the future to find the necessary resources for my life.[24]

The protestations of Christian humility in this proclamation do not obscure the modern person's strong sense of self-awareness or concern for individuality and rights. The *Apology* represented Iosipos's conscious choice of the Enlightenment as a life commitment.

After the publication of the *Apology*, Moisiodax devoted the last eight months of his stay in Vienna to preparing and printing his *Theory of Geography*.[25] The old manuscript of 1767 was entirely revised and brought up to date by the inclusion of the findings of the latest geographical research. This persistent research effort formed the basis for the most important treatise on mathematical geography to appear in Southeastern Europe in the eighteenth century. Moisiodax's concern that the book should be abreast of scientific research found vivid expression in the mass of explanatory comments, bibliographical references, and scientific observations documenting the text and testifying to the serious research on which it was based. Iosipos himself provides much evidence about his research, so that it is possible to assess his professional competence as a scientific geographer. To compose the treatise, he worked systematically at the Imperial Library in Vienna, an experience he warmly acknowledges: "Great gratitude is due to the Imperial Library of Vienna, in which, whenever I frequented it, I was always given the books I asked for willingly and politely, and in which I harvested all the necessary material."[26]

In addition to keeping abreast of the new scientific bibliography, Iosi-

---

[24] Ibid., p. 40.
[25] *Theoria tis Geographias*, p. ix, n.1.
[26] Ibid., p. 168.

pos systematically studied maps and manuscripts.[27] From this broad range of sources he gleaned the evidence on which he based his judgments and conclusions. The importance he attached to keeping the work completely current scientifically can be seen from his attempts to consult the latest publications relevant to his subject. He nevertheless admits with complete scientific honesty to the lack of information when he was unable to gain access to it; thus, with respect to the latest voyage of James Cook, he notes: "How successful was this latest voyage: the matter is completely unclear to me, because in the city in which the printing of the present treatise is being carried out, the description of it is still awaited."[28] In writing this in Vienna in 1781, Moisiodax appears unsure as to Captain Cook's death at Kealakehua Bay two years earlier.

His research was not confined to bibliographical investigation. The empiricism of his method pervades the entire work and registers the Enlightenment's scientific spirit that had inspired Moisiodax. In his text the theoretical principles of mathematical geography are illustrated and tested with reference to the results of geographical exploration, the usefulness of which he never tires of stressing,[29] just as he never refrains from insisting on the need to combine the study of the theoretical principles of geography with the use of visual aids,[30] such as globes of the world and maps.[31] Indeed, to achieve accuracy in his descriptions and to ensure that his readers were properly informed, he made conscientious attempts to see and examine at close hand the mode of operation of astronomical instruments such as the astronomical clock used by sailors; he was, however, unable to find equipment of this kind in the land-locked city of Vienna.[32] These aspects of Moisiodax's work give it not only a lively quality but also historic importance because it is perhaps the only scientific treatise of the Greek Enlightenment that shows, with such immediacy, the scholar at work—collecting, sifting through, and mastering his material to present it to his reader in an organized fashion.

The thirty chapters of the book deal with the basic concepts and elements of mathematical geography; they are followed by a concluding collection of thirty-three problems in mathematical geography that can be solved by reference to a globe of the world,[33] together with the solutions to them, and an "Annex: Concerning the arrangement of the civil year or

[27] Ibid., p. 165, n.1.
[28] Ibid., p. 32, n.
[29] Ibid., pp. 34–36, p. 34, n.1.
[30] Ibid., p. xiv.
[31] Ibid., pp. 163–166: "Concerning geographical plates, a history of cartography."
[32] Ibid., p. 44, n.
[33] Ibid., pp. 133–160.

concerning the calendar in general."[34] This appendix briefly sets out the methods of measuring the year and the problems involved and provides an introduction to the question of the calendar, stressing the reasons and practical needs that dictated the calendar reform of Pope Gregory XIII in 1580. This section of the treatise is based on the relevant works of the French astronomers Blondel and Lalande.

The work, with its empirical methodology, scientific structure, and mathematical language, served obvious ideological ends. This is clear from the emphasis given to the most contentious astronomical problem of the day—certainly as far as Greek thought was concerned—the question of the movement of the Earth. The chapter on this subject is the longest in the book.[35] Moisiodax begins by setting out, in thirteen lines, the arguments of the proponents of the geocentric theory and then devotes ten pages to the arguments for the heliocentric theory, of which he himself was an advocate. In any case he had made his position clear from the outset by stating in the preface to the treatise:

> Everyone who reads this sees clearly that I follow the Moderns, or rather that I follow the Pythagoreans, in what I say about the question: Whether the Earth moves or the Sun. The clarity, the probability, the likelihood of the view that has the Sun at rest and the Earth in motion, and also the vast band of ancient and modern philosophers, with whom the Ancients, when they are contrasted, do not even bear comparison: everything impelled me to approve of the idea that the Sun is stationary. I postpone a more detailed treatment of this subject for the synopsis of Astronomy, if God and the favor of their highnesses the princes permit, and for the present declare to every reader simply that, though I approve of the view of the Moderns, I can neither prove nor disprove this view. Great is the distance between ourselves and the stars, and many are the obstacles in the way of our knowing about the movement either of the Earth or of the Sun. Consequently, any philosopher who deals rationally with these things must, certainly, judge what is more probable, but should never state it as certain. Let every grateful reader then know that, in setting out the arguments for the idea that the Sun is stationary, according to the Moderns, I set before me only one purpose, to inform our people about these things, too, as far as the present commotion permits.[36]

It is apparent that the *Theory of Geography* carried on the struggle that Iosipos had begun with the *Apology* the previous year. The close connection between the two works is revealed by the abundant references in

---

[34] Ibid., p. 167.
[35] Ibid., chap. 28, pp. 106–123.
[36] Ibid., pp. xiv–xv.

the *Apology* to a more extensive treatment of issues that he then raises in the *Theory of Geography* and gives the reader the impression that the two works are complementary. From many points of view, the *Theory of Geography* provides concrete scientific evidence for the theoretical and polemical positions adopted in the *Apology*. The assertion of the philosophy of the moderns and the insistence on scientific knowledge in the earlier work assumes tangible form in the material set out in the treatise of 1781; here, these views are elaborated at greater length and contrasted with traditional knowledge, in what clearly justifies the arguments of the *Apology*.

The continuity between the two works is also attested in the views on language that Iosipos sets out in the preface to the *Geography*. Through the systematic formulation of his arguments in support of the "simple" style—that is, the use of modern Greek as the language of education—he presents his response to the "verbosity" (*glossalgia*) that was also the source of his personal ills. In this way, he deals with yet another outstanding issue left open in the polemic of the *Apology*. He was, of course, well aware that his views were far from conventional. He himself looked upon them as revolutionary and indeed found this to be expected of any pioneering initiative: "Nor do I deny by this that I am being subversive in what I say. Things that are at their beginning are always, inevitably subversive."[37] Nonetheless, he felt that certain truths simply had to be clearly proclaimed, even if they flew in the face of conventional values and touched upon the authority of established figures. Thus, he gives vent fearlessly to his feelings about Voulgaris's contempt for modern Greek, as expressed in the epigrammatic form: "The booklets professing to philosophize in the vulgar tongue are derisory and ought to be whistled at."[38]

> The Great Man, instead of whistling at our simple style, ought to have recommended it, defining the terms according to which it should be regulated, and ought not to have degraded it in a way that not even the language of the Scythians, which he now knows well, should be degraded. When the simple style is pure of foreign words and phrases, it is undoubtedly meaningful and capable of supplying the medium for the exposition of any kind of scholarly material; why, then, should it be reckoned to deserve to be whistled at? . . . It has the particular advantage of being clear which, examined from the vantage point of utility, is worthy of being judged of equal weight to every particular advantage of the ancient language. What is the benefit to young devotees of Philosophy of those fearsome syntactical constructions in which their

---

[37] Ibid., pp. xii–xiii.
[38] E. Voulgaris, *I Logiki ek palaion te kai neoteron syneranistheisa* (Leipzig, 1766), p. 49.

fathers take cover, as though in deep bushes, so as to appear to be making great statements, whereas frequently they are not even making small ones?[39]

Although he rebels and boldly expresses his outbursts, Iosipos seems at the same time to be aware that an all-out, head-on collision with prevailing traditions and conventions of thought could not lead him anywhere. He may have realized that the alternative course of action pursued by Voulgaris and Theotokis—that is, to take refuge in foreign courts—was not open to him. Perhaps he was also acquainted with the story of Anthrakitis. After the rebellion that inspired the *Apology* and his four years of wandering in foreign lands, when return began to appear both desirable and necessary, Iosipos, without compromising in principle, seems finally to realize the need for tactical maneuvering. While declaring his preference for modern science, he appeared in no great hurry to reject the traditional view embraced by the Church. Through this gesture he sought to avoid a head-on collision and left the reader to come of his own accord to the obvious conclusions suggested by the irrefutable scientific arguments set out in the main body of the book. This attitude transpires in the discussion of the thorny question of the calendar in the appendix of the book.[40] He first sets out all the irrefutable scientific reasons for, and social benefits of, the Gregorian calendar reform, according to which the entire question is presented as an elementary but essential rationalization of both daily and public life. He then concludes with some caveats in anticipation of the attack that might be elicited by what were from an Orthodox position the sensitive religious implications of the question:

> Many ask: why does the Eastern Church, although all the Christian peoples of Europe, one after the other, have consented to this arrangement, alone insist on the old arrangement of the year? The reason is one and only one: it is the all-wise economy and prudence by which it is always guided in these matters, and never appears to be in error. The Eastern Church, reflecting that, on the one hand, the Gregorian arrangement is not absolutely neces-

---

[39] *Theoria tis Geographias*, p. xii. The quip about the Scythians and their language was an oblique reference to Voulgaris's residence in Russia, where he prospered as a courtier of Catherine II. Moisiodax's criticism did not remain unanswered by Voulgaris. Many years later, on the occasion of his rejoinder to the strictures against him by the young Athanasios Psalidas in *Kalokinimita* (Vienna, 1795), Evgenios also remembered the criticism of Moisiodax. See *Epistoli tou sophotatou kyriou Evgeniou archiepiskopou proin Slaviniou kai Chersonos* (Trieste, 1797), p. 23: "That we too, in the *Logic* intimated the need for the [ancient] Greek language, and its use in Philosophy; for this reason, Psalidas has now bitingly attacked us with his teeth, as we were once attacked by Moisiodax." Voulgaris's play on the words "Moisiodax" and "odax" (biting with his teeth) was probably not unconnected with the general impression created by Iosipos in the various targets of his criticism.

[40] *Theoria tis Geographias*, pp. 167–195: "Concerning the Arrangement of the Civil Year or Concerning the Calendar in general."

sary, at least in our time, and on the other, that the vulgar masses are easily confused and consider every change in tradition to represent an innovation, and even the dissolution of religion, decided in its wisdom to postpone the correction of the year until the time when it will be necessary. Some of the Europeans, and many of our people who spend time in Europe, think that our Venerable Church insists on the old arrangement of the year simply out of ignorance. What ignorance is this on the part of the Church, when the peasants themselves have begun to sense somewhat the retreat of the equinox? People who say these things are either loose-tongued, and completely lacking in judgment, or have learned to pass judgment on others' affairs as they pass judgment on their own.[41]

Iosipos's intentions could also be detected from another feature of his work. The *Theory of Geography* was the first of his works dedicated to the rulers of the Danubian principalities. With his prospective return in mind, Iosipos seems, from Vienna, to have sought—and secured—the consent of the two reigning princes, Constantinos Mourouzis of Moldavia and Ioannis Alexandros Ypsilandis of Wallachia, to the dedication of his treatise to them. This gesture was completely in keeping with contemporary practice; it would be in no way remarkable in the case of Moisiodax, whose entire earlier career had depended on the goodwill of the powerful. In this light, it is remarkable that none of his previous works had borne a dedication to a Phanariot dignitary. This further indicated the pronounced ideological differences between Iosipos and the power structure of the Principalities, which found expression in his works of 1779–1780. His rapprochement with the princes was, of course, made possible by the fact that, despite the intense criticism he leveled against the social milieu of Moldavia and Wallachia, in both the *Pedagogy* and the *Apology*, he had been careful never to target his arrows on the wielders of princely power themselves. On the contrary, by directing the edge of his criticism at the courtiers and other grandees who stood between the princes and the movement of the Enlightenment, he appeared to imply that they ought to be held responsible for the ills suffered by Moisiodax and all those desiring the reform of Greek culture.[42]

---

[41] Ibid., p. 195.

[42] *Apologia*, p. 82, n.1: "I say what they *ought* here, because our gentlemen, or at least the majority of them, do not even consider it a duty of their estate to assist or to protect schools or those in charge of schools. Once, while I was talking with an official of the prince of Wallachia about the establishment of schools in Wallachia itself, I said that the princely office had a duty, in addition to its others, to concern itself with the schools, to which he responded: Duty? What duty? . . . the rest of his answer being a sardonic laugh. Behold how the good intentions of princes are sometimes subverted or dulled, as is the awareness of their duties that some of the princes themselves have. If they are guardians of their people appointed by God, and if they believe that they are appointed by God, how can

It was, then, to the "lords" themselves, whose goodwill was dulled by the wily courtiers, that Iosipos turned to secure his return and, more important, to find the economic means that he needed over and above the generous support of his merchant friends to complete his program of publication. The works he had ready for publication were designed to complete the survey of the natural sciences inaugurated by the *Theory of Geography*: two complete *Ways of Mathematics*, two corresponding *Ways of Physics*, and an *Abridged Astronomy According to the Moderns*. Of each pair of treatises on mathematics and physics, one was intended for school use, while the other aspired to entertain gentlemen.[43] By offering the powerful a means of access to the culture of the Enlightenment, Iosipos made plain his conviction that the task of educational renewal could not be carried out in isolation, without the reform of the social and political environment. Despite his sharp clash with the social hierarchy of the Principalities five years earlier, Iosipos seems, in the final analysis, to admit that he could not escape from the web of social ties in which he was entangled. Thus, after his outspoken social criticism, he abandoned the path to revolution and returned to the more palatable expectation of reform through education, under the aegis of the prince. As to the aims of his publication program he was completely frank: "And if I find grace, I say, with their Highnesses, I hope that I shall be able fully to inform our public that every science becomes clear when the writer who is writing about it wishes to be clear."[44]

The concurrence of the princes that Moisiodax attempted to elicit by promising in return only the hope of the enlightenment of the Greek people was never to materialize. The publication of the *Geography* was made possible, once again, only by the economic support of the merchants. This time, support for Iosipos's scientific endeavor took the form of neither a grant of aid from some Maecenas nor advance subscriptions to the work, a method he had initiated with his first book in 1761. In his efforts to find subscribers among the trading communities of Hungary Moisiodax was assisted by his fellow-countryman Georgios Hatziathanasiou from Tirnovo in Bulgaria, who collected the money from the subscribers and undertook to distribute the number of copies due each of

---

they not count amongst their other duties the enlightenment of their subjects? Whether the matter is weighed religiously, morally, politically, or in any other way whatsoever, they must inevitably find it to be always thus."

[43] *Theoria tis Geographias*, p. ix. The fact that his program of publication was directed exclusively toward the natural sciences attests to the clarification of his intellectual interests in his maturity, especially when compared with the program announced twenty years earlier in *Ithiki Philosophia*, vol. 1, pp. xxii, xxviii: at that time he was thinking of publishing a grammar as a contribution to the regulation of the Modern Greek language.

[44] *Theoria tis Geographias*, p. ix.

them.⁴⁵ In addition to this, Moisiodax formed a commercial partnership with two wealthy Moschopolite merchants from Pest, his trusted friend and supporter, Naum Moschas, and Naum Dadanis. As terms of this joint commercial venture Moschas and Dadanis would receive half the copies of the book in return for funding its publication.⁴⁶

The significance of this act has not been appreciated by earlier writers on Moisiodax. By adopting this method in the publication of his works, he demonstrated that the modern scientific book was being transformed from an aristocratic pastime into a commercial commodity and an object of investment for profit. In the most tangible and concrete manner, Iosipos's initiative bears witness to the coincidence between the interests of the scholars of the Enlightenment, as producers of this marketable knowledge, and the merchants, not simply as consumers of this knowledge, but as potential financiers of its production and distribution. By entering into a cooperative arrangement and thus formalizing this reciprocity of interests, Moisiodax found for a moment the solution to the perennial financial problem involved in the publication of his works. This step, at the climax of his ideological opposition to the traditional establishment, coincided with the height of his maturity as a writer and scholar. As a consciously chosen course of social action, it made clear the intention of the proponent of modern culture to emancipate himself from the forms of dependence that were impelling him in the direction of compromise. At the same time it revealed his determination to function in society by integrating himself into an alternative order of things that expressed itself in not only new ideological configurations but also new modes of economic activity. It is a measure of the antinomies and discontinuities of the Enlightenment in Southeastern Europe that Iosipos Moisiodax, a pioneer in pointing to this solution to the social impasse of the local intelligentsia, reached the limits of emancipation from the fetters of the traditional corporate structure at the very time when, psychologically, he was on the verge of compromise. After the persecution, wandering, and rebellion, he now sought the road of return.

⁴⁵ Ibid., pp. 212–213.
⁴⁶ Ibid., xv–xvi.

SIX

THE LATER YEARS

AFTER THE PUBLICATION of the *Theory of Geography*, Moisiodax left Vienna for the last time and returned to Bucharest. His overtures to the princes did not, of course, procure for him the finance for his ambitious publication program, but they apparently did at least give him the opportunity to earn his living at court. According to the testimony of an Austrian visitor with excellent knowledge of Wallachian affairs at the time, Iosipos became resident tutor to the beizadés—that is, the sons of the prince of Wallachia, Alexandros Ypsilandis (1774–1782).[1] This indicates both the change in Iosipos's attitude, which was transformed from that of an outspoken critic into that of a courtier, and in the more general cultural climate in the Principalities at this period. The atmosphere of the Enlightenment seems to have influenced collective behavior and mentality to the point where an independent scholar who had just publicly criticized conventional learning and who was known to have clashed with those in authority in the capital of one Principality could be accepted at the court of the other. Indeed, his links with the prince's immediate entourage secured him the sensitive position of tutor to the scions of the dynasty. Thus, despite his revolt, Iosipos eventually failed to attain his social emancipation. He simply transferred his allegiance, and after his earlier patron's demise he became the client of another reforming prince.

Alexandros Ypsilandis's confidence in the author of the *Pedagogy* and the *Apology* was yet another sign of the extent to which the spirit of the Enlightenment had penetrated the circles of Phanariot society in the

---

[1] Franz Joseph Sulzer, *Geschichte des transalpinischen Daciens* (Vienna, 1782), vol. 3, p. 11, refers to a P. Joseph who taught Greek to the sons of the prince of Wallachia. This was probably Moisiodax. A. Camariano Cioran, *Les académies princières de Bucarest et de Jassy et leurs professeurs* (Thessaloniki, 1974), p. 573, n.85, places this event immediately after Iosipos's resignation from the Academy of Jassy in 1777; according to Moisiodax's own testimony, however, he was in Brașov that year, and he most probably left Brașov for his travels in Central Europe. The two possibilities for his period at the court of Alexandros Ypsilandis (1774–1782), therefore, are either immediately after the accession of Ypsilandis, and before Moisiodax had left for Jassy, that is, the years 1774–1776, or after his travels in Central Europe, toward the end of Ypsilandis's rule (1781–1782). His documented presence in Bucharest from 1781 to 1784 argues in favor of the latter. Sulzer's further specification that the Father Joseph in question had recently published one of his works in Vienna makes 1780–1781 the *terminus post quem* for his presence at the court of Wallachia.

Danubian lands. One chief sign of this advance was the program of reform carried out at precisely this period by Alexandros Ypsilandis in Wallachia.[2] Just before Moisiodax was employed as resident tutor, Dimitrios Katartzis, the other major figure of the Enlightenment in the Principalities, had been appointed to the honorific high office of Grand Kloutziaris.[3] A remarkable group of younger scholars had gathered around the aristocratic Katartzis,[4] making Bucharest the most important center of the Greek Enlightenment in the last two decades of the eighteenth century. This was the climate in which Moisiodax found himself after his peregrinations in Europe finally came to an end. His recent researches in Vienna had kept him abreast of modern science, and this, together with the impressions he certainly brought with him of the reforms of Joseph II, might account for the prestige he enjoyed, as indicated by his intellectual impact upon the younger members of the group, particularly those interested in natural philosophy and the investigation of nature.

The removal of Alexandros Ypsilandis from the office of hospodar of Wallachia because of the imprudent adventure of his young sons in Transylvania brought Moisiodax's presence at court to an end. Perhaps his teaching and enthusiasm for the brilliant achievements of Europe stimulated the desire of the two princes, nineteen-year-old Constantinos and seventeen-year-old Dimitrios, to see Europe; as one contemporary observer suggests,[5] this led them, while hunting, to cross the borders and

[2] D. Photeinos, *Istoria tis palai Dakias, ta nyn Transilvanias, Vlachias kai Moldavias* (Vienna, 1818), vol. 2, pp. 352–356, for the first reign of Alexandros Ypsilandis, of whom he notes: "This man issued many good edicts in Wallachia, like no-one else" (p. 354). See also C. Giurescu, "Un remarquable prince phanariote: Alexandre Ypsilanti, voevode de Valachie et de Moldavie," *L'époque phanariote* (Thessaloniki, 1974), pp. 61–69. According to N. Iorga, "Le despotisme éclairé dans les pays roumains au XVIIIème siècle," *Bulletin of the International Committee of Historical Sciences* 9 (1937): 110, Alexander Ypsilandis was the true successor to the two greatest reformers among the Phanariot princes, Nicholas and Constantine Mavrocordatos.

[3] C. Th. Dimaras, *Neoellinikos Diaphotismos* (Athens, 1977), pp. 189–191. The office of Grand Kloutziaris involved the duties of the general overseer of war provisions, but after the reforms of Constantine Mavrocordatos (1746), it had become a purely honorary title. See Jean Louis Carra, *Histoire de la Moldavie*, new ed. (Neuchâtel, 1781), p. 284.

[4] Dimaras, *Neoellinikos Diaphotismos*, pp. 181–187.

[5] See D. Photeinos, *Istoria tis palai Dakias*, vol. 2, pp. 355–356: "But toward the end of this fortunate reign, his two sons, the Beizadedés, wished to enter into European parts, and since their father would not give them permission, lest he attract the suspicion of the Porte and bring its wrath upon himself, they left secretly and came to Transylvania, their escape ending at Vienna." This view is accepted by N. Iorga, "Le despotisme éclairé," p. 144. The motives and final destination of their journey point, I believe, to the influence of Moisiodax's teaching. Another contemporary source, however, A. Komninos-Ypsilandis, *Ta meta tin Alosin (1453–1787)* (Constantinople, 1870), p. 627, proposes a different and less idealistic explanation for their action and hints that the cause of their flight was the pursuit of the pleasures of the flesh.

surrender to the Hapsburg authorities of Transylvania as a protest against their father, who would not grant his permission for the trip. This provoked the suspicions of the Ottoman suzerains and brought about the prince's downfall. The termination of Iosipos's career as court tutor followed as a matter of course.

During the brief rule of Nikolaos Karatzas (1782–1783), Ypsilandis's adversary and persecutor,[6] Moisiodax had little to hope for. In Karatzas's successor, Michael Soutsos, however, it seems he had reason to place greater expectations of support for his work. His earlier, unfulfilled hope of publishing the writings that he had ready for the press was repeated in 1784 when he dedicated his brief *Physiological Notes* to Michael Soutsos. His request of the prince was "to bestow his benevolence on me, and through me to bestow his benevolence generally upon all the schools."[7] His program of publication was the same as that announced in the preface to the *Theory of Geography* three years earlier: "I wish to essay two mathematical ways, one for the use of gentlemen and one for the use of the schools, and likewise two physical ways, one for gentlemen and one for the schools."[8]

He had abandoned the idea of also publishing an *Astronomy According to the Moderns*, announced in 1781, but he still hoped to publish his other writings. What had rekindled his hopes? At this point too, a combination of the fragments of evidence available to us about his life suggests an interesting hypothesis. Iosipos's hopes may possibly have been revived by the intercession of the young Panayiotakis Kodrikas, who had recently arrived in Bucharest as secretary to Michael Soutsos.[9] Kodrikas was a studious youth and a member of Katartzis's intellectual circle. The direction of his scientific interests had undoubtedly been influenced by Moisiodax. It is not implausible to suppose, therefore, that he secured for Iosipos the prince's consent to the dedication of the brief work that was to close his career as a writer. These details perhaps explain Kodrikas's later claim: "I knew the man personally, and I usually conversed with him as my teacher, and finally, at some point I took him under my protection as an author, as was my duty."[10] The "protection" that Kodri-

---

[6] Giurescu, "Un remarquable prince phanariote," p. 67.

[7] Iosipos Moisiodax, *Simeioseis Physiologikai* (Bucharest 1784), p. iv.

[8] Ibid.

[9] C. Th. Dimaras, "Protomi tou Kodrika," in *Phrontismata* (Athens, 1962), pp. 68–69.

[10] P. Kodrikas, *Meleti tis koinis ellinikis dialektou* (Paris, 1818), pp. xxiv–xxv. Kodrikas's assertion met with the following comments from his ideological rivals, in the journal *Ermis o Logios*: "Kodrikas takes leave to speak officially (!) about Moisiodax, because he knew the man (!), and protected him (!) as a writer, as was his duty. Indeed, it was impossible for him to give a better picture of his upbringing and the high level of his education; nevertheless, despite the genteel manner of this declaration by the chancellor concerning his protection, that it does not even approximate to the truth can easily be concluded by anyone who is

kas might have afforded Moisiodax, especially in connection with his work as a writer, points to the conclusion suggested above.

What moved Kodrikas to "protect" Moisiodax may easily be conjectured. The reputation of the experienced scholar and proponent of the Enlightenment undoubtedly held a considerable fascination for the younger members of the learned circle in Bucharest. Kodrikas himself accounts for this: "The man was genuinely erudite. He was an expert in many foreign languages and had been excellently educated in the basic sciences in the academies of Western Europe."[11] It was natural, then, that the younger members of Katartzis's circle should look upon Moisiodax as a teacher. This intellectual relationship is directly attested in the case of two of these younger scholars of the third generation of the neo-Hellenic Enlightenment,[12] and it can be traced indirectly in the work and scientific choices of the most important of the others. Kodrikas was an example of the direct intellectual relationship between disciple and teacher. The evidence for this is supplied by Kodrikas himself, despite the aversion he later expressed for the stance adopted by his former master on the language question.

Rhigas Velestinlis came to the Principalities in the mid-1780s (certainly before 1788), probably as a client of Alexandros Ypsilandis to whom he had been attached after the latter's return to Constantinople in 1782, and formed close links with the local circle of enlightened scholars.[13] His acquaintance with Moisiodax was no doubt facilitated by their common connection with the entourage of Alexandros Ypsilandis; however, the bond between them must have evolved in a short space of time into a deeper and more substantial relationship than would have resulted from the shared experience of service at the court of the powerful. Rhigas's affection and admiration for Moisiodax was eloquently condensed in the reference in the *Great Chart* to the native town of his intellectual mentor. Moisiodax was the only one of Rhigas's contemporaries, and the only personality in later Greek history, to enjoy the distinction of having his name recorded in the *Great Chart* alongside the glorious names of Greek antiquity that were meant to offer a historical panorama of the grandeur of the Greek nation.

---

not unaware how much men who are bedecked with the erudition and education of the late Moisiodax are honored and loved both by the princes and by the leading gentlemen, and by all the powerful men of our nation, and they have no need of the kind of protection that might be offered by Kodrikas. Whatever the case, this boastful proclamation of this protection is worthy neither of goodwill nor of sympathy, but on the contrary, arouses righteous indignation in every noble soul." See *Ermis o Logios* 9 (June 1, 15, 1819): 530–531.

[11] Kodrikas, *Meleti*, p. xxv.

[12] For the "generations" of the Modern Greek Enlightenment cf. P. M. Kitromilides, *Tradition, Enlightenment and Revolution* (Ph.D. diss., Harvard University, 1978), pp. 58–59.

[13] See L. Vranousis, *Rhigas* (Athens, 1953), pp. 17–21, 257–260.

Moisiodax exercised an important influence on Rhigas's intellectual work. In all likelihood he pointed Rhigas's interests in the direction of physics and geography, which were given form shortly afterward in the younger man's own printed works. The *Florilegium of Physics for Sagacious and Studious Greeks* was certainly written in Wallachia in the intellectual climate where Moisiodax was the dominant scientific figure.[14] Moisiodax's influence on Rhigas's thought pervades the entire work.[15] Rhigas's cartographic publications, moreover, implemented the methodological and pedagogical needs stressed by Moisiodax in the *Theory of Geography*, with respect to the proper approach to the study of geographical science.[16] In the formulation of Rhigas's views on language, too, the decisive influence seems to have been that of Moisiodax, who impelled his pupil in the direction of the "simple style," so that his works would be of the greatest possible benefit to the community at large. Above all, however, it was Rhigas's commitment to the enlightenment of his countrymen and to the renewal of culture and society that mark him as the truest of Iosipos's disciples. Rhigas's endeavors and visions formed the natural continuation of and complement to the struggles of Moisiodax.

In addition, Moisiodax exercised a decisive influence on the youthful scientific choices of Panayiotis Kodrikas. The latter's interest in Fontenelle's *Entretiens sur la pluralité des mondes*, which he translated and published in 1794, was probably initially aroused by Moisiodax, who refers to this work in the *Apology* and renders its unusual title in Greek, exactly as it appears in its published form in Kodrikas's translation.[17] Moi-

---

[14] Ibid., p. 33.

[15] A characteristic mark of their intellectual affinity is the way in which Rhigas invokes the scientific explanation of natural phenomena to dispel superstition in connection with, e.g., the belief in vampires. See *Physikis apanthisma* (Vienna, 1790), pp. 106–107, which follows Moisiodax, *Apologia*, pp. 99, 120, and also *Paidagogia*, pp. 100–102.

[16] Iorga formerly asserted that Rhigas's work on maps, and especially his map of Wallachia of 1797, was based on preliminary work by Moisiodax, a view rendered obsolete by recent research. See Camiarano Cioran, *Les académies princières*, pp. 596–597, and G. Laios, "Oi chartes tou Rhiga," *Deltion tis Istorikis kai Ethnologikis Etaireias tis Ellados* 14 (1960): 286–287.

[17] *Apologia*, p. 9, n.2. Kodrikas's translation appeared under the title *Omiliai peri plithyos kosmon tou kyriou Fontenelle* (Vienna, 1794). The first to notice the connection between Kodrikas's rendering of the title and that of Moisiodax was L. Vranousis, *Rhigas*, p. 258, n.2. The authorship of the translation, however, was disputed by Kodrikas's opponents who attributed it to Moisiodax. The rumor was repeated by Korais in a letter to Alexandros Vasileiou, dated February 23, 1803, where he notes that certain "important people" had assured him "that the translation is falsely signed and is the true work of Iosipos Moisiodax." See A. Korais, *Allilographia*, 2: *1799–1809* (Athens, 1966), p. 71. We now know, from the evidence of the manuscripts of Kodrikas, that this view was unjustified. See C. Th. Dimaras, *Phrontismata* (Athens, 1962), p. 71. Korais certainly did not have a particularly good opinion of the translation. Many years later, on November 21, 1816, again in a letter to Vasileiou, he observes that now Kodrikas's style "though considerably mixed, is very differ-

siodax's intellectual influence can also be detected in the scientific work of others among the younger scholars in the circle around Katartzis. The geographical interests of Grigorios Constantas and Daniel Philippidis cannot have failed to be influenced by his promptings. Their joint work, *Novel Geography*, followed Moisiodax's recommendations as to the choice of language used; in some sense it was a complement to the *Theory of Geography* because it mainly covered political and social geography, which was precisely the branch of that science that Moisiodax had felt ought to be left to others.[18] Their empiricism and thoroughness, especially in the description of Greece, would certainly have satisfied Moisiodax because they reflected a practical application of his methodological recommendations. The most faithful follower of Moisiodax's ideas was undoubtedly Daniel Philippidis. Through his two-volume translation of Lalande's *Astronomy*,[19] which had first been introduced into Greek education by Iosipos, Philippidis fulfilled his teacher's earlier pledge to publish a treatise on astronomy "according to the moderns." Philippidis was also directly connected with the intellectual world of Moisiodax by his geographical interests, as attested in his long correspondence with the distinguished French geographer and cartographer Barbié du Bocage,[20] one of which he realized in his important *Geography of Romania*.[21] Finally, we may also include among Moisiodax's intellectual heirs[22] in the Principalities the physician Spyridon Asanis, who published his own Greek translation of the work by the French mathematician Abbé de la Caille, *On Conic Sections*.[23] Iosipos had been the first to introduce the work of the Frenchman into Greek education, in his lectures at Jassy in 1776.[24]

---

ent from the translation of the *Plurality of Worlds*." See *Allilographia*, 3: *1810–1816* (Athens, 1979), p. 522. It should be noted that Korais specifically disapproved of the word *plithys* as a rendering of *pluralité*, as is clear from the exclamation mark he adds after this word.

[18] *Theoria tis Geographias*, p. xiii.

[19] See *Epitomi Astronomias syggrapheisa ypo Ieronymou Lalande . . . metaphrastheisa eis tin kathomiloumenin ellinikin dialekton para D. D. tou Philippidou* (Vienna, 1803), vols. 1–2. Philippidis attended classes by Lalande during his stay in Paris from 1790 to 1794. Moisiodax had used Lalande's work in composing his essay on the question of the calendar. See *Theoria tis Geographias*, p. 167.

[20] Daniel Philippidis, Barbié du Bocage, and Anthimos Gazis, *Allilographia (1794–1819)*, ed. Aik. Coumarianou (Athens, 1966).

[21] Daniel Philippidis, Part I: *Istoria tis Roumounias* (Leipzig, 1816), Part 2: *Geographikon tis Roumounias* (Leipzig, 1816).

[22] For other probable examples of Moisiodax's influence, see Vranousis, *Rhigas*, pp. 258–259, and Dimaras, *Neoellinikos Diaphotismos*, pp. 226–227.

[23] Spyridon Asanis, *Ton konikon tomon analytiki pragmateia syggrapheisa men gallisti para tou abba Caille, ek de tis gallikis eis tin ton Latinon phonin proteron metenechtheisa, methirminefthi idi para tou iatrophilosophou Spyridonos Asanous Kephalinos eis tin aploellinikin* (Vienna, 1803).

[24] See *Apologia*, pp. 37–38.

The scientific spirit encouraged by Iosipos in the aspiring scholars of Bucharest after his return led to his own final venture into publication. In 1784 Iosipos published at the printing workshop of Nikolaos and Ioannis Lazarou, the "new press" of Bucharest, his latest work *Physiological Notes*, which he qualified in a subtitle as being "no more than essays." The slender forty-three-page volume was designed to stimulate curiosity and thus attract the support that would make it possible for Moisiodax to print his unpublished works. Iosipos's own scant economic means ran only to the printing of the few pages of his essay, and the patronage of the young Kodrikas secured for him nothing more than the prince's consent to the dedication of the work. The world of the merchants of Hungary and Vienna was far away and forever lost to Iosipos, who was now at the end of the sixth decade of his life. His hopes were dissipated with it. Another venture in foreign lands seemed completely out of the question in his new circumstances.

In the "forewarning" to the book, Moisiodax for the last time made a confession of his beliefs, which was all the more eloquent for its brevity. This confession was a concise statement composed of three elements: an epigrammatic personal declaration of his unchanged theoretical position, a more general diagnosis of the state of Greek education, and an indication of the proper teaching method.

(a) Position: "I always keep my eyes fixed upon the love of clarity."
(b) Diagnosis: "The inexperience of our people in the mathematical and physical sciences."
(c) Method: "My discourse is especially and primarily directed at those who do not know, and in this its purpose is to show that every obscure, complicated scientific proof can be set out with clarity when the person dealing with it wishes to be clear."[25]

Moisiodax's consistency and unshakeable belief in "sound philosophy" are certainly impressive. The slim volume that rounded off his list of publications nevertheless deserves a little more attention. The evidence it has to offer can be related not only externally but also internally to Iosipos's biography. To date, the discovery of the only known copy has merely shifted the terminus of his writing career by three years. The evidence of the dedication to Michael Soutsos merely confirmed his adherence to the program of publication announced four years earlier in the preface to the *Theory of Geography*. But the neglected pamphlet of Bucharest has more than this to offer. Its pages contain two features that reveal the climate surrounding Iosipos's second stay in Bucharest after his return in 1781. The first feature is his continuing adherence to the

---

[25] *Simeioseis Physiologikai*, p. vii.

intellectual outline of his thought with which we are already familiar. The work is imbued with a desire to give a scientific explanation of natural phenomena, so as to dispel the delusions, superstitions, and fears of the "idiotic people."[26] A notable feature of Moisiodax's attitude remained his emancipation from religious cosmology and the implicit renunciation of the Mosaic interpretation of creation;[27] this was typical of those consciences of the period that were distancing themselves from tradition. The two essays on nature in his final work represent extensions of the scientific concerns of the *Theory of Geography*, to which repeated reference is made.[28] The organization of the finished scientific treatise of his maturity, in which the theoretical axis is formed by the contrast between Ancients and Moderns, is also repeated in the *Notes*.[29] In one respect, in the work of 1784 he goes one step beyond the treatise of 1781 in the complete empiricism of his method.

The first essay in the *Notes* contains the empirical data collected and observed during the period from June 21 to August 3, 1784; they were aimed at interpreting the protracted fog that lasted from June 21 to 24. This unusual phenomenon gave rise among the "idiotic people" to fears of impending disasters, especially earthquakes, which in turn gave Iosipos the incentive for his project of meteorological observation and interpretation during the summer of 1784. He tried to crosscheck his personal observations by questioning "men who came to Bucharest, some of them from Moesia, some from Transylvania, and some from Moldavia."[30] In this way Iosipos attempted to make up for his Viennese research opportunities that were unavailable in Bucharest.

The second, longer essay is concerned with the tides, a contentious problem in natural science at the time because the phenomenon was connected with the debate on the movement of the Earth.[31] Moisiodax linked his examination of the question with the debate about comets, which was of lively concern to the thought of the Enlightenment. Both tides and comets had preoccupied the founders of modern science from Galileo to Newton and constituted staple subjects in the popularizations of modern scientific ideas during the Enlightenment. The appearance of Halley's comet in 1692 and again in 1759 had kindled wide debates, which loomed in the background of Moisiodax's project. The moral and social implica-

---

[26] Ibid., pp. 5, 7.
[27] Ibid., pp. 10–11.
[28] Ibid., pp. 16, 21–22, 31.
[29] Ibid., pp. 16–17, 30, n.2.
[30] Ibid., p. 8.
[31] See Herbert Butterfield, *The Origins of Modern Science, 1300–1800* (London, 1957), p. 70. Cf. Charles Singer, *A Short History of Scientific Ideas to 1900* (Oxford, 1959), p. 324, for the significance of the question in the history of science. Moisiodax refers to the debate in *Apologia*, p. 154.

tions of the debate on comets had been drawn out in the well-known works by Pierre Bayle, *Lettre sur la Comète* (1682) and *Pensées diverses sur la Comète* (1683). Bayle stressed that the appearance of a comet in the firmament was merely a natural phenomenon of no theological significance; therefore, it could not cause any disorders on earth. The arguments developed by the author were directed precisely at the delusions of the "idiotic people" a century before Moisiodax. The question of the tides had occupied Greek scientific thought in the eighteenth century, as can be seen from the debate on the subject between Evgenios Voulgaris and his pupil Theophilos, bishop of Campania.[32] Moisiodax tried to enhance the rational investigation of that controversial natural phenomenon through his empirical approach. In illustrating the theoretical discussion by empirical examples, he refers, among other things, to the *acqua alta* in Venice on March 11, 1784.[33] Moisiodax's reference to tides in the Mediterranean,[34] later finds an echo in Rhigas's criticism of Voltaire's view that there are no tides in that sea.[35]

In addition to the scientific spirit of the Enlightenment that pervades it, the text is marked by a second feature that reveals something of the new situation by which Moisiodax's attitude was formed. This is the truly spectacular turn of his language toward archaism. A comparison of Moisiodax's linguistic practice in the *Notes* with the language theory in the preface to the *Geography* reveals a contradiction eloquent in its implications. The archaizing syntax and vocabulary of the work of 1784 demonstrates that the introductory dedication to the prince meant more than what was required by conventional expediency. The two features combine nicely as evidence for the compromise made by the "disorderly" Iosipos. The language of the *Notes*, with its affected Atticisms and artificial, graceless Hellenism, succeeds only in destroying the lively personal style of Iosipos's earlier works. A little later Katartzis made a similar *volte face*, and in the future, the same road was to be followed by another theoretical adherent of the simple style, and disciple of Moisiodax, Daniel Philippidis.

What dictated this turnabout? For the answer, we have recourse only to hypotheses. These inevitably relate to the mechanisms of social control with which Iosipos had to conform to survive. The *Physiological Notes* reflected the attempt of the unemployed scholar to prove that his views have a practical application, to arouse the interest of the princes and thus secure his livelihood. For this reason he chose to interpret either phenomena that directly affected everyday life, such as the factors contrib-

[32] See *Syllogi anekdoton syggrammaton tou aoidimou Archiepiskopou Evgeniou tou Voulgareos*, ed. G. Ainian (Athens, 1832), vol. 1, pp. 13–40.
[33] *Simeioseis Physiologikai*, p. 34.
[34] *Ibid*.
[35] See Rhigas Velestinlis, *Physikis apanthisma*, p. 64.

uting to weather conditions and the dangers of natural calamities, which demonstrate the usefulness of scientific knowledge, or impressive phenomena like tides and comets, which arouse the curiosity and win the interest of his readers. The nature of the book's contents was probably dictated by the need to elicit the interest of the princes and the public as a means of solving the perennial problem of earning a living. The spectacularly archaic language of the work, however, was designed to guarantee his conformity to social conventions and the demands of social respectability, which he probably judged necessary preconditions for securing the favor of the princes. In writing the work in an archaizing language, nevertheless, Iosipos seemed finally to capitulate to the charges of his opponents, who accused him of not knowing ancient Greek. This was the true significance of weakening his resistance: whereas in the views on language set out in the *Apology* and the *Theory of Geography* he had made it plain to all that he regarded these accusations as unworthy of reply, the compromise now forced upon him by the need to adjust to his circumstances obliged him in his last work to offer a practical refutation of them. The dead language of the essays of 1784 is a symbol of the exhausted fighting spirit of the thwarted crusader.

After the publication of the brief pamphlet on natural science, earlier biographers of Moisiodax lost track of him. The very existence of this last fruit of his scientific labors, which survives in only a single copy, had remained unknown to most contemporaries and also to the pioneers of modern Greek literary history in the nineteenth century.[36] A series of objective and subjective factors made the years immediately following his return to Wallachia a period of decline, despite the reputation he apparently enjoyed amongst local scholars. His detachment from the scientific currents of the Enlightenment, isolation from the Balkan diaspora of merchants in Central Europe, "taming" at the court of the princes, in whose good intentions he reposed his scientific hopes, and finally, increasing disillusionment coming with old age—all these undoubtedly broke his spirit and brought him down to earth in the contradictory reality of the Principalities. At his age—already quite advanced by the standards of the period[37]—a fresh struggle to restore his damaged reputation, comparable with that of 1777–1780, was no longer a realistic option. All this, combined with a particularly sensitive temperament like his own, which al-

---

[36] The only surviving copy is in the Library of the Romanian Academy. It remained unknown to nineteenth-century literary historians and also, until quite recently, escaped the attention of Greek bibliographers. It is noted, however, in Ian Bianu-Nerva Hodoș, *Bibliografia Romanesca veche (1508–1830)* (Bucharest, 1910), vol. 2, p. 300. The complete text is reprinted in P. M. Kitromilides, *Iosipos Moisiodax* (Athens, 1985), pp. 281–321.

[37] Fernand Braudel, *Capitalism and Material Life: 1400–1800* (New York, 1982), pp. 52–53, and Carlo Cipolla, *The Economic History of World Population* (Harmondsworth, 1978), p. 90, and especially David Ogg, *Europe of the Ancien Regime* (London, 1970), pp. 14–19.

ways strongly internalized the external factors, inevitably led to the decline and silence of his last years and to his withdrawal from the scene, with a brief reappearance in 1797, as we shall see. A few years ago C. Th. Dimaras described well the last two decades of Moisiodax's life; he commented that "in 1791, Moisiodax faded away somewhere between Vienna and Bucharest."[38] After so many years of wandering among the Greek diaspora, the centers of the lights, the foreign lands of ideas and dissent, Iosipos seemed now to have crossed the threshold of compromise. Thus, the content of his languor should concern us at the conclusion of his biography. The recent research of Dimaras offers material for hypotheses concerning the last years of Moisiodax's life and suggests that traces of Iosipos should perhaps be sought in connection with a journey in the Greek East by the French Hellenist Jean Baptiste Gaspar d'Ansse de Villoison.

On August 3, 1784, still in Bucharest, Iosipos carried out the meteorological observations that formed the basis for the pamphlet *Physiological Notes*.[39] The work therefore was probably printed in the autumn of 1784. After this, all trace of him is lost. We now know that on Thursday, April 21, 1785, Villoison, at the beginning of a three-year tour of Greek lands to collect inscriptions and manuscripts (1785–1788),[40] visited Mount Athos and came to the Monastery of Vatopedi, where he had an interesting encounter. He himself describes it in the manuscript of his monumental *Voyage historique en Grèce*, which his premature death prevented him from finishing:

> The *skevophylax* [sacristan] was away at that moment, attending to repairs to the college. I was received with open arms by father *Joseph Iosipos* who was called *didaskalos* [teacher] because he had taught the logic of Evgenios and the grammar of Neophytos for six or seven years at the college of Jassy in Moldavia, where the *skevophylax* had been abbot of a *metochion* [dependency] of the monastery of *Vatopedi*. Father Joseph is a wise man, most obliging and most moderate in matters of religion, who agreed with me that the schism was a great evil, above all for the Greeks, had been the ruin of their empire, and now prevented them from being supported by the Christian princes, who were influenced by the *philotimia* [vanity] and *pleonexia* [greed] of the priests of both Churches. He took me initially to see the first library, which is near the Catechumens; it is very well stocked.[41]

---

[38] C. Th. Dimaras, "O protos mathitis mou," *Aphieroma sti mnimi tou Manoli Triandaphyllidi* (Athens, 1960), pp. 98–99.

[39] *Simeioseis Physiologikai*, p. 9.

[40] See Sokratis Kougeas, "To taxidi tou Villoison eis tin Ellada (1784–1786)," in *Aphieroma sti mnimi tou Manoli Triandaphyllidi* (Athens, 1960), pp. 189–203, and especially Renata Lavagnini, ed., *Villoison in Grecia, Note di Viaggio (1784–1786)* (Palermo, 1974), which presents extensive excerpts from Villoison's manuscript.

[41] C. Th. Dimaras, "Eidiseis yia ton Moisiodaka apo ta ystera tou chronia," *O Eranistis*

Villoison's discussions with Father Joseph were not confined to religious matters and the relations of the Eastern and Western churches. After his description of his visits to other monasteries, Villoison recollected his encounter in the Monastery of Vatopedi:

> I forgot to say that at dinner with the monks of *Vatopedi*, the *didaskalos* [teacher] Joseph informed me that in the Morea, in the region called *Tzakonia*, the mountainous and salubrious country of the *Eleftherolakones*, where the women are still *phainomerides* [wear garments open at the side] where the men live a hundred years without illness and only die of old age, and speak Dorian mixed with Italian, and say *emeo* for *emou*, *akekoa*, *uo* instead of *udor*, *bosi* instead of *botrus*, etc., there are three important villages on the mountain: 1st. *Prastos*, 2nd *Kastanitza*, 3rd *Sitina*, and that at ancient Epidauros, opposite *Kolouri* [Salamis], near a village called *Ligourion*, where there was once a city called *Ligis*, there is a very beautiful ancient theater.[42]

Speaking of Villoison's testimony Dimaras suggests that "there are many reasons to believe that this is a description of an encounter between Villoison and Moisiodax." According to Dimaras, Iosipos's presence at Vatopedi, where Villoison might have met him, symbolizes "the return of the subdued prodigal to the place where thirty years before he had taken one of his great steps, that ought to have brought him to an entirely different end."[43]

This is undoubtedly an attractive hypothesis. Iosipos, broken by his unfulfilled struggles and disappointed hopes, chose to return to Vatopedi to indicate his final compromise as clearly as possible. The large monastery on Mount Athos had played host on the surrounding hills to the Athonite Academy, at which he had studied. Now that the school was in decline and Iosipos had abandoned the struggle, might he have returned as a pilgrim or as a member of the brotherhood at Vatopedi? Let us glean from the information given by Villoison all the evidence that argues for identifying Father Joseph of his testimony with Moisiodax.

It cannot be claimed that a careful reading of the evidence with respect to the biographical data recorded by Villoison inspires that feeling of certainty that derives from the convergence of details. We know that Iosipos

---

16 (1980): 148. He publishes the French original from Villoison's manuscript. These excerpts are not included in R. Lavargnini's edition of Villoison's travel notes. The words underlined are in Greek in the original. By the phrase "Katechoumenoi" is meant the narthex of the church. The housing of the library of Vatopedi in this part of the church was attested as early as 1698 in Ioannis Komninos, *Proskynitarion tou Agiou Orous tou Athonos*, ed. by Ioustinos Simonopetritis (1701; reprint, Karyes, 1984), p. 53.

[42] Dimaras, "Eidiseis," p. 149. The evidence for the Tsakonians, recorded for the first time in this note, reappears in Villoison's commentary to the prolegomena in his edition of *Homeri Ilias ad veteris codicis Veneti fidem recensita* (Venice, 1788), pp. xlix–l.

[43] Dimaras, "Eidiseis," p. 148.

did not teach for a period of six to seven years at Jassy, nor did he teach the *Logic* of Evgenios Voulgaris, far less the *Grammar* of Neophytos Kafsokalyvitis. Furthermore, the discussion over dinner at Vatopedi reveals that Villoison's interlocutor was acquainted with Epidauros in the Peloponnese, a detail which, as far as we know at present, was outside Iosipos's experience. It may, moreover, be regarded as extremely doubtful whether Moisiodax would have been in a position to describe to Villoison, in such great detail, the topography of the area around Epidauros, as recorded in the notes of the French visitor. Despite all these doubts, however, there remains very strong internal evidence supporting the identification: the substantive content of the discussion between Villoison and Father Joseph. The religious moderation, which the philhellene Professor Alter had also discerned during Moisiodax's last stay in Vienna; the sorrow at the severance of the Greek nation from Europe, which he never tired of reiterating from the time he published the *Moral Philosophy*; and the remorseless criticism of the moral corruption of the clergy— all these form a network of views that point persuasively enough to Moisiodax.

The verification of Dimaras's hypothesis therefore offers a research challenge for the biographer of Moisiodax. With this in mind, I visited the monastery of Vatopedi to test, with the aid of all surviving archival material, the hypothesis that Moisiodax after his many years of wandering returned to Vatopedi in 1785, either as a simple pilgrim, in accordance with the custom of the age, or as a regular member of the brotherhood.[44] My attempt to check the evidence brought me into contact with the rich deposit of information on eighteenth-century Greek cultural life that has been preserved in the records of Vatopedi.

An investigation of the manuscripts produced considerable evidence on the question raised by Dimaras's discovery. In *Codex A'* of the correspondence of the Monastery are preserved two letters from the monk Joseph to the Sacristan of Vatopedi, Stephanos, dated to 1777.[45] The second of these letters, of December 25, 1777, refers to problems relating to the administration of the Monastery of Golia, a *metochion* (dependency) of Vatopedi in Jassy,[46] and calls upon the sacristan to intervene to

[44] It has not been possible to verify whether Moisiodax was enrolled into the brotherhood of the Monastery of Vatopedi because the surviving register of monks in the monastery begins in the year 1829. The archivist informed me during my visit to the monastery in July 1984 that no earlier lists survive covering the period in which we are interested.

[45] Monastery of Vatopedi Archive, *Codex A*, fols. 38ʳ⁻ᵛ (June 27, 1777) and 40ʳ–41ᵛ (December 25, 1777).

[46] The Monastery of Golia, dedicated to the Ascension, was built at the end of the sixteenth century by the Moldavian boyar Ioannis Golia, who was grand logothetes to the prince of Moldavia, John the Brave (1572–1574). In 1606, Golia's widow Anna and his son Michael dedicated the monastery and all its property to Vatopedi, and their action was confirmed by prince Jeremiah Movila (1600–1606). See T. Bodogae, *Ajutoarele româneşti*

rescue it from the maladministration of the prior Panaretos. These two letters formed the prelude to the involvement of Joseph himself in the affairs of the Monastery of Golia which, judging by the frequency of the correspondence, seems to have seriously concerned the brotherhood at Vatopedi from 1780 to 1800. One letter in this correspondence, dated June 17, 1784, is of particular interest in testing the hypothesis suggested by Villoison's testimony. This letter was addressed to the holy fathers of the "Sacred and Royal Monastery of Vatopedi" by Dimitrios and Georgios, sons of the "the late Manolakis" Lupu, "son of Bogdan." It contains the following passage:

> When our teacher, Master Joseph, came there (we greatly regretted his departure) we did not hesitate to pay the devout respects due to your reverences, declaring to you that while we were staying in our monastery of Golia here, we saw a deed of donation of our great-grandfather Lupu. . . .[47]

The monk Joseph, then, whose interest in Golia had already been expressed in the letters of 1777, seems to have succeeded in the immediately following period in having himself transferred to the *metochion*, where he also acted as teacher of the children of the Moldavian nobility. From the letter of the brothers Lupu, it seems that these scions of the boyar aristocracy resided at the Monastery of Golia to attend the classes given by Joseph, who was now known as "teacher."[48] The monk of the Monastery of Golia uses this same appellation, Joseph the teacher, in signing another letter, of June 13, 1790, to Germanos, the prior of Vatopedi.[49]

All this information gives rise to a number of questions regarding the identity of the teacher Joseph, whom Villoison met at Vatopedi. The teacher Joseph left Jassy for Vatopedi in the summer of 1784. He was therefore probably at the monastery when Villoison arrived there in April 1785. Until 1790, at least, the teacher Joseph is attested as a member of

---

la mânăstirile din Stântul Munte Athos (Sibiu, 1940), pp. 119–120. The Monastery of Golia, then a metochion of Vatopedi, was renovated and its church brilliantly decorated by prince Basil Lupu (1634–1653) and his son Stephen (1659–1661). In 1738 it was devastated by an earthquake that struck Jassy, and in 1754 the prior Gerasimos renovated it "from the foundations." In the eighteenth century, the Monastery of Golia, one of the most impressive buildings in the center of Jassy, is mentioned with admiration by the contemporary narrative poet Caisarios Dapontes.

[47] Monastery of Vatopedi Archive, *Codex A*, fol. 84ʳ.

[48] The information that there was a school in operation in the Monastery of Golia is important; it necessitates the revision of the hitherto prevailing view, accepted by the historian of the monastery, that in contrast with other Romanian monasteries Golia, under the leadership of the Greek priors, contributed nothing of importance to the cultural life of Moldavia. See Radu Popa, *Monastirea Golia* (Bucharest, 1966), p. 9.

[49] Monastery of Vatopedi Archive, *Codex A*, fol. 203 (13 July 1790).

the brotherhood of Vatopedi. This evidence is not irreconcilable with the testimony of Villoison. The period of "six or seven years" of teaching in Moldavia coincides with the dates 1777–1784 specified in the letters from the teacher Joseph. If we assume that after his letters of 1777 he taught at Golia from 1778 until his departure in 1784, we have the six years referred to by Villoison. This points away from Moisiodax because these years coincided with his long period of wandering in foreign countries (1777–1781).

The content of the teaching mentioned by Villoison, too, points away from Moisiodax, who himself gives us precise details of his teaching program. In contrast, the content of the lessons ascribed to Joseph of Vatopedi was closer to the general educational practice of the period. The *Grammar* of Neophytos Kafsokalyvitis was widely used as a teaching aid in the schools of Moldavia and Wallachia, and consequently very probably used by Joseph in his lessons at the Monastery of Golia.[50] Furthermore, the teaching of the *Logic* of Evgenios Voulgaris was an equally fundamental feature of the curriculum of schools not only in the Principalities but also in the entire Greek East until the beginning of the nineteenth century; the work continued to circulate in manuscript copies, too—many of which have been preserved in monastic libraries—for decades after it was printed in 1766.[51] The universal acclaim of Voulgaris's philosophical handbook accounts for the scandal provoked by Moisiodax's refusal to teach Voulgaris's *Logic* at Jassy when he was director of the Academy and makes it probable that Joseph of Vatopedi did teach it at the Monastery of Golia. The teaching of Voulgaris's *Logic*, possibly the connecting link between Joseph and the Enlightenment, may explain his moderate stance on the controversial ideological questions that he discussed with Villoison. Finally, a point of perhaps decisive significance for the solution to the problem is the clerical rank of Joseph of Golia: clearly from the letters the teacher Joseph was an ordained priest (hieromonk) from 1777, whereas Moisiodax never advanced beyond the rank of deacon. These observations seem to indicate that we should see in the person of the teacher Joseph, whom Villoison encountered at Vatopedi, a second Iosipos, who was also, in his own way, an exponent of the Enlightenment. In this case, the importance of Villoison's testimony lies in the fact that it enables us to set the hitherto unknown monk and teacher, whom we have culled from the archives at Vatopedi, within the movement of the Enlightenment. The second Joseph of Golia and Vatopedi

---

[50] See Camariano Cioran, *Les académies princières*, p. 150.

[51] Ibid., pp. 196–198, with many references to manuscripts of the *Logic* that were used for teaching purposes in Romania. An indication of the wide propagation of manuscripts of Voulgaris's *Logic* in monastic libraries throughout the Greek East is provided by Codex 15 (199) of the Monastery of Kykkos in Cyprus, dating from the end of the eighteenth century.

could in turn easily be identified, I think, with the late eighteenth-century teacher of the monastery of Vatopedi, Joseph the Peloponnesian, whom Manuel Gedeon includes among the monks of Athos noted for their learning.[52]

If we accept the existence of a second Iosipos, this might explain an eloquent silence in Villoison's testimony. It is clear from the inscription "ex dono auctoris" in the copy of Moisiodax's edition of *In Nicoclem* in Villoison's library that the French scholar had at one time met Moisiodax (see Chapter 5). Yet there is no mention of this gift in his description of the meeting at Vatopedi. It is reasonable, I believe, to conclude that the meeting with Moisiodax and the presentation of the *In Nicoclem* probably occurred when the work first appeared in 1779 in Venice, where Villoison was also residing at the time. If they had already become acquainted in Venice in 1779, however, why did Villoison, referring to their second meeting in 1785, give no indication of this? And why, indeed, did he apparently fail to recognize in the person of father Joseph, of whom, moreover, he includes a number of biographical details, the worthy scholar whom he had met in Venice? If, despite the doubts left by the new archival evidence, we still insist on identifying Moisiodax with the Joseph of Villoison's testimony, who must certainly now be identified with the teacher Joseph of the four letters in *Codex A'* of Vatopedi, then we shall have to revise Moisiodax's biography at a number of essential points. In my opinion, a revision of this nature would be unwarranted by the available evidence.

Regardless of whether Moisiodax returned to the place from which his intellectual struggles had been initiated, the silence of his last years was certainly persistent. A brief reappearance in Bucharest was no more than an episode that confirmed his move to the sidelines in his old age. In 1797, between March and December, Iosipos Moisiodax was once again a member of the teaching staff of the Academy in Bucharest, with a monthly salary of fifty talers, whereas the salary of the school's headmaster, Lambros Photiadis, was three times greater.[53] His reemergence at this period should perhaps be connected with his old patron Alexandros Ypsilandis's last, brief return to the throne of Wallachia in 1796–1797.[54] This final gesture of the Phanariot prince was designed to help his sons' old tutor secure a livelihood, a problem that appears to have remained unsolved until the end of his life.

The year of Moisiodax's death, like that of his birth, is not accurately known. Georgios Zaviras, who, from 1790 to 1804 collected biographical

---

[52] See Manuel I. Gedeon, *O Athos* (Constantinople, 1885), pp. 224–225.

[53] D. B. Oikonomidis, "Lambros Photiadis (1752–1805)," *Epetiris tou Mesaionikou Archeiou* 3 (1950): 118.

[54] D. Photeinos, *Istoria tis palai Dakias*, vol. 2, pp. 378–379.

data on the Greek scholars of the Ottoman period to compile his history of modern Greek literature, notes of Iosipos: "This wise man is at present living in Bucharest, in Wallachia, but in what condition, I know not."[55] Zaviras, himself a Greek merchant of Hungary, who was acquainted with Moisiodax's work and owned copies of his books,[56] had probably also met the man personally and would certainly have had relatively accurate information from colleagues who had made his acquaintance. He refers to Iosipos and his struggles sympathetically and even includes extracts from the *Apology* in his manuscript. When Zaviras was writing, Moisiodax, at an advanced age by contemporary standards, was still alive in Bucharest.

From the capital of Wallachia, we may assume that he followed the reverberations of the French Revolution in Southeastern Europe,[57] and in his old age he could have felt the emotion aroused by the news from Paris in the liberal spirits of the entire continent. Iosipos perhaps experienced the stirring events through a final sorrow: the execution in Belgrade in 1798 of his beloved pupil, Rhigas Velestinlis, for initiating and leading a revolutionary plot to overthrow Ottoman despotism and unite all subject nationalities in a republic modeled on the French constitution of 1793. Did Iosipos, then, have the opportunity to see Rhigas's *Great Chart*, with its reference to Cernavoda and its mention of his own name? This, too, remains one minor question mark connected with his biography.

A later statement in the Viennese Greek literary journal *Ermis o Logios* places Iosipos's death in 1800, when he was seventy-five years old.[58] Certainly, at the opening of the nineteenth century, while his teacher, Evgenios Voulgaris, was still alive in Russia and the Greek Enlightenment was reaching its climax, the deacon Iosipos Moisiodax had discharged the common human debt. The place "where they laid him," like so many other signposts of his passage, is unknown.

[55] G. Zaviras, *Nea Ellas* (Athens, 1872), p. 353.
[56] András Graf, *Katalogos tis en Voudapesti Vivliothikis tou Georgiou Zavira* (Budapest, 1935), p. 27. Zaviras possessed almost all the works of Moisiodax: vols. 1 and 2 of the *Moral Philosophy*, the *Pedagogy*, *Apology*, and *Theory of Geography*.
[57] See P. Eliade, *De l'influence française sur l'esprit publique en Roumanie* (Paris, 1898), pp. 193–197; N. Iorga, *Histoire des relations entre la France et les Roumains* (Paris, 1918), pp. 120–135; and especially Germaine Lebel, *La France et les principautés danubiennes* (Paris, 1955), pp. 295–307, for the echo of the French Revolution in the Principalities. The survey by L. S. Stavrianos, *The Balkans since 1453* (New York, 1958), pp. 198–213, offers a more general account.
[58] *Ermis o Logios* 2 (March 15, 1812): 86.

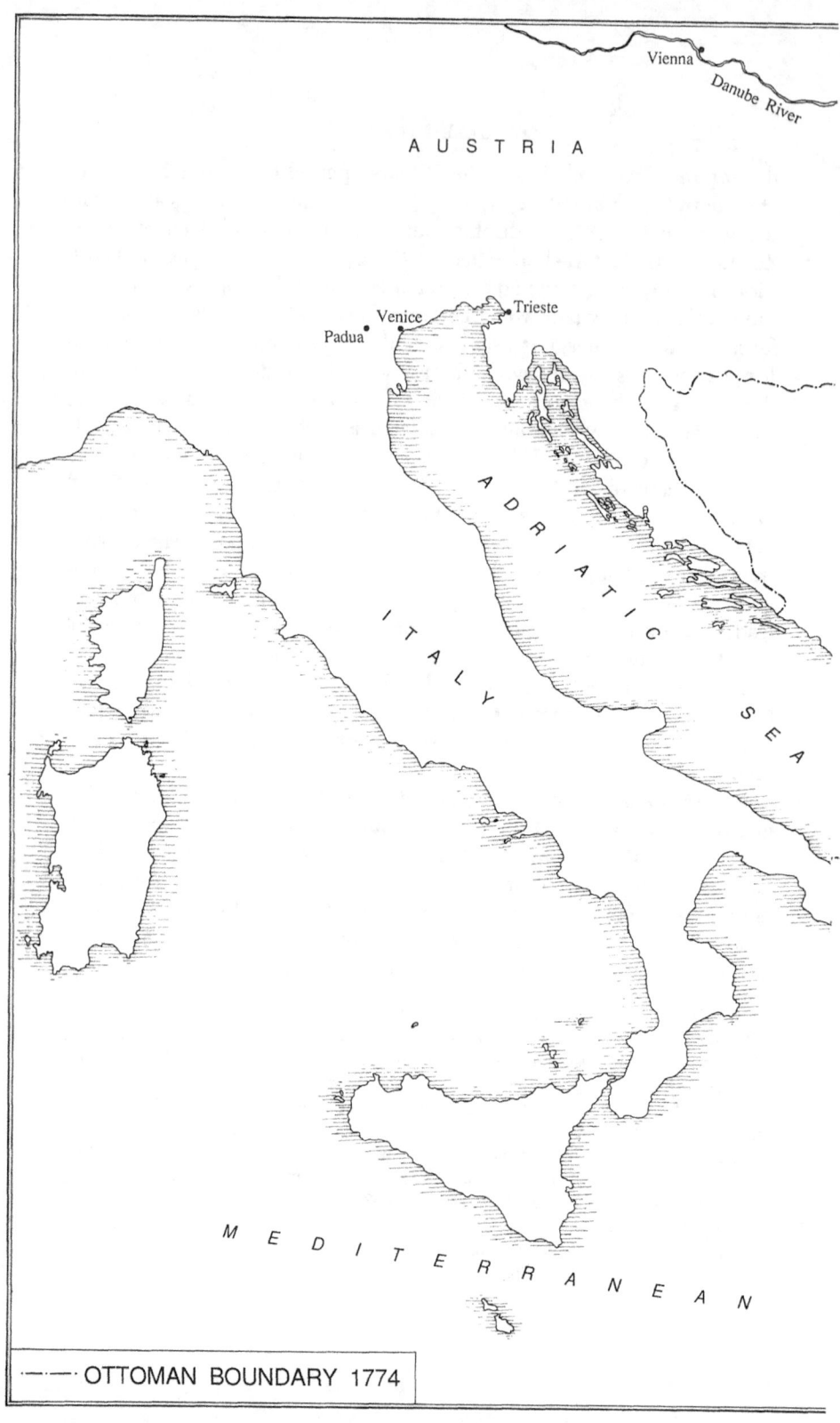

Moisiodax's peregrinations in Southeastern Europe. The map indicates places where Moisiodax's presence is documented in surviving sources.

1. Moisiodax's signature, both in Italian and in Greek. Istituto Ellenico, Venice, Old Archive, Busta 34, Notebook for the year 1759: *Riceveri tenuto dal Clarissimo Signor Nicolò Zuccalà* (5 May 1759).

2. Moisiodax's patron, Prince Gregorios Ghikas of Moldavia (1764–1767, 1774–1777). Engraved frontispiece in N. Theotokis, *Seira enos kai pentikonta ypomnimatiston eis tin Oktateuchon* (Leipzig, 1772).

3. Moisiodax's patron, Prince Alexandros Ypsilandis of Wallachia (1774–1782, 1796–1797). Late-eighteenth-century engraving. Portrait Archive, Centre for Neohellenic Research, National Hellenic Research Foundation, Athens.

ΗΘΙΚΗ ΦΙΛΟΣΟΦΙΑ

ΜΕΤΑΦΡΑΣΘΕΙΣΑ

ΕΚ ΤΟΥ ΙΤΑΛΙΚΟΥ ΙΔΙΩΜΑΤΟΣ,

ΠΑΡΑ

ΙΩΣΗΠΟΥ ΙΕΡΟΔΙΑΚΟΝΟΥ

ΤΟΥ ΜΟΙΣΙΟΔΑΚΟΣ,

ΚΑΙ ΑΦΙΕΡΩΘΕΙΣΑ

Τῷ Παμιερωτάτῳ, Σοφολογιωτάτῳ, ᾧ Θεοπροβλήτῳ Μητροπολίτῃ τῆς Σμύρνης.

ΚΥΡΙΩ, ΚΥΡΙΩ,

ΝΕΟΦΥΤΩ, ΤΩ ΕΚ ΛΕΡΟΥ.

ΤΟΜΟΣ ΠΡΩΤΟΣ.

ΕΝΕΤΙΗΣΙ, 1761.

Παρὰ Ἀμπωμίῳ τῷ Βόρτολι.

CON LICENZA DE' SUPERIORI, E PRIVILEGIO.

4. Title page to Iosipos Moisiodax, *Moral Philosophy*, vol. I (Venice, 1761). Istituto Ellenico, Venice.

ΠΡΑΓΜΑΤΕΙΆ
ΠΕΡΊ ΠΑΙΔΩΝ ΑΓΩΓΗΣ,
Η'
ΠΑΙΔΑΓΩΓΙΑ,
ΣΥΝΤΕΘΕΙΣΑ ΠΑΡΑ'
ΙΩΣΗΠΟΥ ΤΟΥ ΜΟΙΣΙΟΔΑΚΟΣ,
Καὶ τυπωθεῖσα δαπάνῃ Φιλοτίμῳ τῷ Ἐντιμοτάτῳ
καὶ Χρησιμωτάτῳ ἐν πραγματείαις,
ΚΥΡΊΟΥ ΚΥΡΊΟΥ
ΘΕΟΔΩ'ΡΟΥ
ΕΜΜΑΝΟΤΗΛΟΥ ΓΚΙΚΟΥ ΤΟΥ
Α'ΠΟ ΜΟΣΧΟΠΟΛΕΩΣ.

✢ ✢ ✢

αψοθ'. ΕΝΕΤΙΉΣΙ, 1779.

Παρὰ Νικολάῳ Γλυκεῖ τῷ ἐξ Ἰωαννίνων.
CON LICENZA DE' SUPERIORI.

5. Title page to Iosipos Moisiodax, *Pedagogy* (Venice, 1779). Marciana Library, Venice.

ΙΩΣΗΠΟΥ
ΤΟΥ͂ ΜΟΙΣΙΟ´ΔΑΚΟΣ.

Παραλλαγὴ τῦ πρὸς Νικοκλέα λόγυ περὶ Βασιλείας τῦ Ἰσοκράτυς,

Η᾽ ΚΕΦΑ´ΛΑΙΑ ΠΟΛΙΤΙΚΑ᾽,

Μεταπεφρασμένα παρὰ τῦ αὐτῦ Γαλλιςί.

TRANSFORMATION
De l'Oraison d'Isocrate sûr l art de regner pour Nicoclés,

Faite par

JOSEPH MYSSIODAX,
OU CHAPITRES POLITICS,

Traduits par le même en Francois.

αψοθ´. Ε᾽ΝΕΤΙ´ΗΣΙ, 1779.

Παρὰ Δημητρίῳ Θεοδοσίυ τῷ ἐξ Ἰωαννίνων.

E. Φ.

7765

6. Title page to Iosipos Moisiodax, *In Nicoclem* (Venice, 1779). National Library of Greece, Athens.

7. Title page to Iosipos Moisiodax, *Apology* (Vienna, 1780). National Library of Greece, Athens.

8. Title page to Iosipos Moisiodax, *Theory of Geography* (Vienna, 1781). Private collection, Athens.

ΙΩΣΗΠΟΥ ΤΟΥ ΜΟΙΣΙΟΔΑΚΟΣ

Σημειώσεις Φυσιολογικαί,
Αἵτινες διευθύνονται Πανυποκλιτικῶς πρὸς

ΤΟΝ

Ὑψηλότατον, Γαληνότατον, κ̄ Φιλομουσότατον
Αὐθέντην κ̄ Ἡγεμόνα Πάσης Οὐγγροβλαχίας

ΚΥΡΙΟΝ ΚΥΡΙΟΝ

ΙΩΑΝΝΗΝ ΜΙΧΑΗΛΟΝ ΚΩΝΣΤΑΝ-
ΤΙΝΟΥ ΣΟΥΤΖΟΝ ΒΟΕΒΟΔΑΝ,

Λόγῳ ἁπλῶς Δοκιμίων.

Ἐν τῇ νέᾳ Τυπογραφίᾳ τοῦ Βουκουρεσίου.

ἐν Ἔτει 1784.

Παρὰ Νικολάῳ κ̄ Ἰωάννῃ Λαζάρου.

9. Title page to Iosipos Moisiodax, *Physiological Notes* (Bucharest, 1784). Library of the Romanian Academy, Bucharest.

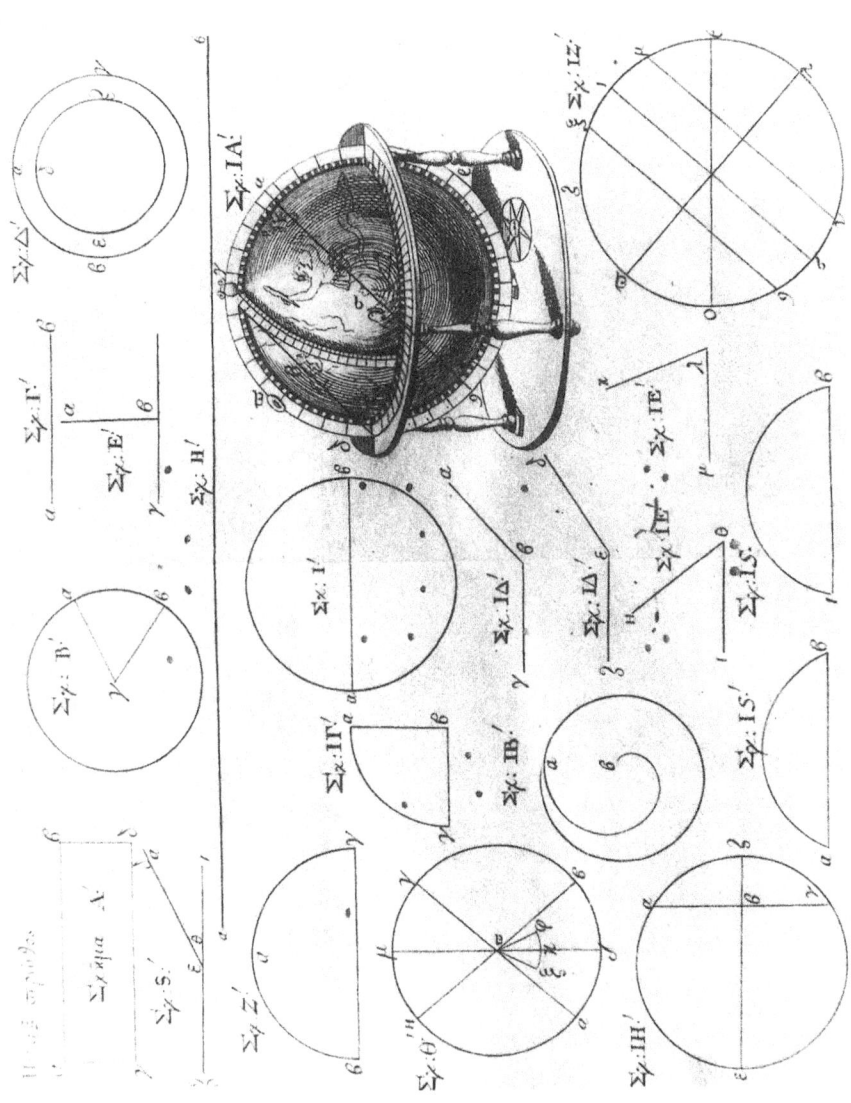

10. Mathematical plate from Iosipos Moisiodax, *Theory of Geography* (Vienna, 1781).

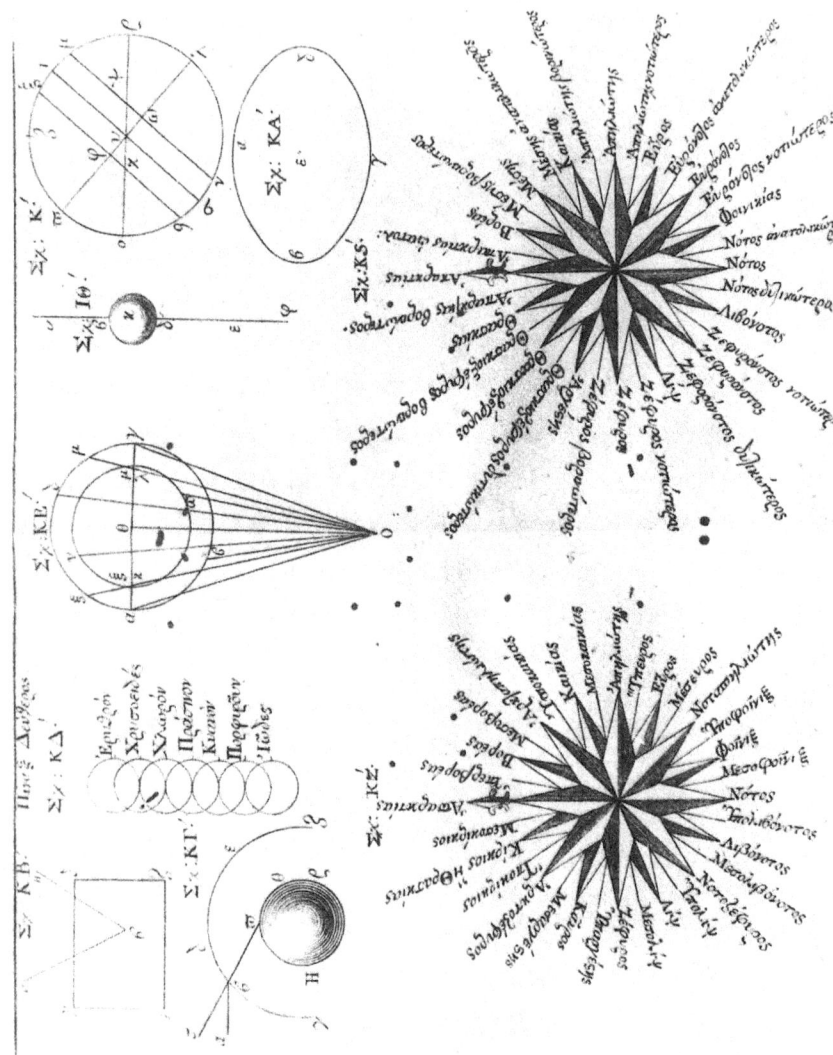

11. Mathematical plate from Iosipos Moisiodax, *Theory of Geography* (Vienna, 1781).

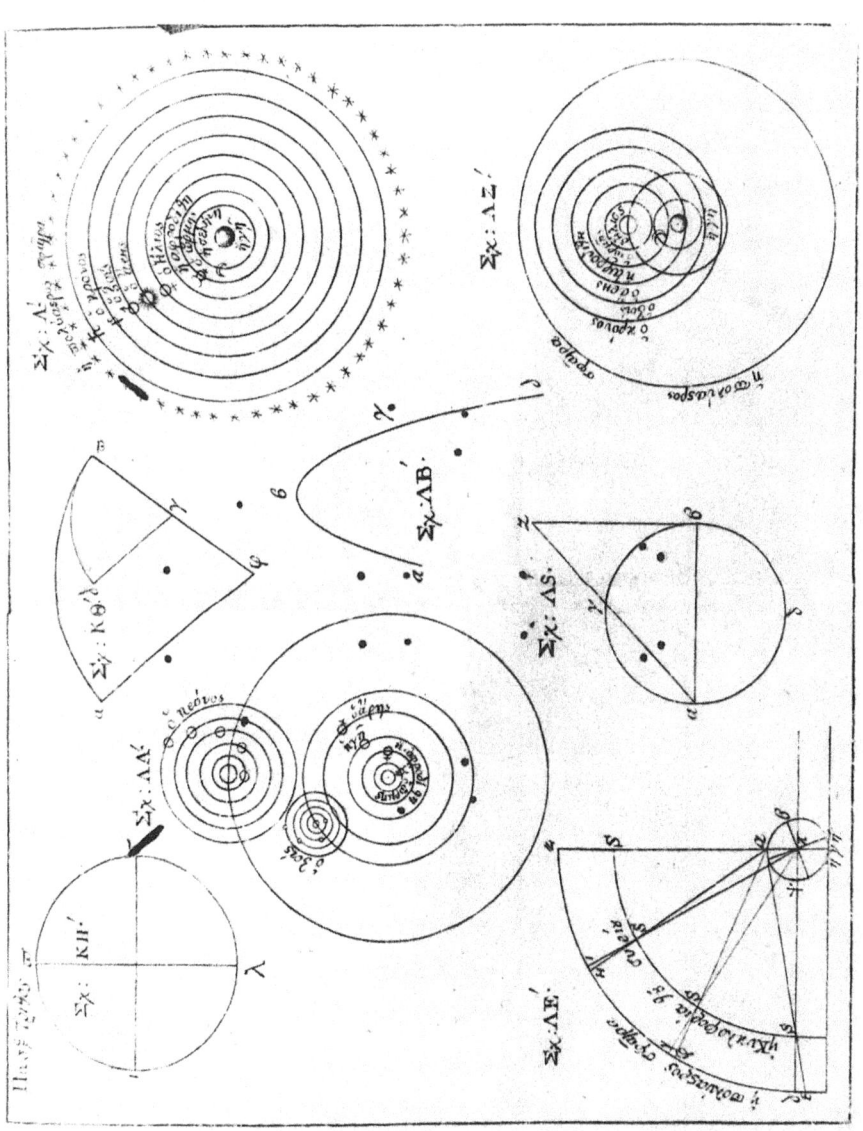

12. Mathematical plate from Iosipos Moisiodax, *Theory of Geography* (Vienna, 1781).

PART TWO

THE COHERENCE OF A VISION

Being inspired by zeal for the true enlightenment of Hellas
. . .
(*Apology*, 1780)

. . . I speak with great liberty.
(*Moral Philosophy*, 1761)

SEVEN

ANCIENTS AND MODERNS

THE THEORETICAL parameters of Moisiodax's thought were determined by the quarrel of the Ancients and Moderns. This intellectual dispute had set its seal on the history of European culture in the seventeenth century,[1] though the prehistory of the conflict may be traced much earlier to the controversies arising out of the emergence of humanism during the Renaissance.[2] The object of the debate was to demonstrate the superiority of the cultural achievements of either the ancient or the modern world. During the course of the seventeenth century the skirmishes between the supporters of the Ancients and the Moderns caused great turmoil in the fields of literature, art, and science, particularly in France and England, the two countries where the achievements of modern civilization made continuous evaluation and comparison inevitable. Many leading intellectuals in the two countries were directly involved in the debate, although the literary polemic was for the most part the work of lesser pamphleteers. The leading representatives of literature, philosophy, and science, who revitalized the European cultural tradition in the seventeenth century, were involved in the dispute only indirectly by escaping the bonds of authority and seeking new means of creative expression beyond accepted conventions.

Despite Jonathan Swift's pleas in favor of the Ancients in *The Battle of the Books* (1704), the dawn of the century of Enlightenment saw the tide turn in favor of the Moderns. The value of classical civilization, however,

---

[1] For a general survey, see Gilbert Highet, *The Classical Tradition: Greek and Roman Influences on Western Literature* (New York, 1949), pp. 261–288. For the climate of the dispute in the eighteenth century, see J. B. Bury, *The Idea of Progress: An Inquiry into Its Origins and Growth* (London, 1920), pp. 78–97. Cf. especially the classic study by Richard F. Jones, *Ancients and Moderns: A Study of the Rise of the Scientific Movement in Seventeenth-Century England* (Gloucester, Mass., 1961), pp. 119–147; and also H. Butterfield, *The Origins of Modern Science: 1300–1800* (London, 1957), pp. 213–218. For the contribution of the dispute to the emergence of the Enlightenment, see Peter Gay, *The Enlightenment: An Interpretation*. Vol. I: *The Rise of Modern Paganism* (New York, 1966), pp. 279–321.

[2] See especially Hans Baron, *The Crisis of the Early Italian Renaissance* (Princeton, 1966), pp. 192–196, 229–232, 329–331, 420–426, 430–435. See also C. Vasoli, "La première querelle des 'anciens' et des 'modernes' aux origines de la Renaissance," in *Classical Influences on European Culture A.D. 1500–1700*, ed. R. R. Bolgar (Cambridge, 1976), pp. 67–80. The older work by Hubert Gillot, *La querelle des anciens et des modernes en France* (Nancy, 1914), pp. 30–49, 50–67, is still of interest.

was no longer denied, as the more extreme members of the modernist party had earlier tried to do. Progress toward Enlightenment was founded on this balance, which was well expressed by Montesquieu.[3] The decisive intellectual preoccupation that eventually made possible the settlement of the dispute was the gradual consolidation in European thought of the theory of progress. This was largely the outcome of the scientific revolution of the seventeenth century, which gave firm evidence to the dynamism of modern thought, over and above the affected excesses and the rhetorical witticisms of literary circles. In the sphere of political theory, however, the ancient models retained their attractiveness. As a succession of theorists from Fénélon to Mably made plain, the classical paradigm of civic virtue remained the most effective standard of political criticism. This accounts for the fact that radical republicanism from the Renaissance to the Enlightenment remained a stranger to the theory of progress and, in contrast, continued to adhere to the cyclical theory of history.[4]

In the Greek context, the quarrel that had agitated European culture made itself felt with a certain time lag only after the turn of the eighteenth century, when the debate in Europe had been essentially exhausted. Echoes of the controversy were first heard in early synopses of Greek literature and sketches of the history of philosophy, such as those by Dimitrios Prokopiou and Evgenios Voulgaris.[5] The evidence afforded by these works and certain other indications suggest that Greek intellectuals were aware of the significance of the dispute from the very outset of the Enlightenment movement. The earliest manifestation of the dispute in Greek literature was the remarkable work by Nicholas Mavrokordatos, *Philotheos's Parerga*, which unequivocally proclaimed the superiority of the Moderns.[6] It was typical of the intellectual climate of Hellenism in the first decades of the eighteenth century, however, that this work remained unpublished until 1800. Voulgaris, despite extolling the contribution made to the progress of philosophy by the critics of scholastic Aristotelianism, remained entrenched behind his eclecticism and

---

[3] Montesquieu, *Oeuvres complètes* (Paris, 1846), pp. 622–624.

[4] Cf. John Pocock, *The Machiavellian Moment: Florentine Political Thought and the Atlantic Republican Tradition* (Princeton, 1975), pp. 218, 493.

[5] See Dimitrios Prokopiou, "Epitetmimeni eparithmisis ton kata ton parelthonta aiona logion Graikon kai peri tinon en to nyn aioni anthounton," in *Bibliotheca Graeca*, ed. Johannes Fabricius, vol. 11 (Hamburg, 1722), pp. 769–804, and Evgenios Voulgaris, *I Logiki* (Leipzig, 1766), pp. 1ff., esp. pp. 37–45 (Proeisodiodis aphigisis peri archis kai proodou tis kata philosophian enstaseos). For the importance of these two sources with regard to the quarrel of the Ancients and Moderns, see Nikos K. Psimmenos, "I Epitetmimeni eparithmisi tou Dimitriou Prokopiou os pigi gnosis tis neoellinikis philosophias," *Ipirotika Chronika* 24 (1982): 204–248.

[6] Nikolaos Mavrokordatos, *Philotheou Parerga*, ed. Gr. Constantas (Vienna, 1800), p. 54.

archaic language and avoided openly declaring himself at variance with "the solemn matter of Antiquity."[7] As a result, Iosipos Moisiodax was essentially the first critic to make the cultural problems posed by the quarrel of the Ancients and Moderns an issue of public debate within the Greek intellectual community.

At this point, as at so many others, Iosipos spoke out freely on ideological issues and precipitated confrontations with conventional intellectual attitudes in his social environment. His involvement in the quarrel of the Ancients and Moderns, the last historical phase of which he belatedly inaugurated in modern Greek culture, was to form the main axis of his thought during the creative twenty-year period from the publication of the *Moral Philosophy* to the *Theory of Geography*. In the prolegomena to the *Moral Philosophy*, Iosipos censured the cultural backwardness of contemporary Greek society and stressed its educational needs. He based his diagnosis on a twofold comparison: first, he contrasted the deficiencies of Greek society with the achievements of Europe; second, he set this partial contrast within a more general comparison of Ancients and Moderns.

In the diagnosis offered in this manifesto for cultural change, Moisiodax was not content with merely pointing out the problem with all its fatal contradictions; instead, he went on to indicate the cure. The problem was crucially located in the position occupied by antiquity in modern Greek education and culture: "At the present day Greece nurtures and feeds two faults that are most unbecoming to her glorious reputation. She is dominated overwhelmingly by deference to and neglect of antiquity. The former has bred in her that powerful presumption that everything which was invented or cultivated by the ancients is noble, is accurate; and the latter has resulted in the scarcity, or rather the nonexistence, of ancient texts."[8] Adherence to the forms of ancient learning and unquestioning acceptance of the authority of tradition—that is, the excessive "deference" to antiquity—was, in Moisiodax's view, responsible for the disastrous ignorance of the substance of classical literature that amounted to "neglect" of ancient civilization in modern Greek education and culture. Inadequate knowledge of the substance accounted for the inability of the partisans of the Ancients to form a proper assessment, and hence their prejudice rose against the Moderns. Precisely this shortsightedness made Iosipos indignant because, through his studies in Europe, he himself had come to different conclusions that once more he expressed without restraint: "Let the truth be proclaimed, however, even though it sometimes stings. Europe at the present day, partly through proper ad-

---

[7] E. Voulgaris, *I Logiki*, p. 45.
[8] *Ithiki Philosophia*, vol. 1, pp. xvi–xvii.

ministration, and partly through the proclivity toward learning of the rulers of the various countries, surpasses in wisdom even ancient Greece."[9]

This assertion of the superiority of modern Europe over ancient Greece places Moisiodax firmly in the camp of the Moderns in their quarrel with the Ancients. His conviction formed the premise of his judgment regarding the needs of modern Greek culture. The conclusion, with which he proposed the cure, was imbued with all the impatience of a man who found himself surrounded by unexpected inflexibility in the face of something he perceived as self-evident and inevitably rose in revolt: "Let there be an end, in the name of the Lord, let there be an end to the deference that takes away from her the ability to judge and to the neglect that strips her of the very possessions of which she disposes! Greece does, does need Europe. Since at the present day the one abounds in and the other is deprived of the worthiest lights of learning."[10] Iosipos's appeal for a reorientation toward contemporary European civilization and his pronouncement that this was the appropriate model for the cultural reform of Hellenism, as against the traditional subservience to antiquity, situate the quarrel of the Ancients and Moderns at the heart of the cultural debate in which he was the protagonist. Moisiodax's argument ignited the controversy, making public a debate about the respective merits of the two cultural models that was already taking shape in modern Greek thought. We have already noted the consequences that Moisiodax himself suffered for his outspokenness.

Iosipos's standpoint in the quarrel was a necessary but not sufficient condition of his philosophical self-definition as an exponent of the Enlightenment. The dispute antedated the Enlightenment; it was not, therefore, its distinctive feature. The characteristic philosophical basis of the Enlightenment was the transition to epistemological empiricism.[11] This bold departure, which rejected the legitimacy of metaphysics as an object of philosophical speculation and established the external perceptible world as the proper object of human inquiry, was the foundation of the philosophy of the Enlightenment. This was precisely the object of the "sound philosophy" that Moisiodax embraced and strove to propagate through his teaching and writing.

Twenty years after the publication of the *Moral Philosophy*, he clarified his philosophical position in the *Apology*. As a result of his experiences in the intervening period, the broader cultural criticism of his first

---

[9] *Ibid.*, p. xx. For a fuller analysis of Moisiodax's pertinent arguments, see P. M. Kitromilides, "The Last Battle of the Ancients and Moderns: Ancient Greece and Modern Europe in the Neohellenic Revival," *Modern Greek Studies Yearbook*, 1 (1985): 79–91.

[10] *Ithiki Philosophia*, vol. 1, p. xxi. Cf. *Apologia*, p. 166.

[11] Cf. Ernst Cassirer, *The Philosophy of the Enlightenment* (Princeton, 1951), pp. 37–47, 93–98.

work had now become more specifically focused on the question of the superiority of modern science over Aristotelian physics. At the same time, his argument turned sharply in the direction of social criticism, as reflected in his insinuations concerning the motives of the enemies of modern thought.

The introductory section of the *Apology* presents Moisiodax's scientific and philosophical beliefs through a review of modern scientific progress and its confrontation with the obstacles erected by and the reactions from the followers of Aristotelianism. This text is important as a statement in modern Greek of the *topoi* of Enlightenment epistemology. Moisiodax proclaims his opposition to not only the scholastic tradition of Aristotelian logic and metaphysics but also its neo-Aristotelian offshoots and sings the praises of modern natural philosophy. In this framework mathematics and empirical science appeared the necessary foundation on which to erect "sound philosophy." Citing examples and invoking the great names of modern science to document his position, Moisiodax recalls the atmosphere of D'Alembert's "Discours préliminaire" to the *Encyclopédie*: he depicts the pantheon of the Enlightenment, chief among them the three founders of modern knowledge, who delivered the coups de grace to lingering scholastic Aristotelianism—Descartes, Galileo, and Newton. The figure of "incomparable glory" in these pages was of course Newton, "a man of natural genius and profundity . . . convinced by long years of experience how necessary mathematics is to physics."[12]

The evolution of Moisiodax's thought between the prolegomena to the *Moral Philosophy* and the *Apology* signified the character of his philosophical ideas. The intellectual courage and enthusiasm with which he spoke out in favor of the natural philosophy of the Enlightenment may occasionally obscure the fact that in several important respects he remained within the framework of Christian rationalism, an integral part of the moderate Enlightenment. His choice of Muratori's work indicates this: an impeccable Christian frame of reference provided the legitimate context for the reorientation from scholastic logic and metaphysics to a philosophy of human praxis and a moral individualism that acknowledged the secular priorities of self-preservation, bodily health, and earthly happiness as valid goals of human life. Moisiodax's philosophical position unfolded along these lines: his transition from Muratori to the Christian rationalism of the German Enlightenment, which is perceptible in the *Apology*, was a natural development. In that text, the "philosophia Leibnitio-Wolffiana" provided the spiritual underpinning of Iosipos's ideas:

[12] *Apologia*, p. 13; see pp. 10–15 for the survey of modern science. Cf. D'Alembert, *Discours préliminaire* (Paris, 1894), pp. 92–113.

he was aware of Leibniz's monadology,[13] and he adopted a broadly Wolffian position in his discussion of the definition and division of metaphysics as part of his own conception of "sound philosophy."[14] In this respect his work reflected the influence exercised by Wolff's philosophy in Central and Southeastern Europe—an influence that was further propagated and popularized by the works of Wolff's disciple Christian Friedrich Baumeister, which were translated into Greek and used in the Principalities.[15] Moisiodax retained this general philosophical framework without particularly caring either to prove or disprove it. Although he did not question its basic tenets, his own attitude regarding fundamental metaphysical issues deep down apparently tended toward a form of agnosticism: accept the doctrines of the faith because there is no way of knowing about them. The patience he urged upon his readers concerning these things betrays his ultimate agnosticism.[16] His original argument for his choice of Muratori's work on account of its focus on ethical questions retained its force in view of all the practical problems—basically issues of academic, social, and political morality—that shaped the question of knowledge as presented in the *Apology*. This cardinal foundation of his secular outlook on philosophical issues combined with his scepticism specifically about the possibility of knowledge in metaphysical questions to form the preconditions of his conception of the proper task of "sound philosophy"—the study of nature and the external world through mathematical, observational, and experimental methods. The stress on this methodological aspect of sound philosophy was programmatic and intentional: it underlined the point that Aristotelianism could not be identified with sound philosophy because it rejected the use of mathematics in physics. Moisiodax wished to leave no doubt about the opposition between his conception of sound philosophy and the Aristotelian tradition; thus, he further emphasized that mathematics was the essential epistemological preliminary of sound philosophy and that the empirical investigation of nature was its true substantive content. That is why, despite his admiration for Descartes and Leibniz, the real hero of the *Apology* was Newton. This also explains why, despite the formal framework of Wolffian rationalism, the substantive philosophical content of his thought was largely drawn from French Encyclopedism: the *Apology*'s emphasis on natural philosophy and utilitarianism makes this evident.

[13] *Apologia*, pp. 151–152, n.6.

[14] Ibid., pp. 103–106. Cf. P. C. Noutsos, "Iosipos Moisiodax: Orismos kai diairesi tis metaphysikis," *Dodoni* 11 (1982): 185–192.

[15] See Emanuel Turczunski, *Die deutsch-griechischen Kulturbeziehungen bis zur Berufung König Ottos* (Munich, 1959), pp. 168–169, 173–174, 185–186, 204–205.

[16] E.g., *Paidagogia*, p. 106.

Moisiodax's text is pervaded with the scientific optimism of the theory of progress. The triumph of modern science, it was clear to his eyes, had shaped the intellectual climate within which the Moderns prevailed in their quarrel with the Ancients. In this context Moisiodax set his concern for the intellectual reconstruction of Hellenism as well; he alluded to those who had preceded him in the endeavor to introduce modern philosophy and science into Greek education, Manassis Iliadis, Nikolaos Zerzoulis, and Evgenios Voulgaris and then sketched his own attempts.[17] On this basis, Iosipos unequivocally and daringly described the problem of Greek culture, distilled into three epigrammatic conclusions: first, "the present wretched condition" of Greek education; second, his diagnosis of the necessity of cultural change that he judged the "most pressing need of Hellas";[18] and third, the optimistic detection of the possibilities for progress—"men have an innate desire to learn."[19]

Why then should the attempts at reform have proved so difficult that Iosipos was imbued with pessimism and dejection about his own personal fate? The answer lies in his suspicions of and the oblique allusions he had made as early as 1765 to the motives of the Ancients' supporters in their campaign against modern science: their attitude was not simply the product of intellectual ossification and ideological obscurantism. It arose from fear that their ignorance would be discovered, trepidation that they might lose the vested privileges secured to them by their monopoly over the educational system, and finally concern at undermining the mechanisms of ideological control that followed upon the slightest deviation from reproducing conventional wisdom. For precisely this reason, it appeared to Iosipos, the followers of Aristotelianism were ready to stigmatize the followers of the Moderns by charging them with heresy and atheism. Moisiodax was not the first to meet with the kind of treatment he had received at the hands of the Reverend Such-and-such in 1765; he probably had in mind the precedent of Methodios Anthrakitis, too, in hinting at the motives leading to his being accused of pro-Catholic sentiments: "But I say that it is not zeal for the faith that moves men of this sort actively to oppose modern philosophy, or to dissuade the youth from entering the Academies of Europe. What then is the cause? Let whoever wishes divine it."[20]

His awareness of the sociopolitical implications of the dispute in Greek culture did not diminish the importance Iosipos attached to its substantive scientific content. After the more generalized polemic of the *Apol-*

---

[17] *Apologia*, pp. 25–27.
[18] Ibid., p. 18.
[19] Ibid., p. 23.
[20] Ibid., p. 167n.

ogy, he returned in the *Theory of Geography* to a systematic attempt to reconstruct prevailing Greek concepts of natural phenomena on the model of modern science. The quarrel of the Ancients and Moderns formed the axis around which he organized the material of his most important scientific treatise (see Chapter 5). In developing his subject, he methodically set out side by side the arguments used by both parties on each scientific question with which he was dealing so that the superiority of the Moderns would become apparent through a simple comparison. He does this, for example, when dealing with the hotly disputed issue of the movement of the Earth. Having set forth the arguments of the Ptolemaic school against the movement of the Earth, he appends the counterarguments of the followers of Copernicus in a long footnote and then gives a detailed analysis of the arguments of the Moderns in support of the view that the Earth revolves around the Sun and its own axis.[21]

As an ideological document, the treatise forms a succinct statement of the quarrel of the Ancients and Moderns in the field of theoretical geography. Although he placed himself firmly in the camp of the Moderns, Iosipos was not dogmatic in assessing the Ancients' contribution to scientific knowledge. When the opportunity arose, he unhesitatingly reproves groundless criticisms or errors committed by the Moderns in their evaluation of the Ancients. He frequently also hints at the reasons for these excesses. The attitude of the Moderns and their prejudices against the Ancients might have been owing to ignorance and spite, but they were also owing to the inadequacy of the Modern Greeks themselves, the heirs of the Ancients. In his apportionment of responsibility Moisiodax was, as usual, severe. As to the responsibilities of the Modern Greeks, he notes: "Some of the Moderns, who contrive in everything to belittle the achievements of the Greeks, the reason being that there is not today a single Greek fit to comb their wig as it should be combed, attribute the invention of the armillary sphere to the Babylonians or the Egyptians."[22]

Another serious source of the negative attitude of the Moderns toward the Ancients was plain ignorance: "A myriad mistakes of this kind are to be found amongst the Moderns, arising from their ignorance of the Greek language; one plagiarizes from the other, and they transmit amongst themselves the mistakes of others, and they are not merely ignorant of the truth, but frequently insult the truth."[23] Ignorance, however, could be combined with both rancor and plagiarism of the Ancients' knowledge without even the appropriate acknowledgment. Moisiodax, heir to the

---

[21] *Theoria tis Geographias*, pp. 107–108: the arguments of the Ptolemaic school; note pp. 108–110: the reply of the Copernicans; pp. 109–123: the arguments of the Moderns.

[22] Ibid., p. 2, n.

[23] Ibid., p. 54, n.1.

tradition of Greek letters of which the Orthodox Church had been the guardian in the Greek East and equipped with the scientific knowledge of enlightened Europe, offers a fine example of scientific criticism with regard to the nomenclature of the winds:

> I suspect that the Moderns tend to be somewhat impertinent in their judgment in this matter, as in many others that refer to our ancient ancestors.... The purity of the Greek terminology that flourishes in all the names of the winds, the extreme ignorance that obscured the vision of all the nations of the West, whether before or even during the age of Charlemagne, finally, the very short voyages made by the nations of the West at that time: all these things convince us with good reason that our ancient ancestors were either aware of or used the names of the thirty-two winds, and that it is primarily they who should be reckoned the creators of the above classification of the winds. Everyone can see from this, I think, no less than from other things, that the Moderns, who otherwise owe every fruit of their erudition (the same claim may reasonably be made about everything else in which they now take so much pride) to the seeds sown by our good and noble ancestors, nevertheless, like kicking asses, are not merely ungrateful, but even show contempt.[24]

With these assertions, the committed innovator of Modern Greek culture revealed that he was capable of balanced and scrupulous scientific judgment. The *Theory of Geography* exemplifies the maturity and self-awareness of the responsible worker of science.

The nuances of Moisiodax's position on the worth of antiquity reflected the complexity of the Modern Greek attitude toward the classical tradition and the delicate balance that the Enlightenment had to preserve in the Greek context in appraising the merits of ancient civilization. The delicacy of the Enlightenment's stance stemmed from two sources: on the one hand, the value of Greek antiquity had to be defended against the wholesale rejection of pagan learning by Orthodox fundamentalism. In acknowledging the achievements of the Ancients, the Greek Enlightenment preserved its distance from the extreme tenets of Christian theology against profane philosophy. On the other hand, the affirmation of antiquity had to be circumspect and reserved lest it appeared a concession to the theological version of Aristotelianism, which was impregnated with the danger of resubmerging philosophy to theology. This explains why the Greek Enlightenment, in spite of its general receptivity to classical civilization, never managed to develop a unified posture on antiq-

[24] Ibid., pp. 81–82, n.2.

uity and did not quite idealize it until rather late—after Aristotelianism had been safely discredited in scientific thought and political struggles dictated new ideological uses of ancient models. Moisiodax's qualified attitude toward the Ancients reflected the antinomies of this entire cultural dilemma.

EIGHT

SCIENCE AS A VOCATION

THE STANCE adopted by Moisiodax in the quarrel of the Ancients and Moderns, a partial expression of his broader philosophical and scientific convictions, epitomizes the intellectual outlook of a champion of the new natural science of the Enlightenment. His attitude was shaped by a number of intellectual presuppositions that formed the shared basis on which the "natural philosopher" of the Enlightenment worked. The more general intellectual predilections that determined his standpoint in the dispute shaped his scientific and educational identity. Thus his recognition of the contribution of the Ancients to the progress of civilization and knowledge in certain fields, his espousal of Cartesian rationalism and acceptance of the theory of progress as the logical principle underlying the history of mankind, and finally his belief in the brilliant prospects of science—all these were shared tenets of the party of the Moderns that made Moisiodax one of their number.[1]

With this turn of mind Iosipos approached the issues in the natural sciences that formed his primary theoretical interest. There can be little or no doubt that these interests shaped his intellectual self-definition, which he saw as the professional vocation of the "natural philosopher." The ideal of "sound philosophy" that he proclaimed as the touchstone of his intellectual life essentially meant modern science in contradistinction to the traditional academic content of philosophy—that is, to scholastic logic and metaphysics. His work as both writer and teacher can best be appreciated, therefore, as part of the emergence of the idea of modern science in Greek thought. His intellectual identity may be properly recaptured and appraised in the perspective of the history of science.[2] To this end, the evidence supplied by Moisiodax's writings could be used as the basis of an attempt to locate him within the intellectual climate of the natural philosophy of the Enlightenment.

[1] Cf. J. B. Bury, *The Idea of Progress* (London, 1920), pp. 78–97.

[2] The sketchy treatment of Moisiodax's work in the existing studies of science in the Modern Greek Enlightenment is obvious, for example, in M. Stephanidis, *Ai physikai epistimai en Elladi pro tis Epanastaseos* (Athens, 1926), pp. 16–17. An attempt to place Moisiodax's ideas within the perspective of the history of science is made in P. M. Kitromilides, "The Idea of Science in the Modern Greek Enlightenment," in *Greek Studies in the Philosophy and History of Science*, ed. P. Nicolacopoulos (Dordrecht, 1990), pp. 187–200, esp. 192–195.

The testimony of his works is sufficiently clear to support an interpretative enterprise of this kind. In both the *Apology* and the *Theory of Geography* his expositions are accompanied by a plethora of references to scientific sources; thus, it is relatively easy to detect the origins of his ideas and evaluate his position with reference to the trends and debates in European science during his time. Furthermore, in Moisiodax's case, the historian of science finds himself faced with a happy combination of circumstances that makes it possible to trace the development of his scientific views: the surviving 1767 manuscript of the *Theory of Geography*, which contains the first draft of the treatise, can be compared with the printed version of the text that followed in 1781. The final form of the work reflects the evolution of Iosipos's scientific outlook in the tumultuous intervening years, which had been marked by his clash with his social and political environment and his renewed contact with European culture.

It is revealing of the scientific options preferred by Moisiodax that, of the publishing program in the field of the natural sciences that he repeatedly announced, when circumstances and setbacks permitted, he ultimately produced only one complete publication—his treatise on geography. This indicates his abandonment of abstract mathematical thought in favor of fields of research in which observation and empirical data could be marshaled to check abstract conceptual structures. This shift of emphasis places Moisiodax in the climate of eighteenth-century science[3] and sets him apart from his teacher Evgenios Voulgaris, who remained an adherent of the earlier tradition of abstract thought; the main emphasis in his scientific work being on mathematics.[4]

In shifting his position, Moisiodax was following the trend that was leaving Descartes behind and establishing Galileo and Newton as the leading figures in the field of natural science.[5] This orientation, detectable in Iosipos's scientific work, determined the content of his lectures at the Academy in Jassy, which were presented systematically in the first draft of the geography, as preserved in the 1767 manuscript. When Moisiodax first appeared on the scene, European scientific thought was still feeling the effects of the resistance to the theories of Galileo and Newton,

---

[3] Cf. P. Hazard, *European Thought in the Eighteenth Century* (Gloucester, Mass., 1973), pp. 130–144.

[4] For brief appraisals of Voulgaris's scientific thought, see G. P. Henderson, *The Revival of Greek Thought* (Albany, N.Y., 1970), pp. 64–69, and Kitromilides, "The Idea of Science," pp. 190–192.

[5] Cf. A. Rupert Hall, *The Revolution in Science: 1500–1750* (London, 1983), pp. 113–114, and for the new scientific climate of the later seventeenth and eighteenth centuries, pp. 256–284. On Moisiodax's own appraisals of the contributions of Galileo and Newton to the rise of modern science, see *Apologia*, pp. 154–159, with references to specific scientific discoveries in the notes.

not so much from the adherents of the traditional geocentric theory, but from the supporters of the Cartesian theory of the universe, for which Fontenelle, during his long life, remained a militant propagandist.[6] Moisiodax's alignments in the contests of European science made him a pioneer in the context of Greek scientific thought. Those of his predecessors who had dealt with questions of geography and cosmography had ranged themselves with the Ptolemaic tradition; thus, Moisiodax refers to Chrysanthos Notaras and Kosmas Balanos when he wishes to give examples of the system he regarded as obsolete.[7] Even Evgenios Voulgaris remained circumspect in his public declarations on these matters and sought for compromise by proclaiming his adherence to the Tychonic system.[8] Only Nikiphoros Theotokis, in his *Elements of Physics*, published in 1766, had dared to express in print his preference for the heliocentric theory; even then, he referred to it noncommittally as "the view of the Moderns."[9] In the 1760s, therefore, when Moisiodax made it clear that he stood in Newton's camp he was breaking in a significant way with the prevailing paradigm of "normal science" in contemporary Greek scientific thought that, toward the end of the eighteenth and the beginning of the nineteenth centuries, produced attempts to refute the heliocentric theory and witnessed the persecution of those who embraced and taught it.[10] It is worth noting, as an indication of the intellectual climate of the

---

[6] See the introduction by Robert Shackleton to his edition of the works of Fontenelle, *Entretiens sur la pluralité des mondes—Digression sur les anciens et les modernes* (Oxford, 1955), pp. 2–6, 20–28.

[7] *Theoria tis Geographias*, p. 83, n.1, and 108, n.1.

[8] E. Voulgaris, *Peri systimatos tou Pantos epitomos ekthesis* (Vienna, 1805), p. 63. Cf. H. Butterfield, *The Origins of Modern Science* (London, 1957), p. 71, for the Tychonic system as a compromise in the history of science.

[9] Nikiphoros Theotokis, *Stoicheia physikis* (Leipzig, 1766), vol. 1, "To entefxomeno," fol. *6ʳ, and pp. 47–64, 64–87.

[10] As late as 1797 Moisiodax's former classmate at the Athonite Academy, Sergios Makraios, produced a *Trophy against the Followers of Copernicus*, in which he marshalled arguments from ancient Greek astronomy against the heliocentric theory of the universe. The dispute continued up to the eve of the Greek War of Independence. It is referred to by Korais in a letter to Dorotheos Proïos of November 16, 1816, where he also diagnoses its causes: "It was with sorrow that I read what you write concerning the anti-philosophers, about whom I had some knowledge even before your letter. It is not their zeal for religion that stirs them up against the movement of the earth, but rather they are afraid that the rotation of the sphere may move and overturn the reputation they have so unworthily acquired." See A. Korais, *Allilographia*, vol. 3: *1810–1816* (Athens, 1979), p. 514. In an unpublished text, in codex 6262 of the Monastery of Saint Panteleimon on Mount Athos, we read the following: "The teacher of the school in Kydonies was accused of teaching the astronomical system of Copernicus and Pythagoras." See P. M. Kitromilides, "Ideologikes synepeies tis koinonikis diamachis sti Smyrni (1809–1810)," *Deltio Kentrou Mikrasiatikon Spoudon* 3 (1982): 29. For a general survey of the debate in the Modern Greek Enlighten-

time, that the translation of Newton's work attempted by Nikolaos Zerzoulis, remained unpublished, and today even the whereabouts of the manuscript is unknown.[11] This is the background against which Moisiodax's espousal of Newton's views should be assessed.

The evolution of Moisiodax's thought between the first and second versions of his geography demonstrates how he had consolidated and enriched his scientific views. The two versions have essentially the same structure—regarding the arrangement, division, and content of the chapters. The identity between the chapters is complete, and the divergence suggested by a comparison of the respective tables of contents is only apparent. For example, Chapter 1 of the printed version—"Concerning the circles of a sphere"—is missing from the manuscript, but the material it contains is set out by way of introduction to the text before the numbered chapters begin.[12] From Chapter 1 of the manuscript and Chapter 2 of the printed version, respectively ("Concerning the horizon") to Chapters 26 and 28 respectively, there is complete identity, except that chapter 24 of the manuscript ("Concerning the size of the surface of the Earth") becomes chapter 26 in the printed version. The importance attached by Iosipos to the material in the two final chapters of the treatise—Chapters 25 and 26 of the manuscript, "Concerning the shape of the Earth" and "Concerning whether the Earth moves or does not move"—is clear from the fact that it is developed at greater length in the printed version, which necessitates the subdivision of the material into a larger number of chapters. Thus, in the published text the chapter "Concerning the shape of the Earth" is expanded into two chapters: "Concerning the shape of the Earth, that it is spherical" is supplemented by the additional chapter "Concerning the true shape of the Earth," which contains further specifications and clarifications, based on the latest findings of scientific research. By adding the explanatory qualification "that it is spherical" to the title of the relevant chapter in the final version he underlines a fundamental dimension of the published text that distinguishes it from the manuscript: the author's ideological intentions are now openly expressed, without the restraints still operating at the time of the composition and dictating a certain moderation of tone. It should not be for-

---

ment, see P. Kondylis, *O Neoellinikos Diaphotismos. Oi philosophikes idees* (Athens, 1988), pp. 109–128.

[11] Linos G. Benakis, "Apo tin istoria tou metavyzantinou aristotelismou ston elliniko choro. Amphisvitisi kai yperaspisi tou philosophou ston 18° aiona. Nikolaos Zerzoulis—Dorotheos Lesvios," *Philosophia* 7 (1977): 420–421. Among Moisiodax's contemporaries, Christodoulos Pamblekis stated in print but anonymously his Newtonian views in the same year that saw the publication of the *Theory of Geography*. See *I Alithis Politiki* (Venice, 1781), pp. 123, 125 (translator's notes to the text).

[12] Ms. *Theoria tis Geographias*, fols. 1–3.

gotten that the original version of the work was intended to be dedicated to the Patriarch of Jerusalem (see Chapter 3).

The ideological intentions of the work can be seen quite clearly from reworking and expanding the material in the chapter "Concerning whether the Earth moves or does not move." As noted earlier (see Chapter 5), this chapter is the longest in the printed version of the *Theory of Geography*—an indication of the importance Iosipos attached to the subject. Comparing it with the manuscript reveals the importance of this feature even more strikingly. The single chapter in the manuscript is expanded into three in the printed text. A chapter bearing exactly the same title in both the manuscript and the final version sets out and contrasts the arguments of the Ancients and Moderns on the subject. To this is added, in the printed version, a chapter, "concerning the view of Tycho and the Tychonists," which deals in greater detail with the material in the last three pages of the manuscript chapter on the movement of the earth.[13] Finally, the printed version's additional chapter "Concerning the view of René Descartes and the Cartesians" is completely missing from the manuscript. This addition is significant because it underscores Moisiodax's desire to align himself totally with Newtonian science. The account of the Cartesian theory of the universe was given merely to make his survey exhaustive. Iosipos alludes to the general abandonment of this theory caused by the progress of scientific research and criticizes the stubborn adherence of the French astronomers and geographers to the Cartesian system (possibly an allusion to Fontenelle) by noting that this was due to an "excess of patriotic zeal."[14] The reminder that national ambitions have no place in scientific thought and can only create obstacles in the path of its advancement was an indirect, but eloquent warning to his fellow compatriots. The oblique allusion to the occasional outbursts of fanaticism on the part of the Greek Ptolemaists was unmistakeable.

When he published the *Theory of Geography*, Iosipos knew from bitter experience that the most effective way to attain his ideological objectives would be through convincing, well-founded arguments, not through the mere partisan polemic of his enemies. He accordingly abided by strict scientific reasoning in the statement of his theories. A good example of this aspect of his method is the way in which he formulates the most contentious of the scientific problems that concern him:

[13] Ms. *Theoria tis Geographias*, fols. 72–74.

[14] *Theoria tis Geographias*, p. 131, n.1. On the hold of Cartesianism on French scientific thought, cf. Ernst Cassirer, *The Philosophy of the Enlightenment* (Princeton, 1951), pp. 80–81, and on French reactions to Newtonian physics, cf. Ira O. Wade, *The Structure and Form of the French Enlightenment*, Vol., 1: *Esprit philosophique* (Princeton, 1977), 138–139.

> Whether: the Earth moves or the Sun, is an ancient dispute, almost as old as philosophy itself. The ancient Peripatetics, and the brigades of Western monks, without even a single exception, hold the belief that the Earth is stationary, and moreover that it lies at the very middle of the universe and is the center of the entire order of things. The Pythagoreans, on the other hand, and along with the Pythagoreans all the academies of modern philosophers, on the contrary assign to the Earth two movements, one about its axis, which produces days and nights, and one about the Sun, which produces years.[15]

A second element in his method is his insistence on the distinction between scientific knowledge and religion. Greek education was caught in a complex web, with seams of such sensitivity and power that Iosipos knew well that the disassociation of the two was a basic precondition for the unbiased practice of science in Greek society. In his attitude he expresses the classic demand of the Enlightenment: "The Holy Spirit instructs initiates of the Holy Scriptures and of our supernatural religion, but it does not at the same time instruct either builders, or goldsmiths, or stone-masons, and consequently no mathematicians either: why? The reason is locked away in the deeply unknown darkness of the supernatural will of God, and we timorous humans are therefore unable to know it."[16] Without this distinction, no progress would be possible. The passages of the Scriptures invoked by the Ptolemaists were "in accord with the superstitions held by the men of that time, especially the Jews, a boorish, uneducated nation, by nature prone to error in matters relating to the senses. When the Scripture philosophizes, this is invariably the manner in which it philosophizes, and no philosopher who has learned to view matters through reason, can deny it."[17]

Only after the achievement of this more general independence for the practice of science would it be possible to implement the proper scientific method in research into natural phenomena. This method used two techniques: inductive reasoning in logically evaluating the material, and empiricism in collecting the data. The choice of inductive reasoning basically reverts to the quarrel of the Ancients and Moderns and represents a condensation at the methodological level of the historical logic that dictated its outcome:

> A priori arguments we call those that are derived from the natural principles of things themselves, as when, for example, it is required that you infer all the phenomena connected with man from man's existence and rationality.

---

[15] *Theoria tis Geographias*, pp. 106–7.
[16] Ibid., p. 62, n.1.
[17] Ibid., pp. 110–111.

The ancients, and especially Aristotle, sought to argue in this fashion in almost all things: and this is the main reason why their philosophy, as I note in the second note on page 7 of the first part of my apology, did not make much progress in its theorems. A posteriori arguments we call those that are drawn from observations of things. For example, it was observed that all bodies attract each other in proportion to their mass and the distance between them. From this it was deduced that it was necessary for a force to be located in bodies by which they are obliged mutually to attract each other. Every great advance in which philosophy today rejoices is attributable to this manner of philosophizing.[18]

The adoption of empiricism as both an epistemological position and a research technique was tantamount to an intellectual revolution; it opened up new roads for the evolution of science in the eighteenth century. Iosipos's response to the demand was unequivocal: "The senses must be accounted sure judges of phenomena."[19] His entire work bears the stamp of his attempt to put this into practice. His empiricism can be perceived in the pedagogical method he proposes for the study of geography: "All those coming to geography should equip themselves with globes, which can be acquired by those who live near the sea from Venice or from other coastal cities, and by those who live in Wallachia and Moldavia from Vienna, or from Leipzig."[20] For precisely this reason the thirty-three problems included in the published version of the *Theory of Geography* and intended to consolidate knowledge of the subject, are exercises solvable with the use of a globe.

The empirical method emerges even more graphically, however, from his references to the accounts of geographical discoveries made by explorers and navigators as evidence against which to check and confirm the findings of theoretical geography. It is indicative of Moisiodax's method that he had recourse to the evidence of Captain Cook's voyages in resolving a number of contentious problems in theoretical geography.[21] While discussing the calculation of geographical latitude and longitude to determine the precise shape of the Earth, Moisiodax critically examined the views of Maupertuis on the subject. He first compared them with the relevant views of Newton and Huygens and then proceeded to check the theoretical propositions empirically on the basis of the evidence afforded by the latest geographical explorations:

[18] Ibid., pp. 92–93, n.5.
[19] Ibid., p. 111.
[20] Ibid., p. xiv.
[21] For the importance of Cook's voyages, especially with regard to the development of cartography, see C. Singer, *A Short History of Scientific Ideas to 1900* (Oxford, 1959), pp. 320–321, 395.

I read the travels of the admirable Jacques Cook (that is, his travels in the southern seas), a man generally admitted to be most experienced in naval science, and with justice adjudged superior to any other sea-man, and in them I found every other detail referring to navigation, but did not find even a hint that he took latitude and longitude according to the views of Maupertuis. The critical reader can, I think, infer from this that the view of the French astronomer and geographer is neither easy to maintain, nor necessarily maintainable.[22]

Moisiodax's scepticism concerning Maupertuis was, of course, unfounded, and his juxtaposition of the views of Newton with those of the eminent French mathematician, who tried to confirm them empirically through geographical measurements, betrayed his misunderstanding of the issue.[23] His admiration for Captain Cook, however, the earliest mention in Greek of the great navigator of the South Seas, represented just one more instance of the fascination and excitement provoked throughout Europe by Cook's voyages and discoveries.[24]

The seafarers and explorers thus become the heroes of the new science:

The countless toils and dangers undergone by all these men in their own particular voyages, and the intention of almost all of them to increase human knowledge, whether on matters of Natural History, or Astronomy, or Geography, make these men deserving of the respect of all and worthy to be praised in every book referring in any way to their discoveries. Whoever reads the publications of the voyages of these men, and especially the more recent of them, cannot fail to adjudge them common benefactors of the human race, and consequently to inscribe them, each in his own way, on the tablets of immortality.[25]

Iosipos attempted to conform to these models in his own painstaking researches in the Imperial Library in Vienna, in his careful study of geographical maps and astronomical instruments, and in his unremitting ef-

[22] *Theoria tis Geographias*, p. 106, n. The recording of the captain's name as Jacques in the text indicates that Moisiodax's information probably derived from a French source. In the *Apology*, p. 159, n.1, however, Moisiodax had referred in detail to Maupertuis's measurements in the Arctic, without questioning his findings.

[23] On the relevant background, see Thomas L. Hankins, *Science and the Enlightenment* (Cambridge, 1985), pp. 37–39.

[24] On the wider interest that was echoed in Moisiodax's attitude, see P. Marshall and G. Williams, *The Great Map of Mankind* (Cambridge, Mass., 1982), pp. 268–290, and Bernard Smith, *European Vision and the South Pacific* (New Haven, 1985), pp. 114–118, 137–138. More specifically on Captain Cook's fame on the continent of Europe, see Bernard Smith, "Cook's Posthumous Reputation," in *Captain James Cook and his Times*, ed. R. Fisher and H. Johnson (Vancouver, 1979), pp. 159–185.

[25] *Theoria tis Geographias*, pp. 95–96, continuation of p. 94, n.1.

forts to keep himself completely up to date. These research endeavors are reflected in the copious documentation of the printed version of the *Theory of Geography*. This is also one crucial difference between the manuscript and the published version of the work: the expanded documentation offers a moving illustration of the labors of the scholar, revealing the researcher "at work," in the excitement of his quest.

His interest in geographical discoveries and his use of the evidence supplied by them to further scientific understanding links Moisiodax with the heightened curiosity of the eighteenth century. The major advance of eighteenth-century empirical science was founded upon a desire to become acquainted with the wider world and the secrets of nature. The hallmark of the science of the Enlightenment was precisely the redirection of attention and interest away from the abstract to the experimental and descriptive sciences, from astronomy and theoretical physics to experimental physics, natural history, and chemistry.[26] This had been Diderot's agenda for natural philosophy, and Iosipos appears to have been the earliest representative of this outlook in Greek scientific thought. In this orientation of Moisiodax's thought can be seen the influence of Poleni's instruction in "experimental philosophy" at Padua.[27] Iosipos's involvement with theoretical geography and the progress of navigation links him directly with the fever of interest in these questions within eighteenth-century scientific thought.[28] Until his final pamphlet on natural science published in 1784, which reflected in so many ways his personal capitulation, he retained his belief in both empirical science and the observation of nature and continued to strive for outlets through which he could implement it in systematic empirical research.[29]

The final component of Moisiodax's scientific identity was his utilitarian view of the relationship between science and society. The advance of scientific knowledge was desirable basically because of its direct contribution to improving the conditions of life and civilization. In his eyes, technological advance, at least to some extent, justifies scientific inquiry. Both Katartzis and Moisiodax were exponents of this practical utilitarianism in the Greek Enlightenment. His espousal of this view identified Moisiodax with the spirit of the age: practical utility was the fundamental

[26] Cf. Ernst Cassirer, *The Philosophy of the Enlightenment* (Princeton, 1951), pp. 73–80, and Charles C. Gillespie, *The Edge of Objectivity: An Essay in the History of Scientific Ideas* (Princeton, 1960), pp. 169–170. On the practical applications, see T. L. Hankins, *Science and the Enlightenment*, pp. 46–157.

[27] Cf. Marialaura Soppelsa, *Genesi del metodo Galileiano e tramonto dell'Aristotelismo nella Scuola di Padova* (Padua, 1974), pp. 141–154.

[28] Cf. Eric G. Forbes, "Mathematic Cosmography," in *The Ferment of Knowledge: Studies in the Historiography of Eighteenth-Century Science* (Cambridge, 1980), pp. 437–444.

[29] See chapter 6, for the researches on which the *Simeioseis Physiologikai* was based.

expectation of science, and the achievement of this was its justification.[30] "Only he who has never seen, has never traveled through Europe can be ignorant of the countless, the essential, the useful benefits that Europe enjoys, by virtue of Newtonian philosophy, in machines, in buildings, in many other kinds of things which facilitate life."[31] Observations such as these seem to justify the optimism of the Enlightenment: science was transformed into a philosophy of history and provided the foundation for the theory of progress.

[30] Cf. Forbes, "Mathematic Cosmography," pp. 446–448.
[31] *Apologia*, p. 15.

NINE

PEDAGOGY AS SOCIAL CRITICISM

THE GENERAL REFORM envisaged by Iosipos for Greek culture was to be informed by the ideals of modern science and "sound philosophy." The specific mechanisms and methods of the reform were proposed within the context of the pedagogical views he had culled from the work of John Locke and adapted to the realities of Greek educational practice.[1] In setting forth his pedagogical theory, Moisiodax subjected the methods and content of contemporary Greek education to critical examination. He did not confine himself to this, however; the problem of education and the issues involved in the upbringing of children were dealt with as one aspect of the more general social problem that he perceived in the Greek reality of his time. This theoretical approach to raising children corresponded with Dimitrios Katartzis's view. Shortly after the publication of Moisiodax's *Pedagogy*, in his essay on education Katartzis voiced the same social preoccupations and the same intellectual concerns, though in a much more radical linguistic medium.[2] He was not as bold as Iosipos in the area of social action, however, and never made his opinions public. The reception given Moisiodax's views in their shared social environment cannot be unconnected with the reasons for Katartzis's silence.

---

[1] E. Kriaras, "I Paidagogia tou Moisiodakos kai i schesi tis me to paidagogiko syggramma tou Locke," *Byzantinisch-Neugriechische Jahrbücher* 17 (1943): 135–153. The systematic identification of the borrowings by Moisiodax from Locke's *Some Thoughts Concerning Education* in this important study corrects the confusion in N. A. Bostantzis, *Paidagogikai ideai Iosipou tou Moisiodakos* (Athens, 1941). Another contribution transferring Locke's ideas on education into the pedagogical philosophy of the Greek Enlightenment was that of Gabriel Kallonas (1724–1795), in his *Paidagogia periechousa pany ophelimous nouthesias te kai oion di kanonas peri tou pos dei anatrephesthai ta paidia* (Vienna, 1800). A pupil of Voulgaris at the Athonite Academy, and later parish priest to the Greek communities in Vienna, Pest, and other Hungarian cities, Gabriel Kallonas expresses the same social world as Moisiodax. The first two parts of Kallonas's *Paidagogia* consist of a translation of Locke's treatise on education, while the third is a translation of the first part of the work *El Criticón* by the Spanish educationalist Balthazar Gracián. See E. Kriaras, "Gavriil Kallonas, metaphrastis ergon tou Locke kai tou Gracián," *Ellinika* 13 (1954): 294–314, and A. Camariano Cioran, *Les académies princières de Bucarest et de Jassy et leurs professeurs* (Thessaloniki, 1974), pp. 268–271.

[2] Dimitrios Katartzis, "Schedio tis agogis ton paidion Romion kai Vlachon, pou prepei na genetai meta logou sta koina kai spitika scholeia," *Ta Evriskomena*, ed. C. Th. Dimaras (Athens, 1970), pp. 24–41.

The social implications of Iosipos's theoretical concerns lend his views on education a vitality that distinguishes them from the commonplaces of European educational theory in the period of the Enlightenment, which had been to a considerable extent formulated under the influence of John Locke's *Some Thoughts Concerning Education*, in the French translation by Pierre Coste. Locke's treatise on education was the product of a long tradition of pedagogical humanism, the roots of which went back to the thought of Quintilian; Montaigne and Comenius were its modern representatives. This educational philosophy emphasized the value of encouragement, rejected punishment as a means of creating motivation for learning, stressed the need to cultivate character as more important than erudition, and drew a correlation between the effectiveness of the curriculum and the extent to which it was adapted to the needs of the individual child. Locke's ideas had been incorporated into the common heritage of European pedagogical thought through their popularization in the *Traité de l'éducation des enfants* by the Swiss pastor Jean Pierre de Crouçaz, a well-known supporter of Descartes and Locke in the philosophical disputes of the period.[3] By following this stream of educational theory, Iosipos appears, in this field as in that of natural science, to be in harmony with the mainstream of the Enlightenment.

Moisiodax's educational criticism operates on four levels. First, it deals with social relations within the family, the initial context of the child's upbringing. Second, the critique considers relations between the family and education and, more specifically, the attitude of the family to the practitioners of education—the teachers—and includes a description of what should be acceptable conduct on the part of the latter. Moisiodax's development of his arguments in both these spheres of educational analysis owes a considerable debt to Locke. Third, Iosipos turns to the content of education and the methods of imparting knowledge. Here his ac-

---

[3] The work was published in 1693 and translated into French in 1696. On the French translations and propagation of the work on the continent, see *The Educational Writings of John Locke*, ed. by James L. Axtell (Cambridge, 1968), pp. 88–97, 101–104, citing European editions of the text. The two Greek adaptations by Moisiodax and Kallonas indicate another line of research on the role of the text in the development of European pedagogical thought. For the views of Locke on education, cf. M. Cranston, *John Locke: A Biography* (London, 1957), pp. 239–245. For the influence of Locke on the educational thought of the Enlightenment, see Peter Gay, *The Enlightenment: An Interpretation*, Vol. 2: *The Science of Freedom* (New York, 1969), pp. 501–516. The importance of Locke's pedagogical treatise in European thought is acknowledged by C. Koumas, *Syndagma Philosophias* (Vienna, 1818), vol. 1, p. 21. Koumas, an experienced educator himself, noted that Locke's "psychological researches, his rules on method, and his work on education" secured him "eternal glory." The treatise on education by J. P. Crouçaz that popularized Locke's views was published in two volumes in the Hague in 1722. See H. O. Christophersen, *A Bibliographical Introduction to the Study of John Locke* (Oslo, 1930), p. 126.

count focuses more specifically on Modern Greek educational practice. The material presented in his educational treatise is organized on these three levels, as becomes clear simply from reading the table of contents. From this point of view, Iosipos adopts a consistently professional approach to his subject: he attempts to examine it in a rounded manner and present all aspects of it, without being overly discursive, throughout confining his argument within the technical requirements of the field. In addition to the professional concerns of his educational theory, however, as defined by Locke's principles, Iosipos added to his analysis a dimension that connected education with its social milieu. Thus, on the fourth level, he examines upbringing and education as social phenomena; his scrutiny of the relationship between education and society transmutes educational theory into social analysis.

The theoretical basis for the arguments used by Moisiodax in his examination of the upbringing of children in the family and the relationship of the family to education is to be sought in the basic epistemological arguments marshaled by Locke against the existence of innate ideas and in the view that experience is the sole source of knowledge. Iosipos's formulation of these views introduced into Greek thought the idea of the human mind as a tabula rasa: "When a child is first born, it resembles, as Aristotle says, a clean slate or paper, which does not have even a single letter, but which in time receives every letter, that is every imprint, every idea."[4] His alignment with the proponents of philosophical empiricism is also indicated by another famous metaphor, borrowed by the educational theory of the Enlightenment from the history of epistemology: young children "are like soft wax, which responds indiscriminately to any molding, and can be brought just as skillfully to evil as to good." Moisiodax's ideas at this point appear close to the sensationalist psychology expounded in the article on "Education" in Diderot's *Encyclopédie*.[5]

Although these philosophical ideas in Moisiodax's work are not original, their transference into the Greek language marks a memorable moment in the symbolic advance of Modern Greek thought toward its emancipation from the medieval tradition. The incorporation of these images into the symbolism and vocabulary of collective communication gradually endowed Greek culture with the conceptual equipment through which it could be linked to the cultural climate of modernity.

This was the background to Iosipos's exhortations to parents regarding

---

[4] *Paidagogia*, pp. 15–16. Cf. Aaron, John Locke, pp. 114–115.

[5] *Paidagogia*, p. 17. Cf. *Encyclopédie ou Dictionnaire raisonnée des sciences, des arts et des métiers*, vol. 5 (Paris, 1755), pp. 397–403. On the significance of the metaphors of the clean slate and wax, see Margaret J. M. Ezell, "John Locke's Images of Childhood: Early Eighteenth-Century Response to Some Thoughts Concerning Education," *Eighteenth-Century Studies* 17 (Winter 1983–1984): 139–155, esp. 151.

the raising of their children. He warned them of the damaging effects on children's character of being brought up by domestic nurses and uneducated servants; he also warned parents of the destructive effects of excessive tenderness and the lack of discipline, seriousness, and even severity in regulating their own attitude toward their children. At the same time, however, he recommends the avoidance of the extreme distance that some parents kept from their children, to the point where they were excluded from the common family table. Moisiodax nevertheless states quite categorically the reasons why children should not take part in dinner parties and wedding feasts, hunting, card playing, and other pastimes, during which they might be exposed to examples and stimuli that would upset the integrity and balance of the development of the body, character, and brain and thereby undermine the primary aim of upbringing. By thus placing the child and its specific needs at the center of his educational thinking, Moisiodax echoes in Greek thought a broader preoccupation of contemporary European culture, reflected in the discovery of the child.[6]

In the same spirit, Moisiodax advises parents on the dress of their children and on the imposition of disciplinary punishments for misconduct. In these matters, too, the guiding principle is still the achievement of balance, through which the child might attain integrity and eventual maturity. To avoid jeopardizing the achievement of this goal, Iosipos warns that the reins of discipline should not be slackened when the children leave their childhood behind and enter adolescence and early adulthood: this is the time when passions erupt, the period of gravest danger. To convey his belief in the need for uninterrupted growth under sound pedagogical guidance, Moisiodax introduced into his text another famous image, which had a considerable prehistory as a symbol in European literature and ideology: "Young men resemble ships that sail on wild oceans, and which are beset during the voyage by many, wild Symplegades. Passions, appetites, desires: all these form so many winds which ceaselessly blow against them and attempt to sink them to the depths of evil living."[7] With this simile, his account of the problems of youth becomes a specific example of his more general diagnosis of the existential condition of mankind: "The present life is an ocean which is continually buffeted by adventures, and man is like the ships that sail on stormy oceans."[8] To prevent young people from being plunged to the depths of "evil-living" by these storms, parents were called upon to shelter them and protect them from "sycophants, parasites and similarly from all parties of wickedness."

---

[6] Cf. Philippe Ariès, *L'enfant et la vie familiale sous l'ancien régime* (Paris, 1973), pp. 53–74.

[7] *Paidagogia*, p. 32.

[8] Ibid., p. 11.

Moisiodax's analysis at this point and the examples by which he tried to document his message transport us directly to the Phanariot society of Wallachia and Moldavia, the criticism of which was constantly his broader aim. For the moment, however, we must dwell on exposing the educational measures by which Iosipos attempted to safeguard the healthy development of the youthful personality. In this difficult task the helmsman-father depends completely on the cooperation of the teacher.

The most crucial factor in education, after the conduct of the parents and the formation of social relations in the bosom of the family, is the role played by the teacher. In his treatment of this subject, Iosipos examines two dimensions of the teacher's role in the process of upbringing: the first refers to relations between the family and the practitioner of education, and the second covers the teacher's own approach to his work. From Iosipos's standpoint these questions formed the most sensitive element in the entire nexus of relations involved in education. His personal involvement comes to the surface; his argument conveys a loaded quality, and his analysis reflects the immediacy of concrete historical evidence. Here we have not the educational theorist but the experienced educator, whose writing is guided by his sharpened sensitivity and critical eye.

On the basis of both theoretical principles of education and personal experience, Moisiodax was able unhesitatingly to recommend to parents the kind of person suitable as the teacher of their children. In Iosipos's judgment, that teacher should possess five qualities. First, the credible teacher should be capable of cultivating morals and molding the malleable character of the children at the same time as he imparts knowledge. Second, the teacher should be young, free of arrogance and inflexibility, and therefore able to approach the children and respond to their needs without any preconceptions or other ulterior considerations. Third, Iosipos warns, with characteristic realism and sensitivity, that the teacher should be a person whose appearance will not alarm the child. This advice was an indirect criticism of the aged clerics' involvement in teaching with disastrous effects on the way the young pupils responded to their teaching and consequently on the effectiveness of their instruction. Moisiodax makes no attempt to conceal the recollections of terror with which his own experiences as a child at school had left him (see Chapter 1). The fourth and fifth pieces of advice demonstrate Moisiodax's opposition to the content of traditional schooling: he recommends that parents avoid teachers who teach only grammar and Aristotelian physics and prefer those who offer the knowledge of modern science with its practical benefits. The five characteristics of the teacher outlined by Moisiodax form in essence a summary declaration of the principles and aims of his new educational philosophy.[9]

[9] *Paidagogia*, pp. 56–60.

This new kind of teacher required appropriate treatment from the parents. Iosipos defined it clearly and realistically: "Favor, honor, generosity, salary, these are the main rewards for the willingness to teach."[10] Arrogance toward the teacher, any attempt to belittle him, the withholding of his salary, and the slanderous imputation to him of mistakes and shortcomings all meet with Iosipos's categorical opposition. In his vigorous condemnation of this kind of behavior toward the exponents of education, Iosipos offers further evidence of the contemporary forms of social conduct that aroused his conscience.

Iosipos naturally did not stop at his recommendations for the correct treatment of teachers. He added a description of the proper attitude to be adopted by the practitioners of education themselves and of their comportment as instructors. The omission of this dimension—the relationship between teacher and society—would have reduced Moisiodax's pedagogical argument to a narrow, self-interested claim on behalf of his guild. For Iosipos, however, the ethos and mission of the educator constituted a much higher ideal. The work of the teacher, education, was "among the most difficult of arts,"[11] the practice of which required not only erudition and knowledge but also a deep acquaintance with human nature: "The expert educator is therefore required to have, as well as learning, a competent knowledge of human qualities and peculiarities."[12] Only those who know the human soul can become true teachers. To achieve this they have to approach their pupils with humanity, integrity, and constancy so as to win their respect without arousing fear or encouraging impudence. In his exhortations to the teacher, Iosipos moves from general principles of conduct to specific recommendations for teaching. He suggests ways in which instruction and learning could be transformed from the dry, oppressive process that he had known into a pleasant, attractive experience; thus, knowledge might be consolidated, and a love of learning cultivated. He also tackles the difficult problem of discipline and the imposition of corrective punishments on disobedient pupils. While indicating his own preference for control by exhortation, he did not completely rule out the use of corporal punishment: "As the ultimate aid, there remains a fierce beating."[13] He hastens to add, however, that neither criticism nor corporal punishment should be imposed in a spirit of vengeance. In these points he faithfully followed Locke and the pedagogical views of the Enlightenment.

To this outline of the teacher's task, Iosipos added two further dimensions that pointed to the ideological foundation of his views on education.

[10] Ibid., p. 61.
[11] Ibid., p. 70.
[12] Ibid., p. 72.
[13] Ibid., p. 91.

It was an integral part of the task of education to rid the children of the crudeness of character and tendency to lie inculcated in them by their social surroundings: "rustic rudeness" and "mendacity" were for Moisiodax components of the social reality that education was called upon to erase in order to open to human beings the road to civilization. Another equally important aspect of the teacher's work was to overcome the superstition and gullibility that the children brought with them. Education should aim at undermining the deception nurtured by the "headless ideas" that obfuscated human thought: "There is no place on the entire surface of the earth in which are not heard a myriad false, monstrous statements, which are validated by ignorance, simplicity, superstition, by habitual usage."[14] Educational theory, confronting the climate of delusion and conventional mythology, was thus transformed into a tool of social criticism.

The purpose of the latter was to cultivate the virtues of social coexistence and to confine religion within its proper domain by teaching its principles in the framework of what was rationally acceptable. In advancing these ideas Moisiodax proceeded beyond professional educational theory to a declaration of ideological principles. It is worth noting, however, that in his reference to the teaching of the principles of religion, he significantly modified Locke's views and substituted for them the standard Orthodox doctrines on the trinitarian nature of God, the incarnation, and the sacraments.[15] Basically, however, with regard to the question of religion, Moisiodax recommends the avoidance of too much debate: "It is enough for us to believe, then, and if we do not comprehend all that we are commanded to believe, patience is required."[16] Behind the protestations of Orthodoxy one cannot but detect the agnosticism and indifference of the free-thinker. In this respect Moisiodax departed significantly from Locke's piety in defining the goals of education.

The final area of concern with the problems of education that attracted Moisiodax's attention was its substantive content. At this level his critique is general and straightforward. It is also entirely predictable to the student of his thought: Iosipos submitted the entire spectrum of studies in the Greek schools to an exhaustive and rationally based critique; he demanded the complete revision of the curriculum and its replacement by what was essentially the curriculum of the Enlightenment. In his analysis he relied on Locke only for formulating the general guiding princi-

[14] Ibid., p. 100.

[15] Ibid., pp. 104–105. Contrast J. Locke, *Some Thoughts Concerning Education*, in *The Educational Writings of John Locke*, pp. 241–244.

[16] *Paidagogia*, p. 106

ples and referred in minute detail to the actual practice of contemporary Greek education, on the basis of his first-hand experience.

For Iosipos the problem of Greek education was all-embracing, vitally urgent. Once more, the starting point for his presentation of the problem was personal experience:

> An attentive glance at the schools, both private and public, and it seems to me that the truth, which I wish to proclaim, is everywhere clear, and informs all discerning observers. And in truth, I shudder every time I call to mind those Atlantean toils, those endless terms in which I spent my poor youth at different gymnasia, being taught the grammatical forms of Greek. . . . But what is this unpleasant truth that I wish to declare? That the teachers must change their style of teaching and abandon the well-trodden path.[17]

In Iosipos's judgment, total change was needed in Greek education. First, a radical reform was required in the manner in which the study of the Greek language was introduced, through the teaching of grammar. Critically examining the system of language teaching, Iosipos concludes that the strict grammatical approach on which Greek education was based taught nothing but "things either difficult to comprehend, or useless, or unnecessary for beginners."[18] Accordingly, the last chapters of the *Pedagogy* sought to suggest an alternative method for teaching Greek, a method aimed at replacing the arid learning of grammar with instruction in texts that would lead to a meaningful contact with the humanistic content of classical literature. He stresses the need to understand the meaning of the material being taught and condemns the insistence on the memorization of dead forms. Children who learn by heart "resemble parrots that recite, but in no way understand what they are reciting."[19] For the teaching of grammar to be more effective, he emphasizes that the presentation of the material must be simplified and rationalized. He also makes plain his view that the formalism that had for centuries tortured generations of Greek students ought finally to be abandoned. This required the creative intervention of the teacher. His task was to interpose himself between the rules of grammar and the pupil's efforts and make them intelligible, by expressing them in language understandable by the children:

> Many rules are given in Laskaris, some obscure, some complicated, some exhaustively long and some completely superfluous. The teacher is therefore required to illuminate the first, unravel the second, abbreviate the overlong, and skip over the superfluous; indeed, I infer that the teacher should

[17] Ibid., pp. 108, 109.
[18] Ibid., p. 110.
[19] Ibid., p. 111.

gather together an abridged version of the most essential verbal rules and expound this in the simple language, which is more readily understood by the children. Alack, what a heavy burden you are placing upon us! The teacher may reply: Yes, my most learned friend, I, too, see your heavy burden, but how else is your zeal as a teacher to manifest itself? How else can you fulfill the duties of your teaching vocation?[20]

This was the ethos of the new educational philosophy advanced by Iosipos. The simplification and rationalization of teaching required for implementing this educational ethos could be realized if "sound philosophy" became the guiding principle of the task of education.[21] The reference to sound philosophy demonstrates the essential unity of Iosipos's position with respect to the problem of Modern Greek education and culture: sound philosophy was not only the model for cultural reform but also the foundation of the new pedagogy. The Enlightenment and its basis in rationalist philosophy formed the unifying framework of his criticism.

From the examination of grammatical education, Iosipos extended his critique to the canon of the texts taught in the schools. He unequivocally rejected all the established texts for teaching ancient Greek—namely, the manuals of grammar by Manuel Chrysoloras and Theodoros Gazis, and the manuals of syntax by Neophytos Kafsokalyvitis and Ananias Parios—as counterproductive and useless.[22] His critique, logically founded upon arguments borrowed from educational theory and teaching practice, was never reduced to the level of mere ideological polemic. Iosipos even ventures to suggest abandoning the works of the Church Fathers and other religious writings as teaching texts because, as he notes, "The church fathers do not write in standard Greek, but in a scriptural manner: that is, they adapt their speech to the style of the Scriptures."[23] Iosipos recommended an alternative selection of works, including Aesop and Lucian, to arouse the interest of young children, and Herodian, Arrian and Xenophon, Demosthenes and Thucydides. In the study of these texts, "it is of no advantage to read them mechanically, as is everywhere the custom today: that is, comprehension alone is not enough: what is required is the understanding of the moral content of the most significant

---

[20] Ibid., p. 118. Constantinos Laskaris (1434–1501) was the author of the first printed Greek book, *Epitomi ton okto tou logou meron* (Milan, 1476), which was widely reprinted and extensively used as a textbook of grammar in Greek schools until the nineteenth century.

[21] Ibid., pp. 127–128.

[22] Ibid., pp. 130, 142–143. On these works and especially on Neophytos Kafsokalyvitis cf. the judgment of Moisiodax's contemporary, the French classicist D'Ansse de Villoison in *Homeri Ilias ad veteris codicis Veneti fidem recensita* (Venice, 1788), p. xiii.

[23] Ibid., p. 135.

sections or passages, or the particular character of each author."²⁴ Thus, the desideratum was a real acquaintance with the spirit of classical culture, not the mechanical use of the text as a basis for grammatical exercises. The selection of the ancient historians, in particular, offered a direct taste of classical civilization that could make it a real and immediate intellectual experience for the pupil.

The achievement of this substantive knowledge of the classical texts called for a change in the method by which they were interpreted. At this point, too, Iosipos differed radically from conventional practice: "I come to say unusual things about this, too. First, I say there must be a complete end to the writing down of synonyms and swarms of words."²⁵ Iosipos demands the abandonment of the interpretation of ancient works that involved writing large numbers of synonyms above each word and the replacement of that practice with rendering in Modern Greek the meaning of the text. This would effectively cultivate the pupil's understanding and judgment, which, according to Iosipos, should be broadened by practice in free translation and the writing of essays and compositions; these he considered exercises that gave scope for creativity and the use of the critical faculties, though Iosipos warmly recommended that the likely tendency of the pupil to exaggerate, adopt a pompous tone, and be ostentatious should be discouraged. An example of the new approach to the ancient texts was presumably furnished by his own free translation of Isocrates' speech *In Nicoclem*, which he published the same year, together with his *Pedagogy*.

The arguments on which Iosipos based his criticism of the educational practice of his day were nothing less than a diagnosis of the needs of Greek society. The kind of education offered by the Greek schools was adjudged by him to be useless and irrelevant to real social needs that he perceived around him, wherever he turned his gaze:

> And in truth the present fortune of Greece is completely deficient, and the Greek, whether of noble birth or of some other status, is hedged about by want as soon as he advances beyond childhood. When a young man spends seven or eight years with grammar, paying excessive attention to detail . . . , if his desire to learn is not completely frozen, he still is left with no time or resources. He is completely deprived of ethics, natural science, and many other useful sciences, and having learned, totally unnecessarily, to call bread "arton" and wine "oinon," he still sees "arton" and "oinon" in the same way as he saw them before he was initiated into the mysteries of excess.²⁶

---

²⁴ Ibid., p. 136.

²⁵ Ibid., p. 138. In his opposition to the writing of synonyms in interpreting ancient texts, Moisiodax was following the pedagogical tradition of the Greek students of the schools of Venice and Padua, who were the first to engage in a critique of education in the Greek East.

²⁶ *Paidagogia*, p. 143.

Irony at this point becomes an element in the author's argumentation and gives more effective expression to his message. His reasoning remained constantly focused on the social needs that education had to meet:

> The needs of our society certainly demand . . . good Turkish, since this is the dialect of our rulers; good Italian or French, because these are today the most widely spoken of the European dialects; good vernacular Greek, because this is today our spoken language, through which in due course, some will speak in public, some will pass judgment in courts, some will express among their fellow countrymen their every need, their every concept. An accurate knowledge of ancient Greek is a great advantage to be sought after; but for the princes it is not merely useless, but also harmful: for what reason? Because through its verbosity it precludes law, ethics, geography, and many other ideas, in which moreover, members of ruling houses ought to excel.[27]

The perception of education as an integral part of the broader social environment and the recognition that the purposes of learning must address specific social needs were components of Moisiodax's utilitarianism. In this respect, too, his pedagogical theory showed close affinity with the ideas of the article "Education" in Diderot's *Encyclopédie*. This aspect of his pedagogical thought cut across the other levels of his analysis of educational reality, broadening it into a general critique of social practices and conventions. In his examination of the role of the family in bringing up children, his criticism resided in his astute observations on the "parties of wickedness" who skilfully undermine the serious nurture of the youth by using the weapons of flattery and sycophancy:

> And how long (they cry), how long is the *Kokoni* or the *Tzelebis* to study? And they directly imply by this that much study is excessive, and inappropriate for gentlemen: that an hour of study in the morning and another in the evening is enough for them; that gentlemen, as gentlemen, need wealth and honors, not a lot of study, and they then cite the example of "such and such" or "so and so" who, without a lot of study, have reached the rank of Banos or Logothetis, have become magnates, rich, powerful, great. They then recite the worst insults against the poor teachers to the parents, claiming that they upset the children and will make them deficient.[28]

These observations open a window on the Phanariot society of the Danubian principalities. They reveal the social relations and the collective mentality and behavior that the new pedagogy had to confront. The character of the social milieu and the constraints and obstacles it placed upon the task of the exponent of "sound philosophy" help account for Moisiodax's rebellion and collision with his environment. The dynamic of the

---

[27] Ibid., pp. 157–158.
[28] Ibid., p. 50. "*Kokoni*" and "*Tzelebis*" were terms of affection addressed to the offspring of prominent families among the Phanariots.

clash was essentially social; it articulated the rejection by the independent intellectual of an entire nexus of ways of life and class relations. His own inflexibility in this confrontation meant almost inevitably that he would be crushed by the mechanisms of social control.

Moisiodax was fully aware of the contradiction between his own stands and the workings of Phanariot society. This awareness was eloquently expressed in the context of his analysis of the relations between family and teacher, at the second level of his educational critique:

> Those who are educated men (I do not include here those servile characters who through their slavish subservience besmirch their profession), all are free men in status, and free men of distinguished character, who automatically pay to each man the honor due to him. When the teacher undertakes to attend to the education of a child of noble birth, he does not divest himself of his good freedom, for which he has shed so much sweat, and over which, if he cares about his own blood, or the price of his life, he would not compromise at all.[29]

The intellectual's freedom is the product of his own personal strivings and determines his place in society: this statement may be interpreted as an indication of Moisiodax's espousal of the social principles of liberalism. On this basis he was apparently prepared to confront the semifeudal world of the Phanariot society in the Danubian principalities. In a way, this attitude epitomized the conflict between the worlds of personal achievement and social ascription.[30] His sense of the freedom of the intellectual naturally also constituted an ideological position that could, and in his case did, bring its advocate into conflict with the prevailing norms around him. The free intellectual, as an exponent of the principles of the Enlightenment, not only rejected traditional education, through his embroilment in the criticism of the Ancients by the Moderns, but stigmatized the whole range of beliefs and prejudices with which his rational values inevitably came into conflict: "Spells, vampires, hypnoses, interpretations of dreams, prophesies, witchcraft, ghosts, premonitions of epidemic disasters drawn from dreams, earthquakes, comets, eclipses and so forth: all these belong to the category of headless ideas."[31] These "headless ideas" shaped the cultural climate that made possible the exis-

---

[29] Ibid., p. 63.

[30] Cf. Chapter 4. Moisiodax's educational criticism, that is, operated socially, to some extent, in a parallel way to the educational and philosophical ideas of John Locke. Moisiodax, however, differed from Locke on the crucial question of public versus private education. Whereas Locke prefers private education in the home, Moisiodax asserts that education in public, "common" schools is preferable. See *Paidagogia*, pp. 66–67, and contrast Locke, *Some Thoughts concerning Education*, pp. 165–171.

[31] *Paidagogia*, p. 100.

tence of not only the "parties of wickedness" that cultivated and skilfully exploited them but also what in Moisiodax's opinion was the major and most dangerous factor standing in the way of cultural and educational progress—religious fanaticism, which was responsible for "those useless expenditures on religion, so many of which are undertaken by any one man that ten or twenty together might suffice to endow a splendid academy; but I do not proceed further in a contention so thorny that it cannot but make me bleed."[32]

Moisiodax attempted to undermine superstition and delusion by appealing to right reason and science, to modern "physiology," "because only modern 'physiology' has the great advantage of stigmatizing headless ideas of this sort, of being a substitute for them and attempting to purge them."[33] Upon this scientific basis he founded the ethos of both the new education and the new world that he visualized: the world of individual integrity, personal endeavor, and creative expression. These values determined both the approach to the child and the self-definition of the teacher.[34] At the same time they produced a utilitarian world guided by an awareness of the social purpose of education. For the new ethos to consolidate itself and function, it was necessary to overcome certain social and political obstacles, whose existence transforms education into essentially a political problem: "And in truth, a man cannot expound how much irregularity and difficulty is created for the state by an uneducated and base man: especially when together with his roughness, he combines power and authority."[35] To appreciate fully Moisiodax's response to the problem of education, it is necessary to examine the broader political framework of his thought.

[32] Ibid., p. 6.
[33] Ibid., p. 102.
[34] Ibid., pp. 85–86.
[35] Ibid., p. 4.

TEN

IMAGES OF THE POLITY

THE CONVENTIONAL VIEW of Moisiodax's political thought connects him with the theory of enlightened absolutism, predominant in Phanariot circles; it constituted the political expression of the earlier phase of the Greek Enlightenment. Dimitrios Katartzis presented the classic statement of this political orientation in the intellectual circles within which Moisiodax moved during the twenty years of his maturity. A high official at the Phanariot court of Wallachia and a pioneering exponent of the reforming spirit, which he hoped might be translated into action through the political choices of enlightened princes, Katartzis was responsible for the maturest statement in Greek of the ideology of enlightened absolutism. More advanced in his views on language, Katartzis shared Moisiodax's social utilitarianism and encyclopedism and his stance in the quarrel of the Ancients and Moderns. Reasonably, then, the two have also been identified with regard to their political preferences. Iosipos's psychological makeup and social experience, however, led him along paths that distanced him from the position adopted by Katartzis on the political question. In my analysis I intend to evaluate the available evidence and propose a new interpretation of the formation of Moisiodax's political thought that distinguishes him radically from Katartzis and links him with an alternative tradition of political speculation.

A first reading of the texts seems to provide considerable evidence in support of the conventional view of the nature of Moisiodax's political thought. This evidence can be divided into three categories. First, Moisiodax's written addresses and appeals to Phanariot princes locate him firmly in the political climate of his time.[1] These works depict Moisiodax as a rational exponent of the anticipation of social and cultural reform based on the goodwill of the prince. In this sphere, neither Moisiodax's appeals nor the expectations of Greek men of letters generally differed in any essential respects from the hopes cultivated by representatives of the Enlightenment such as Voltaire and Diderot, with regard to the potential of "enlightened monarchy." This is the typical optimism of the intellectual, who rarely succeeds in shaking off the mostly naive conviction that

---

[1] See, for example, *Theoria tis Geographias*, preface, and *Simeioseis Physiologikai*, pp. iii–vi.

he will be able to direct political action through his philanthropic and enlightened advice. In eighteenth-century Balkan society, within the oppressively narrow margins left by Ottoman domination, these hopes seemed to be the only outlet for those men of letters who dreamed of change and progress. The general social reality, however, revealed them to be fragile, a source more often of disappointment than vindication.

The second category of evidence regarding Moisiodax's political orientation comprises his references to the models of enlightened absolutism, which are found scattered throughout his works. We may select some relevant passages, beginning with the prolegomena to the *Moral Philosophy*, where he mentions the achievements of the enlightened Russian monarchy. Moisiodax, following an already long tradition of Greek and Balkan writers, singled out and extolled the example of Peter the Great, who reformed an entire nation.[2] The 1765 inaugural lecture at the Princely Academy in Jassy, "Concerning philosophy in general," ends with an apostrophe to Prince Grigorios Ghikas, celebrating the union of philosophy and power that had made his reign a "golden age" in Moldavia.[3] References to the Phanariot dynastic families and intimations of what was expected of whoever rose to the princely dignity are scattered throughout the *Apology*. There are also, of course, references to the great model of enlightened monarchy of the period, the Hapsburg Empire, which formed an example for the neighboring world of the Principalities. The empress Maria Theresa is referred to as "most mighty and most charitable."[4] Wherever reference is made to enlightened absolutism, its justification is based on the association of this particular form of political authority with protection of the sciences and advancement of learning. The absolute monarch's espousal of the aspiration to cultural change marked him out as a champion of progress and provided the raison d'être for his power. At the same time, endorsement of absolutism depended upon its conduct toward learning and its practitioners. This attitude toward absolutism emerges characteristically in Moisiodax's appraisal of the treatment of the Danish astronomer Tycho Brahe by the princes whose subject he was: "Rudolph, on the one hand, by virtue of the truly regal sense of honor that he displayed toward Kepler, toward

---

[2] *Ithiki Philosophia*, vol. 1, p. xxxi.

[3] *Apologia*, p. 130.

[4] Ibid., p. 158. For the influence of the Hapsburg monarchy, and especially of the system known as "Josephinism," at the courts of the Principalities of East Central Europe, see T. Blanning, *Joseph II and Enlightened Despotism* (London, 1970), pp. 111–112, and R. Okey, *Eastern Europe, 1740–1980: Feudalism to Communism* (London, 1982), p. 58. See also K. Hitchins, *The Rumanian National Movement in Transylvania: 1780–1849* (Cambridge, Mass., 1969), pp. 67, 69, 73, 103, 113–114, and Emanuel Turczynski, *Die deutsch-griechischen Kulturbeziehungen bis zur Berufung König Ottos* (Munich, 1959), pp. 222–224, on the impact of Josephinism on Greek culture in the broader "Danube region."

Tycho, and toward other men of wisdom, lives for eternity in the writings of Philosophy and History. The persecutor of Tycho, in contrast, remains confounded in the great crowd of those princes who have achieved nothing."[5] The justification of absolutism, then, depends on its contribution to the advancement of science and the recognition of the reforming mission of education. Of his patron, Grigorios Ghikas, Moisiodax notes:

> Sound administration and well-being delight his hosts of subjects, while the glorious works of his fulsome providence give him a good reputation with everyone. Fountains, hospitals, aqueducts, monasteries, churches: all do honor to his highness, a worthy successor to his forebears, and all weave for him the garland of remembrance. Renown needed no other end, to extend the trumpeting of his great glory, save the crowning jewel of his achievements: I mean the newly built museum of Philosophy.[6]

The same diagnosis, linking the justification of monarchy with the implementation of a reform program, can be made on the basis of the third and most important piece of evidence that connects Moisiodax politically with the theory of enlightened absolutism. The evidence in question is his only explicitly political text, the free translation of Isocrates' *In Nicoclem*. The choice of this particular text connects Moisiodax, as we have already noted (see Chapter 7), with the tradition of political literature known in the history of political thought as *speculum principum* ("mirror for princes"). With Plato's *Politicus* as its conceptual point of departure, this paraenetic literature attempted to hold up paradigms of political morality to princes, with the aim of inducing them to regulate their behavior accordingly. The genre flourished particularly in the Hellenistic and Byzantine periods, encouraged, of course, by the prevailing monarchical political context, which understandably sought in this literature its political justification. One of its most distinguished and earliest representatives was Isocrates, whose works were widely used by the later exponents of paraenetic literature as support for their own arguments. This tradition of political discourse provided the backbone of Byzantine political thought, and despite some republican challenges such as that of Gemistos-Pletho during the Palaeologan Renaissance, it lingered on as the dominant form of political ideology in post-Byzantine culture. In the late seventeenth and early eighteenth centuries, the "mirror for princes" tradition in Greek literature revived, prompted by the existence of Orthodox princes in the Danubian lands, who encouraged this kind of political expression. Under prince Şerban Cantacuzeno (1678–1688) and the

---

[5] *Theoria tis Geographias*, pp. 123–124, n.2. Cf. *Apologia*, p. 157, n.1. On Tycho's adventures, see A. R. Hall, *The Revolution in Science, 1500–1750* (London, 1983), pp. 137–138.

[6] *Apologia*, pp. 130–131.

great patron of culture Constantine Brancoveanu (1688–1714), the Hellenistic and Byzantine paraenetic literature became the court ideology in Wallachia. Moisiodax's work can thus be set within a literary tradition that, in his immediate cultural environment, was represented by Sevastos Kyminitis, Chrysanthos Notaras, Alexandros Mavrokordatos, Anthimos Iviritis (metropolitan of Hungary-Wallachia), Nikolaos Mavrokordatos, and Neophytos Kafsokalyvitis.[7] Iosipos's immediate predecessor in the political use of Isocrates' text was Sevastos Kyminitis (1625–1702), who in the 1690s taught Greek literature at the newly founded Academy of Bucharest, even before the first Phanariots ascended to the throne of the Principalities. Kyminitis taught a broad range of the classics of Byzantine "mirror for princes" literature, including standard texts by Synesius of Cyrene, Agapetus Diaconus, and Archbishop Theophylact of Bulgaria.[8] Isocrates' *In Nicoclem* occupied a prominent place in this paraenetic literature and, along with other speeches by the Athenian orator, was paraphrased by Kyminitis into Modern Greek.[9] The work was thus well established in the canon of texts taught in the academic curriculum of the Principalities several decades before Moisiodax turned to it. Iosipos's political use of the text to some extent represents the ideological transformation of the entire tradition, in that his exhortations contributed to the transition from the moral edification of the prince to the ideal of reforming authority: "When commands, customs and laws do not conform to public stability, or when they are scarcely useful, there should

---

[7] See K. Kinini "Le discours à Nicoclès par Misiodax," *Ellinika* 29 (1976): 105–106, and V. Georgescu, *Political Ideas and the Enlightenment in the Romanian Principalities (1750–1831)* (New York, 1971), pp. 61–62, for the incorporation of Greek paraenetic literature into Romanian political thought. See also A. Duțu, "Le miroir des princes dans la culture roumaine," *Revue des études Sud-Est européennes* 6 (1968): 439–479; and for a more thorough treatment, A. Duțu, *Les livres de sagesse dans la culture roumaine. Introduction à l'histoire des mentalités Sud-Est européennes* (Bucharest, 1971), pp. 99–153. Despite the author's extensive collection of source material, he does not refer to Moisiodax's version of *In Nicoclem*, but does mention an unpublished Romanian translation of the *Moral Philosophy* by V. Vîrnav (1825).

[8] A. Camariano Cioran, *Les académies princières de Bucharest et de Jassy et leurs professeurs* (Thessaloniki, 1974), pp. 367–369. On the importance of these sources in Byzantine political thought, see Ernest Barker, *Social and Political Thought in Byzantium* (Oxford, 1961), pp. 2, 54–63, 145–150. A full list of Kyminitis's writings has been compiled by A. Papadopoulos-Kerameus in Eudoxiu de Hurmuzaki, *Documente privitoare la Istoria Românilor*, Vol. 13: *Texte Grecești* (Bucharest, 1909), pp. xv–xxvii.

[9] According to A. Papadopoulos-Kerameus, *Documente privitoare*, p. xix, item no. 37, a copy of the text had survived in the Myrides Codex of Sumela Monastery in the Pontos. The whereabouts of the Codex after the dissolution of the monastery and the dispersal of its library are unknown. It would be quite interesting, were this manuscript recovered, to compare Kyminitis's version with Moisiodax's paraphrase of Isocrates. The comparison could be revealing about the transmission of the text and the sources of Moisiodax's rendering.

be no hesitation in changing them. It is an act of excessive piety, which indeed is frequently harmful, to preserve old traditions merely because they happen to be old traditions."[10] The anticipation of reform constituted the political justification of absolutism in the thought of the Enlightenment; at the same time it provided the yardstick by which it was measured. The Modern Greek and French renderings of Isocrates' exhortations to King Nicocles of Salamis in Cyprus represented for Iosipos a distillation of the hopes that formed the rationale behind his orientation toward enlightened monarchy. Because this orientation presupposed the fulfillment of certain expectations, however, his political position remained a conditional choice.

Nevertheless, Iosipos's expectations of enlightened monarchy nurtured another vision, which attested to the breadth of his reforming ideas. The historical example of Russia, where the will of enlightened despotism had succeeded in making the Russians within the space of a few generations "the competitors of the leading nations of Europe in wisdom and civility,"[11] gave Iosipos the hope that the beneficent, almost miraculous influence of the "lights" would also help to humanize and civilize the fearsome Ottoman despotism and transform it into a factor for civilization and reform in the vast empire. If Greek society proved receptive to the gifts of enlightened Europe, perhaps these would "alleviate the burden of tyranny" with their beneficial influence:

> Is not, then, the harshness of a prince (even the severest, or wildest) softened more by the educated man than by the uneducated servant? In this case we should not despair of the receptivity of the wielders of power to learning. They too are human beings, and therefore endowed with the same desire to learn on which we are nurtured as well. They are merely in need of guides; they want examples to follow.[12]

The recognition of the humanity of the "wielders of power," which endowed them in Moisiodax's eyes with an equal capability of approaching the goods of civilization, indicated his emancipation from the intolerance of traditional religious distinctions. The vertical cleavages that sprang from the dogmatic exclusivity of Orthodox teaching had ceased to operate in his thought, while the new exclusivities of national alignments had not yet begun to operate. Meanwhile, the cosmopolitan humanism of the Enlightenment afforded a basis for envisaging the solution to the political problem of Southeastern Europe through a cultural revolution that would

---

[10] *Parallagi pros Nicoclea*, p. 13.
[11] *Ithiki Philosophia*, vol. 1, p. xxxi.
[12] Ibid., p. xxx.

bridge the gap between the Ottoman wielders of authority and the enslaved.

Moisiodax was fully aware that these ideas transcended the traditional barriers behind which, in accord with the dictates of conventional values, the collective identity was entrenched. His awareness of his emancipation from accepted tradition was sufficiently acute for him to realize that his idea "to many would appear strange, the product of the imagination."[13] Nevertheless, he did not hesitate to state it publicly, essentially as a political program:

> If we devote ourselves wholeheartedly to mathematics and to physics, it is possible that not only will learning find some recognition with the wielders of power, but also that our nation will find through it a certain comfort with them. . . . I believe that they too are human beings, by nature longing to know, and that, since they are born in Greece and breathe Greek air, that they too have the same intelligence as other Greeks; nor do they lack in good taste, at least as much as is required for them not to express displeasure at the most important lessons of Philosophy, or not to dishonor those who profess these things.[14]

During the twenty years of his maturity, the anticipation that it would prove possible to civilize the wielders of power never left Moisiodax. It is worth noting that his specific view on the potential of the Ottoman monarchy extended dialectically his political attitude toward enlightened absolutism. Whereas in the case of absolutism in general, the cultural achievements of the despot formed the touchstone by which he was to be either vindicated or censured, in the particular case of the Ottoman empire, the exercise and relations of power were themselves to be reformed as a result of cultural change instigated from below by the subjects. In both cases, politics and culture were elements of the same historical logic.

Moisiodax's hopes that the Ottoman rulers were capable of benefiting from philosophy and scientific learning were based on tangible examples, not merely the pious aspirations of the visionary intellectual. Some indications were furnished by the interest shown by erudite Muslim clerics in learning about astronomy and geography from Chrysanthos Notaras, the patriarch of Jerusalem; by the Turkish translation of Corydaleus's *Logic* by Nikolaos Kritias, at the urging of an Ottoman official; and by the great interest in geography, astronomy, and French culture evinced by the Sultan Mustafa III himself, "a mind most serious and by nature most

---

[13] *Apologia*, p. 28.
[14] Ibid.

curious."[15] According to Moisiodax, these examples were good omens for the prospects of learning and eventually even the advent of the Enlightenment in the Ottoman empire.

Moisiodax's optimistic assessment may be explained with reference to two factors. The first of these was the recognition of the humanity of the powers that be and their ability to broaden their intellectual horizons. In stating this view, Moisiodax appears as heir to Phanariot thinking, particularly in the form in which it had been expressed by Nikolaos Mavrokordatos and survived in the courts and learned circles of the Principalities.[16] Nikolaos Mavrokordatos was the most authentic exponent of the cosmopolitan humanism of the early Enlightenment in the thought of Southeastern Europe, and in this respect Moisiodax can be counted one of his true intellectual successors. The second factor that explains Moisiodax's thought was his personal experience. Himself a Hellenized Balkan, he discovered, through his education, that Greek culture was the instrument of his social mobility, intellectual growth, and awareness of his own individuality. The network of Greek schools, education, and language, as channels of social communication in the Balkans, secured the cultural unity of the region. On this foundation it was possible to erect the culture of the Enlightenment, against the background of which the benefits reaped by Iosipos from his individual struggles and sacrifices could be shared by all. This vision inspired in him the most noble sentiments: "I recommend nothing more than Sound Philosophy, which, in addition to other things, is rich in its power to win over all the nations, bringing them to the knowledge that human beings, as human beings, are all brethren, all deserving mutual love."[17] Here the ideal of sound philosophy transcends its epistemological purpose and becomes the source of a social morality, the content of which was cosmopolitan humanism. The political views of Moisiodax's disciple Rhigas Velestinlis, a genuine representative of revolutionary civic humanism in Southeastern Europe during the 1790s, were the products of precisely these intellectual and ethical values.

This wide horizon had been attained by living the life of the mind. The intensity and immediacy of his intellectual values enabled Moisiodax to

---

[15] Ibid., pp. 29–30. See also Evgenios Voulgaris, *Stochasmoi eis tous parontas krisimous kairous tou Othomanikou kratous* (Kerkyra, 1854), p. 20. The Turkish translation of Aristotle is mentioned by D. Katartzis, *Ta Evriskomena*, ed. C. Th. Dimaras (Athens, 1970), p. 62. The Sultan Moustafa III (1757–1774) is not mentioned by name by Moisiodax, though the identification is certain because he is described as the brother and predecessor of the "now most charitably ruling" Abdulhamit I (1774–1789). Moustafa was the father of the reformer Sultan Selim III (1789–1807).

[16] Nikolaos Mavrokordatos, *Philotheou Parerga*, ed. Grigorios Constantas (Vienna, 1800), pp. 24–25.

[17] *Apologia*, p. 33.

dream and rebel; for him, intellectual life was neither a source of inhibitions nor a means of controlling social behavior, as it was for other scholars more effectively integrated into their social environment; on the contrary, intellectual life provided the practical experience of emancipation and a stimulus to criticism. In his own experience of emancipation, which sprang from the life of the mind, lay the roots of the radical difference between the stance adopted by Iosipos and the political theory prevailing in his milieu.

For Moisiodax, the essence of the life of the mind was twofold: first, it defined a specific social situation within the overall social division of labor; second, it entailed a distinctive ethos that vindicated its practitioners before the conscience of the community. Together these two features formed the content of the personal emancipation of the educated individual. A decisive factor in determining the social situation of this new type of educated individual was his disassociation from the corporate social ties of traditional society. This found its expression in Iosipos's lively sense of the freedom that education brings to the scholar. The sense of social emancipation nurtured an awareness of one's individuality and personal autonomy. As a result of this attitude toward society, Iosipos was predisposed politically to seek a system of free institutions within which his social being could find functional expression. This attitude might explain the distance he gradually moved from the conventional realities of his society and its monarchical political expression. His quest was rooted in the double crisis of the 1770s, the broader crisis in the political legitimacy of the Phanariot regime in the Principalities, and his own conflict with the society of Jassy. Both crises, as we have seen, had revealed, naked to his eyes, the vanity of his expectations of enlightened absolutism.

In this context, the self-definition of the "educated man" was transformed from a mere free individual into a "disorderly" learned man. His disorderliness, which underlay his conflict with various forms of convention and social status in his social environment, also inclined Iosipos to aspire to a regime of free institutions and tolerance in which the disorderly individual would be able to find that orderliness of life unattainable within the restrictive environment of any authoritarian regime, however "enlightened." The mainstream of Enlightenment political thought could offer Moisiodax a solution to his quest: the political system of England, which the analyses of Voltaire and Montesquieu had elevated into the ideal of liberal minds throughout the European continent, afforded a model to which he might very naturally turn after his disillusionment with enlightened monarchy. Moisiodax's own admiration for the English was, moreover, unbounded:

The English, a nation in all things punctilious and veracious, and first among all the nations of Europe, which pays most attention today to new discoveries, have proved to be an example to all the others in such things, and consequently rather to be approved, with regard both to the natural sciences and to the instruments of the natural sciences. Those Greek devotees of science who live on the coasts, in Smyrna, for example, in Constantinople, or in Thessaloniki, all have the opportunity to procure English globes through English traders who reside in the said cities for purposes of commerce, and who do not disdain to render a service fitting to philhellenism, which the English always and everywhere profess.[18]

Commerce, their distinctive social ethic (punctiliousness and veracity), and their commitment to modern science were the characteristics that in Moisiodax's eyes made the English "the foremost of all the European nations." These were precisely the characteristics that the entire European Enlightenment admired in the island society of Britain. For the Greek observer the English were further vindicated by their philhellenism.[19] It appears, however, that for Iosipos all this was not enough to make the English political system the appropriate model for the regime that might provide a suitable political framework in which to implement the new political ethic of freedom.

Moisiodax's eventual dissent from the theory and values of enlightened despotism was of a more radical nature and inclined him toward the school of political thought that sought the model of freedom in the non-monarchical states of the European world. Around the republican systems of Switzerland, the Dutch United Provinces, and the older Italian aristocracies, especially that of Venice, there had been articulated in the seventeenth and particularly the eighteenth centuries a republican ideology that kept alive an alternative vision of political life, even during the apogee of absolutism.[20] This vision, which did not subside in the face of the dynamic progress of absolutism toward its final triumph, provided a

---

[18] *Theoria tis Geographias*, pp. 162–163, n.2. Cf. p. 32, n.1, and the comments of Daniel Philippidis and Grigorios Constantas, *Neoteriki Geographia* (Vienna, 1791), p. 95, who express the same climate of opinion as Moisiodax.

[19] The favorable disposition of the Greeks toward the English before the French Revolution was also noted by Korais, who connected it with the dignified attitude of the English toward the "barbarous court" that tyrannized the Greeks. See A. Korais, *Mémoire sur l'état actuel de la civilisation dans la Grèce* (Paris, 1803), p. 43.

[20] See Franco Venturi, *Utopia and Reform in the Enlightenment* (Cambridge, 1971), pp. 18–46. Nannerl O. Keohane, *Philosophy and the State in France* (Princeton, 1980), pp. 383–385, 417–419. And on the prestige still enjoyed by the Venetian model, see W. J. Bowsma, *Venice and the Defence of Republican Liberty* (Berkeley, 1968), pp. 624–628. For a concise survey of the historical terrain, cf. Yves Durand, *Les républiques au temps des monarchies* (Paris, 1973), esp. pp. 5–12, 67, 179–204.

refuge for the proponents of political dissent and social criticism. After the decline of Venice and Holland in the eighteenth century, the model of the Helvetic city-republics and rural cantons and their relentless struggles against the pressures of absolutism on the western and eastern borders of their confederacy kept alive the vision of freedom, equality, and civic virtue.[21] From a turn of the argument in the *Apology* it seems that this model, the source of inspiration and hope to the citizen of Geneva, Jean-Jacques Rousseau, provided Moisiodax with the paradigm that might meet the requirements of his political sensitivity:

> Helvetia is the name of the whole of that part of the Alps that is inhabited and administered by the nation the ancients, both Greeks and Romans, called *Helvetii*, who were later called *Suisses* by the French and *Suizzeri* by the Italians. The whole nation is governed aristocratically, and the entire aristocracy is formed of ten-and-three other, partial aristocracies, commonly called *Cantons* or *Cantoni*; these, though each being self-governing bodies, are at the same time members of a broader unit, forming together the overall aristocracy. This is also the case with the aristocracy of the Belgians, the Batavians or the Dutch. This nation was once upon a time under the suzerainty of the ancient dukes of Austria, but being dissatisfied with the rule of some of the Austrian governors, it seceded at the beginning of the fourteenth century and, confronting them thereafter, always with perseverance, it succeeded with difficulty in ensuring its freedom after sixty battles. Likewise, it fought for its freedom against the duke of Burgundy Charles, called *le Téméraire*, who, about the end of the fifteenth century moved against them in order to subject them, but who in the end was completely destroyed at their victorious hands. Both the private and public weal of these Swiss was and continues to be famous among all the nations of Europe. Frugal and freedom loving, they never desired to expand, nor did they ever suffer to be ruled by a king, but all of them submit to the authority of their laws, which protect the weak against the tyranny of the strong, and they all enjoy an equality the like of which is not to be found in the other aristocracies of Europe.[22]

The historical significance of this political option to which Moisiodax seems to turn at the climax of his conflict with his social environment has hitherto been completely ignored by all students of his thought. In fact, it cannot be emphasized enough. His gravitation toward the Swiss model of frugality, equality, sovereignty of the law, hostility to monarchy, and

---

[21] Cf. Ira O. Wade, *The Structure and Form of the French Enlightenment*, Vol. 2: *Esprit révolutionaire* (Princeton, 1977), pp. 331, 334, 359, concerning the admiration in which the model of Swiss freedom was held by the more radical representatives of the political thought of the Enlightenment, such as Raynal and Mably. See also Durand, *Les républiques*, pp. 202–203.

[22] *Apologia*, pp. 181–182, n.3.

an unquenchable, invincible desire for freedom linked Iosipos with the tradition of republican thinking that kept alive the ideological heritage of the civic humanism of the Renaissance in modern Europe and prepared the theoretical ground for the radicalism of the French Revolution. From this point of view, Moisiodax occupies a unique and crucial position in the political thought of Southeastern Europe. A careful study of the formation of his political thought can reveal the intellectual grounds of the favorable predisposition he eventually adopted toward the republican tradition. The influences to which he was exposed during his "wandering" in Central Europe, from 1777 to 1781, at a time when the ferment of Josephinism was giving rise to the circulation of a wide range of ideological concerns, did not fail to challenge the model of enlightened monarchy from the vantage point of radical republicanism. These ideological debates with which Moisiodax probably came in contact could be considered so many stimuli sustaining his predisposition toward republicanism.[23]

The specific source of Moisiodax's information and ideas about Swiss society and institutions could be traced by considering some pertinent texts available in his intellectual environment. One source of political theory that can be assumed to have been accessible to him besides the texts of classical Greek and Byzantine literature, was Réal de Curban's *Science du Gouvernement*, the first two volumes of which were later (in 1784–1786) translated into Greek by Katartzis.[24] This indicates that the work was known in the Phanariot intellectual circles of Bucharest at the time Moisiodax was living there. The second volume of the work, which is essentially a survey of the political history and political geography of the several countries of modern Europe,[25] includes a section on the political system of Switzerland.[26] After considering the political and religious history of Switzerland and noting the social mores and military forces of the Swiss, the section surveys in detail the cantons and other component parts of the Helvetic confederation. It ends with an account of the external relations of Switzerland and an appraisal of the forms of

---

[23] On the context of these debates and their radical leanings, cf. Charles O'Brien, *Ideas of Religious Toleration at the Time of Joseph II: A Study of the Enlightenment among Catholics in Austria* (Philadelphia, 1969), esp. pp. 58–68, and E. Wangermann, *From Joseph II to the Jacobin Trials* (Oxford, 1969), pp. 20–25.

[24] See D. Katartzis, *Ta Evriskomena* (Athens, 1970), pp. 311–329, 417–426.

[25] Gaspard de Réal de Curban, *La science du gouvernement*, vol. 2: *Contenant le gouvernement de France, la Constitution relativement aux Traités jusqu'au dernier d'Aix-la-Chapelle inclusivement, l'Entendue, les Moeurs, les Forces, le Nombre des Habitants, les Revenues, les Loix de chaque État de l'Europe, consideré en particulier* (Aix-la-Chapelle, 1761).

[26] Ibid., pp. 385–433. Cf. D. Katartzis, *Ta Evriskomena*, p. 421: the contents of chapter 8 of this volume, dealing with the "Commonwealth of the Swiss."

government of the various cantons: seven cantons are found to have a mixture of aristocratic and democratic government, and six feature a purely democratic constitution. After a note on the public law of the Swiss the section concludes with some general reflections on the Swiss political system.

Réal de Curban, as a loyal servant of the king of France, was not particularly favorable to the Swiss, although he preserved a noteworthy detachment in his description. Réal judged their system of government with its republican forms and its decentralized confederate structure to be a paradox,[27] something of an anomaly in Europe at the height of absolutism. Yet he did not fail to note the love of liberty and the zeal for their independence that characterized the Swiss. These traits, he concluded, would guarantee the survival of the Helvetic confederacy for a long time: "The poverty of the country, the mountains of which it is full, the bravery of the Swiss and their love for independence, will preserve perhaps for a long time the Helvetic confederation."[28] A close reading of Réal's text creates a strong impression that Moisiodax's information about Switzerland might have derived from this source. What he did not share, of course, was Réal's promonarchical scepticism. On the contrary, Moisiodax, if he did use Réal's text, turned the Frenchman's descriptive account into the factual basis of his own enthusiasm for the Swiss system as a model of the good republic. There could hardly be better confirmation of Moisiodax's conversion to intellectual and political radicalism than this transvaluation. Réal de Curban's work had been essentially an argument for social hierarchy and absolutism and was directed against the disorder the author associated with the new liberal values.[29] For Katartzis, who had been a Phanariot courtier, this might have been an argument consonant with prevailing social conventions. Besides, he informs the reader in the preface that the translation had been undertaken at the command of his princely master, the Phanariot hospodar of Wallachia, Michael Soutsos.[30] Yet in Moisiodax's hands it was turned on its head. If the argument outlined above is plausible, Réal's conservative argument was read by Moisiodax for his own political purposes, and he gleaned from it just those elements that could best serve him in constructing an alternative vision whereby he could criticize the conventional model of political legitimacy that Katartzis did not dare to question.

The sources of Moisiodax's republican leanings could be traced even further back in his intellectual biography to the climate prevailing at the

[27] Réal de Curban, *La science du gouvernement*, vol. 2, p. 431
[28] Ibid.
[29] Cf. R. R. Palmer, *The Age of the Democratic Revolution*, vol. 1: *The Challenge* (Princeton, 1959), pp. 61–62.
[30] D. Katartzis, *Ta Evriskomena*, pp. 312, 328.

university of Padua during his student years. The *Apology* is permeated with the lively impressions he retained, twenty years later, of his studies there. One might therefore be justified in assuming that the political notions he brought with him from his stay in Padua had an equally formative influence in shaping the overall framework of his political thought. These political concepts were elaborated by speculations on the character of the Venetian constitution and its gradual disintegration during the eighteenth century; on the necessity of law as a cohesive force in a state; on the corruption of regimes and their degeneration into tyranny; and on civic virtue and a public ethos, considered as the basis for viable non-monarchical, republican regimes. These issues, widely discussed in Greek student circles at Padua,[31] consequently formed the broader framework of political thought to which Iosipos was likely to have been exposed during his time there. This conceptual armory formed precisely the legacy of civic humanism that in the eighteenth century informed the political analysis of Montesquieu and Rousseau and later provided the ideological substratum for revolutionary radicalism.[32]

In this perspective we can regard Moisiodax's political thought as the channel through which these ideas were transmitted to the Phanariot culture of the Principalities. It is, of course, historically unsound to assert that Iosipos was the only one expressing these ideas in the Principalities. Ideological curiosity and sensibilities in the bosom of the Greco-Romanian Phanariot society suggest that we should look for other proponents of similar ideas, including contemporary Romanian-speaking intellectuals, who were acquainted with the work of Montesquieu and concerned with the problems of political and social reform.[33] Moisiodax's importance lies in the precocity with which he publicly voiced these republican ideas; this makes him a pioneer. Historically, the most significant aspect of his contribution consisted of the influence his political ideas, no less than his scientific views, exercised on the circle around Katartzis—an influence that was vigorously felt, despite Katartzis's own eventual ideological retraction and silence. From this point of view, primarily the ideas of

---

[31] See A. Stergellis, *Ta dimosievmata ton Ellinon spoudaston tou Panepistimiou tis Padovas ton 17o kai 18o aiona* (Athens, 1970), pp. 72, 75, 86–95. For the broader cultural background to this debate, cf. Frederick Lane, *Venice and History* (Baltimore, 1966), pp. 520ff., esp. pp. 532–536.

[32] See Franco Venturi, *Utopia and Reform in the Enlightenment*, pp. 70–94, and cf. J. G. A. Pocock, *The Machiavellian Moment* (Princeton, 1975), pp. 462–505. On the Greek dimension of this trend, cf. P. M. Kitromilides, "Politikos Oumanismos kai Diaphotismos: symvoli sti dierevnisi tis ideologikis leitourgias tis politikis theorias tou Montesquieu," in *Philosophia kai Politiki* (Athens, 1982), pp. 291–304, where the argument is set out at length.

[33] E.g., Ion Cantacouzino, translator of Montesquieu and Rousseau. Cf. A. Duțu, "La culture roumaine à l'époque des Phanariotes: héritage et nouvelles acquisitions," *L'époque phanariote*, p. 79, and Georgescu, *Political Ideas and the Enlightenment*, pp. 49, 74.

Moisiodax acted as a catalyst in determining the political orientation of a group of younger representatives of the Greek Enlightenment. This group consisted precisely of Moisiodax's disciples, who could be considered the exponents of radical civic humanism in Greek thought. From this circle, too, eventually sprang the revolutionary radicalism of the most faithful of Moisiodax's followers, Rhigas Velestinlis.

A point of clarification is required at this stage of the argument. Since at least the time of Machiavelli, successive varieties and incarnations of the two models of political reasoning—reforming absolutism and the republican polity of free institutions—coexist and alternate in the history of European political thought as forms of polemic against aristocratic feudalism. Opposition to feudalism formed the common ideological denominator of the two models. Precisely this social tension, as we have seen, offered the central axis of Moisiodax's position. In these models—first of reforming enlightened monarchy and then of the republic of law and freedom—he found the weapons of ideological polemic with which to appeal to modern liberal values against the quasi-feudal fetters of his social environment. The transition at the symbolic level of his political discourse registers this constant social quest; consequently, it may be understood to indicate the deeper essential unity of his thought.

To appreciate the true historical dimensions of Moisiodax's flirtation with republican thinking and avoid the danger of mechanistic recourse to anachronistic political interpretations, certain analytical distinctions must be drawn. The roots of his political thought could, of course, be sought in the climate of Padua, through which he was directly connected with the heritage of Renaissance civic humanism. The specificity of his political position, however, was shaped by a choice between the alternatives offered by the ideological tradition with which he was eventually aligned. These alternatives included two political models: first, the ancient model of civic virtue, which subordinated the citizen to the public good, was symbolized by the examples of Sparta and Rome; second, the modern model of the republic of free institutions and the rule of law was patterned on Switzerland and Venice. Totally indicative of Moisiodax's theoretical position he chose the latter, which he could also evaluate empirically on the evidence of contemporary political behavior.[34] This choice

---

[34] In addition to the models of Venice and Switzerland, Moisiodax seems to have been quite well acquainted with the example of the republic of the Netherlands. See *Apologia*, p. 183, n.1: "Belgium or Belgica is the name given to what is more commonly called Holland. Every city of note in this land has within it canals full of water and capable of carrying upon them boats of all sizes and of all kinds, which come and go incessantly, to unload and load the various wares that the Dutch either bring in from abroad or send abroad. These canals were dug and walled at the sides at the beginning of last century, after the Dutch had ended their war with Spain, in 1609, which lasted a total of almost more than forty

extends his position in the quarrel of the Ancients and Moderns, but it also allows us to appraise the character of his political attitude; the revolutionary turn in political thought, which resulted from the contemplation of ancient models and featured in Rousseau and his Jacobin heirs, was foreign to Moisiodax's thought. The latter outcome was realized in the political thought of the Greek Enlightenment by the translation of theory into action by Rhigas and his own radical successors, such as the anonymous patriot who wrote the republican treatise *Hellenic Nomarchy*.

Nevertheless, Moisiodax's contribution to articulating an alternative political ideology with such revolutionary implications is of profound importance. As a result of his introducing such concepts into Greek thought it was possible to envisage an alternative system of political institutions beyond the conventional models of traditional legitimacy. Moisiodax's role as an intermediary between the European republican tradition and Balkan radicalism makes his thought the initial point of dissent in the political thought of the Greek and more generally the Balkan Enlightenment.

The appeal of Moisiodax's ideas in Greek radical circles at the time of the French Revolution is made plain by a hitherto unnoticed fact. On October 16, 1790, a small group of Greek radicals in Vienna issued a proclamation announcing their intention to publish the first Greek gazette to bring news of current affairs and enlightenment to their countrymen. The opening paragraphs of the *Announcement*, which refer to the cultural achievements of ancient Greece to illustrate the pressing needs of Modern Greek society,[35] are taken verbatim from Moisiodax's prolegomena to his edition of Muratori's *Moral Philosophy*. The *Announcement* was written by the brothers Markidis-Pouliou, the protagonists of radicalism among Vienna Greeks;[36] later in the decade they became close

---

years. It is a sight worth seeing, for a man to see the Dutch cities, in which appear the roofs of the buildings, the flags of the ships and the tops of the trees in the avenues, almost all of which are flanked by two rows of trees; all of which transform the vista, whether of the city, or the plain, or the sea itself. When Belgium revolted from Spain, to which it was formerly subject, it had a small population, and was poor and despised, and did not even have buildings, save for poor huts. Its steadfast endurance, and the continuous warfare waged by it, now against the Spanish, now against the Lusitanians or the Portuguese, now against the English, or others, made its inhabitants colonizers of Batavia in the Cape of Good Hope and lords of the Molucca islands, and many other wide lands in India, and also made their cities the equal, in terms of fine buildings, of the leading cities of Europe. I insert this digression simply to inform those who do not know." The descriptive immediacy of this passage may be an indication that Moisiodax, among his many journeys, perhaps visited the Netherlands, probably during his wanderings between 1777 and 1780.

[35] See G. Laios, *O ellinikos typos tis Viennis apo tou 1784 mechri tou 1821* (Athens, 1961), p. 28.

[36] See N. Iorga, "Vienne comme centre des idées de l'Occident et de l'esprit révolutionnaire," *Revue historique du Sud-Est européen* 1 (1924): 23–36.

collaborators with Rhigas's project for overthrowing Ottoman despotism and establishing a republic of the Balkan peoples.[37] From this we might infer that Moisiodax's relationship with Rhigas was not merely individual, based on ethnic and intellectual affinities, but interwoven in a broader web of political associations and radical ideas. The sentiments, therefore, of later representatives of quite advanced ideological positions in the Greek Enlightenment, such as Ioannis Vilaras,[38] who regarded Iosipos as their intellectual precursor, appear completely justified. Equally understandable was the assertion of the defenders of cultural conventions, who considered the reformers, such as Korais, to be merely usurpers of Moisiodax's ideas.[39] It is no coincidence, moreover, that his name came back into currency with striking frequency, when ideological conflict was kindled on the eve of the Greek War of Independence.[40] Moisiodax was apparently aware of the contribution of his ideas to articulating radical dissent, when he described himself in his clash with the various forms of authority and convention as "libertine" and "disorderly."

[37] See L. Vranousis, *Rhigas* (Athens, 1953), pp. 48–53, 64–73.

[38] E. I. Moschonas, ed., *I dimotikistiki antithesi stin koraïki "mesi odo"* (Athens, 1981), p. 161.

[39] Ignatios Skalioras, *Epistoli tis neas philosophias stilifteftiki* (Leipzig, 1817), p. 24.

[40] See, for example, the frequent mentions of it in the periodical *Ermis o Logios* 9 (1819): 475, 498, 525, 530, 531, 577. The following references indicate the spirit in which Moisiodax was remembered: "Iosipos Moisiodax was the first to speak out and write against the condition of our schools," *Ermis o Logios* 9 (1819): 498; "Not one of the Greeks of any importance is unaware that the main aim of Katartzis, of Moisiodax, of Grigorios, of Daniel, of Christopoulos, of Korais, and other erudite men is the same; this aim is the enlightenment of our nation, but experience and reason have shown it to be impossible to achieve this through a language in which we are not raised, and in which we do not live. They have stated, therefore, that we should write and be taught in the living language, and not despise it: and this alone is sufficient to gain these men immortality in the future history of our culture" (ibid., p. 525).

EPILOGUE

THE SIGNIFICANCE of Moisiodax's place in eighteenth-century Greek and more broadly Southeastern European culture hinges on two factors. First, a number of crucial features of the process of cultural change in Balkan society are encapsulated in his experience; second, though his career in this sense embodied wider phenomena, at the same time it exemplified the distinctive quality of an intense individuality that constantly challenges the reader to a dialogue. The example of Moisiodax, seen as a distillation of wider phenomena of cultural change, may be considered to place him at the intersection of the coordinates of eighteenth-century Balkan culture and thought. These coordinates can be investigated at three levels.

The first level of the cultural experience of Balkan society, epitomized by the career of Moisiodax, comprises what might be termed the Balkan dimension of Greek culture. Moisiodax's experience, as a Hellenized intellectual, illustrates the historical process underlying the cultural gospel preached by the other "Moesiodacian," Daniel of Moschopolis, who translated into ideology the practice whereby elements from diverse Balkan ethnic backgrounds were integrated into the community of Greek culture through the channels of both Church and education, which were often identical. The phenomenon attests to the role of Greek education as an instrument of social change and mobility in eighteenth-century Balkan society. This factor helps to account for both the Balkan visions of Rhigas, at the level of political thought, and the inter-Balkan nature of the revolutionary initiatives from 1790 to 1821 at the level of political action.[1] From the perspective of political action, Greek culture, as a conduit of the Enlightenment and more specifically of the revolutionary classicism that constituted its most radical political expression, may be seen as a major factor in initiating processes of political transformation in Balkan society during what has been called the "age of the democratic revolution."[2] As we have seen, Moisiodax was not merely one of the earliest representatives of these phenomena, but he contributed as a political

---

[1] On this subject, cf. N. Todorov, *I valkaniki diastasi tis Epanastasis tou 1821* (Athens, 1982), and also the earlier comments by N. G. Svoronos, "O Dionysios Photeinos kai to istorikon ergon aftou," *Ellinika* 10 (1937–1938): 171–172, 176.

[2] Cf. R. R. Palmer, *The Age of the Democratic Revolution: A Political History of Europe and America, 1765–1800*, 2 vols. (Princeton, 1959–1964). Vol. I: *The Challenge*; Southeastern Europe is dealt with in vol. 2: *The Struggle* (Princeton, 1964), pp. 171–174. The question has been discussed with specific reference to the Balkans by Traian Stoianovich, *A Study in Balkan Civilization* (New York, 1967), pp. 144–154.

thinker to articulating the republican ideas that formed the political mainspring of the entire process.

In addition to this, Moisiodax, as a representative of the phenomenon of cultural Hellenization, embodies another hallmark of Balkan society and the place of Greek culture within it. Fernand Braudel has reminded us that the Balkans formed one area of the Mediterranean world most intensively marked by interpenetrating cultural frontiers.[3] This interpenetration was registered in not only the geographical distribution and dispersal of ethnic groups but also the mobility and initiatives of individuals and the nature of the cultural trends that provided diverse ethnic groups with common denominators of historical existence. These observations make it possible to understand, at the level of long-term historical processes, the particular function of Greek culture. As Braudel observes, Greek culture had been able to survive, clad in the panoply of Orthodox religious doctrine, because, during the critical period of the fifteenth and sixteenth centuries, it proved capable of proffering a dramatic refusal to the West and its religious expression.[4] Following Braudel's line of reasoning, however, we may add that, if the great refusal of the fifteenth and sixteenth centuries ensured the survival of Greek culture, then its vitality was demonstrated in the eighteenth century by reversing this refusal and rejection of the West. According to Braudel, the abilities to select and absorb elements from other cultures and exercise a corresponding influence on them mark the viability of civilizations.[5] The assimilation of the Enlightenment by the Greek culture of the eighteenth century and its transmission to the other ethnic communities of the Balkan peninsula supply testimony to the character of Greek culture as a shared mode of historical existence. The cultural influence of Hellenism was not, of course, restricted to disseminating the Greek language and education; it was also reflected in its capacity to receive into its bosom human resources from other cultures. In his individual experience, Iosipos Moisiodax embodies this entire complex phenomenon: first, his career illustrates the enrichment of Greek culture with manpower from the other Balkan ethnic communities; second, he contributed to the transfusion of Western ideas into the Greek culture of which he had become part; and third, he was zealously active in the transmission of this culture to the other Balkan peoples, especially the Wallachians and Moldavians of the Danubian principalities.[6] Moisiodax's career, then, could be considered

---

[3] Cf. Fernand Braudel, *The Mediterranean and the Mediterranean World in the Age of Philip II* (New York, 1972), vol. 2, pp. 770–771. Braudel relies to a large degree on the earlier, but penetrating work by J. Cvijić, *La péninsule balkanique* (Paris, 1918).

[4] See Braudel, *The Mediterranean*, vol. 2, pp. 769–770.

[5] *Ibid.*, pp. 763–764.

[6] For the dissemination of Romanian translations of his work, see A. Camiarano Cioran,

evidence of the historical role of Greek culture as a unifying factor in eighteenth-century Balkan society. The limits of the extent to which Moisiodax was accepted, as characteristically outlined in the views of Kodrikas, are at the same time the limits of the viability of Greek culture as the shared heritage of the Balkan peoples.

The second level at which Moisiodax's career may be viewed as a representative illustration is that of the supranational phenomenon of the cosmopolitan thought of the Enlightenment. We have seen that, in both his scientific and pedagogical views and his stance in the quarrel of the Ancients and Moderns, Iosipos represented the standard views of the mainstream of the Enlightenment. His position suggests that he had overcome the doubts and reservations felt by other Balkan exponents of the Enlightenment, contemporary with or slightly later than himself, who moved in the same geographical area as he did. Moisiodax translated these views into the Greek language and brought them to consider the problems of Balkan society. Despite his emotional and intellectual commitment to the idea of "Hellas" as a collective definition and his preoccupation with the urgent "needs of the nation," Moisiodax's concerns were not defined in terms of nationalism. On the contrary, he projected the cosmopolitan humanism of the Enlightenment in his account of the problems of the collective body to which he felt he belonged; this collective body was still articulated primarily in religious terms within the framework of the Ottoman empire. Moisiodax's originality resides in his attempts to express his theoretical concerns in the Greek language and to relate them to the specific requirements of Balkan culture and society.[7]

At a third level, finally, Moisiodax's case encapsulates the conflict between the intellectual who espoused heterodox ideology and values and his social environment and more specifically with the prevailing structures of power relations. The heightened expectations of social mobility, which inspire in the intellectual his educational achievements, lead him into direct conflict with his social environment when he becomes conscious of the fact that education is an insufficient factor for the amelioration of his social position. This, the typical experience of Central European intellectuals during the late Enlightenment, added an existential dimension to their predisposition toward dissent and social criticism.[8] In Eastern Europe, where social cleavages were deeper and social conflicts more sharply internalized, the experience was correspondingly more pointed. If the young Herder could complain in 1769 of the setbacks to

---

Les académies princières de Bucharest et de Jassy et leurs professeurs (Thessaloniki, 1974), pp. 582–583.

[7] Cf. René Pomeau, *L'Europe des Lumières* (Paris, 1966), pp. 174–197.

[8] See Elie Kedourie, *Nationalism* (London, 1966), pp. 43–47.

his career on account of such adverse social circumstances,[9] it is hardly surprising that in 1780 Moisiodax was indignant about his "malign" fate. Even Iosipos's intense personal psychological makeup may be explained, to some extent, with reference to the realities of his social environment.

These realities in Eastern Europe were defined primarily by the phenomenon of "refeudalization,"[10] the product of the sixteenth-century economic conjunctures that lasted in the particular region that later became Romania until the twentieth century. In this context, social relations continued to be much more inflexible, the margins of social mobility much more restricted, and, of course, the limits of tolerance of dissent much narrower than in Western or even Central Europe. This accounts for the cautious attitude adopted by some Romanian- and Greek-speaking exponents of the Enlightenment in the Danubian principalities toward the structure of society and their inability to subject to criticism certain glaring social injustices. In the cultural movement conventionally described as the "Romanian Enlightenment" such forms of social criticism remained until quite late rather peripheral in comparison with the dominant preoccupation with historical and ethnic origins and the political status of the Principalities.[11] At the same time the ideological pressures to which they were subjected were such that statements of social criticism, like those of Naum Ramniceanu, for example, remained unpublished in their own time. It should also be remembered that a spirit as open and liberal as Dimitrios Katartzis, who lived in the same geographical area, did not dare to touch upon social questions despite his courageous cultural criticism. In this perspective, the radical nature of the social criticism voiced by Moisiodax and a few of his successors may be appreciated in its true dimensions. The significance of Moisiodax's contribution lies in the early public expression of his criticism: the *terminus ante quem* for this is 1780, at least ten years before the tradition of radical dissent emerged in the ranks of the Greek Enlightenment and the ex-

---

[9] See J. C. Herder, "Journal of My Voyage in the Year 1769," in *J. C. Herder on Social and Political Culture*, trans. F. M. Barnard (Cambridge, 1969), pp. 63–70.

[10] See R. Okey, *Eastern Europe, 1740–1980: Feudalism to Communism* (London, 1982), pp. 18–21. The interpretative approach of the present study owes much to the classic work by Barrington Moore, Jr., *Social Origins of Dictatorship and Democracy* (Boston, 1966), pp. 413–483, which suggests the broader directions for the interpretation of historical change in Eastern Europe in a way directly relevant to the arguments delineated throughout this book. The classic and still unsurpassed study of peasant serfdom in Romania, which illustrates exactly the process of "refeudalization" is David Mitrany, *The Land and the Peasant in Rumania* (London, 1930).

[11] See K. Hitchins, *The Rumanian National Movement in Transylvania, 1780–1849* (Cambridge, Mass., 1969), pp. 71–110, and V. Georgescu, *Political Ideas and the Enlightenment in the Romanian Principalities (1750–1831)*, (New York, 1971), pp. 93–103, on the varieties of social criticism voiced in the Principalities.

pression of similar ideas in the Romanian language under the impact of the French Revolution. It is noteworthy, moreover, that the most articulate of these early statements of social criticism remained anonymous; this indicates the sense of danger felt by those who voiced them. Consequently, Iosipos had to struggle to formulate the language of criticism through which to express his ideas and feelings. This aspect gives his work a particular interest. Through Moisiodax, then, the Enlightenment as a movement of intellectual dissent began to function as social criticism in the culture of Southeastern Europe by drawing attention to the contradictions and injustices in its environment. Political dissent, a specific expression of this mental temper, rejected ideologically validated political models and condemned the predominant power relations that flowed from them.

The foregoing analysis points to a few broader implications of the evidence discussed so far concerning the study of the Enlightenment in the Balkans. Before turning to them, however, a concluding word is in order about the utility of this study's biographical approach as a method of intellectual history. The in-depth exploration and assessment of biographical information in the case of Moisiodax and the pursuit of the several hints contained in his life-story concerning the social preconditions of his intellectual and political choices make plain, I think, the practical effectiveness of biography for a social history of ideas. Considered on their own, as purely textual evidence, Moisiodax's ideas could tell us much about his intentions and projects, but not quite enough for a full interpretation. Moreover, to the extent that his ideas and forms of expression did carry on earlier traditions of discourse, they could also occasionally mislead us as to his purposes. This is illustrated adequately, I believe, by the interpretation of his political thought up to now as simply an argument for enlightened despotism. Biographical details made it possible to place the textual testimony in context and locate it within relevant evidence about the social and cultural environment and its symbolic nuances, thus making possible that fuller understanding—occasionally surprising in new discoveries—sought by interpretation. Biography has supplied the empirical method for context building and thus linked the textual issues with the multiple social and historical variables that ultimately shape them. In the present study, biography brought into focus the geographical and ethnological aspects of cultural life and cultural change in the eighteenth-century Balkans that have hitherto eluded a conventional historiography of ideas concentrating on philosophical or literary issues.[12] In this sense the assessment of the evidence about Moisio-

---

[12] On this aspect of the subject cf. as well P. M. Kitromilides, "Cultural Change and Social Criticism: The Case of Iosipos Moisiodax," *History of European Ideas* 10 (1989): 667–676.

dax's life has turned "ethnobiography" to the service of intellectual history. Finally, in connection with social and ideological conflicts that form the stuff of a social history of ideas, biography provided the prism that revealed their import in the microcosm of personal experience that ultimately shapes intellectual options and orientations and determines their limits. In Moisiodax's case we were able to trace these limits—first with his outspoken social criticism, then with his transient flirtation with republicanism, and finally with his capitulation and domestication at the courts of the princes. By extension, in dealing with other "limiting case studies" the biographical approach could well be a productive way of making conspicuous issues of gender or race that seriously challenge an ever-evolving history of ideas.[13]

Substantively the evidence of Moisiodax's intellectual biography points to at least two aspects of the phenomenon of the Enlightenment in the Balkans that need, I believe, to be seriously reconsidered. One of these aspects involves the whole question of the "national identity" of the Enlightenment in Southeastern Europe. The historiographical association of the period of the Enlightenment with "national revivals" in the Balkans has nurtured the convention always to locate the Enlightenment "in national context"; thus, scholars talk of the Modern Greek Enlightenment, the Romanian Enlightenment, and the Serbian Enlightenment, on the model, presumably, of the French, the German, the Scottish, or the American Enlightenment. The foremost argument for this approach is based on the language used for expressing Enlightenment ideas in particular cultural contexts. This is certainly a powerful and empirically compelling argument. Yet the evidence of biography, which among other things led us to the self-definitions of the exponents of the movements of intellectual change themselves, might suggest a modification of the whole idea of national Enlightenments. The evidence about Moisiodax provides a case in point. He wrote in Greek, and on that count he belongs to the Greek Enlightenment. Living primarily in what is today Romania, he had as well a considerable impact on local intellectual life. A little later the pattern was replicated by Daniel Philippidis and Dionysios Photeinos, who also wrote in Greek but lived in the Principalities and addressed local social and cultural problems in their works. Substantively, if not linguistically, all these authors belong in equal measure to the Romanian Enlightenment. Accordingly, on the ethnobiographical evidence of Moi-

[13] Cf. the discussion by Donald R. Kelley, "What is Happening to the History of Ideas?" *Journal of the History of Ideas* 51, (January 1990): 3–25. Carrying the arguments of this particular article one step further, I might add that biography could provide the key to deciphering the language of the evidence in the various "disciplinary" histories within the wide field of the history of ideas: this suggests how close the fit is between biography as a method and the history of ideas as a broad field of inquiry.

siodax's life-story, a claim might be made for considering the Enlightenment as a broader Southeastern European intellectual phenomenon; this frees it from the rather anachronistic projection of nineteenth-century political frontiers backward into the cultural life of the eighteenth century. Such a view might allow a better appreciation of the ways in which persons from diverse ethnic backgrounds were integrated into a common intellectual movement and of the role of the Greek language and education as a factor of cultural unity as well as a channel of ideological change.

Nevertheless, in the context of the mutability of collective identities, Iosipos, through his socialization into Greek culture, would come to adopt that lively sense of belonging that he expressed in his passionate pleas for the improvement of Hellas. His biography to a considerable degree studies identity formation through crossing linguistic and cultural boundaries. Thus language, the foremost and almost foreordained criterion of nationality according to the nationalist historiography of Eastern Europe, appears to have been a component of collective identity no less fluid and voluntary than any other "subjective" factor.

The understanding of the Enlightenment as a non-nationalist intellectual phenomenon might lead to a fuller, rather surprising appreciation of the extent to which it built on foundations and profited from practices established much earlier by the Orthodox Church. Indeed, if both the categories of nationalist historical thought and the old Voltairean antireligious premises of writing about the Enlightenment are set aside for a moment, we might consider the fact that for a transient historical moment in Southeastern Europe the Enlightenment, as an alternative cultural configuration, appeared destined to carry on the role of Orthodox Christianity as the shared intellectual patrimony of the region. This, essentially, had been Moisiodax's hope, but of course it was preempted by the inexorable dynamism of the rise of nationalism, which in the nineteenth century destroyed both the universalist humanism of the Enlightenment and the ecumenicity of the shared Orthodox spiritual tradition of Southeastern Europe.[14] Nevertheless, it might be interesting as well as revealing in understanding the dynamics of local politics to attempt to rethink the intellectual and political history of the Balkans along the lines of these alternative approaches.

The discussion of Moisiodax's case touches upon a second substantive issue in connection with the character of the Enlightenment in the Balkans: the originality of intellectual phenomena such as those discussed in this study. I am not concerned here to suggest that the Enlightenment

---

[14] Cf. P. M. Kitromilides, "Imagined Communities and the Origins of the National Question in the Balkans," *European History Quarterly* 19, no. 2 (April 1989): 149–192.

as articulated in Balkan culture possessed any kind of theoretical originality. On the contrary, it consisted mainly in the eclectic absorption of influences emanating from a multiplicity of sources. In its arguments it either repeated or modified the basic *topoi* of contemporary European philosophy and science. Moisiodax's texts supply ample evidence to illustrate this point. What is significant, however, is not tracing influences and discovering the occasionally all too obvious *topoi* but rather appreciating the uses to which the exponents of the Balkan Enlightenment put their sources and the arguments they gleaned from them. It is pointless to trace influences in order to conclude that a thinker is unoriginal and therefore of little interest. True, the philosophical and scientific ideas of the major authors of the Greek Enlightenment—including the most important, such as Evgenios Voulgaris, Iosipos Moisiodax, and Veniamin Lesvios—are all derivative. This conclusion is not particularly interesting; nevertheless, some important and even original ideas emerged: not only did they exemplify occasionally surprising range and versatility in borrowing and translating the new philosophical vocabulary, but they also found complex uses for it in initiating a novel understanding of intellectual life in their particular context. The originality ultimately lay in the possibility of criticism that the new philosophical ideas could sustain. Precisely *the questioning of conventions* could be seen as the major premise that held together the diverse strands of criticism—cultural, educational, social, and political—upon which Moisiodax and other representatives of the Enlightenment embarked, turning them into a coherent vision of a new morality in a new society. The Enlightenment in Southeastern Europe should be interpreted and appraised in such a manner. Its inception, its aspirations, and the extent of its eventual successes and failures should be measured against the project of criticism in both a theoretical and a practical sense—and it is with a final word about Moisiodax as a critic that this study should conclude.

Moisiodax's criticism, readily explicable in sociological terms, found its outlet in a personal psychology so intense that it would certainly be an oversimplification to end our interpretation with the account of the complex social phenomena of which his experience was the product. Over and above the socially determined attitudes and behavior stands the conscious human personality, *striving for self-definition in relation to the social environment*. Moisiodax's experience is a classic example of the formation of personal identity through reflection and observation; the individual judges himself by evaluating the judgments of others.[15] An essential element in this process is the search for the "ego-ideal," which forms the focal point for constructing the personality and defining indi-

---

[15] Cf. Eric H. Erikson, *Identity, Youth and Crisis* (New York, 1968), p. 22.

vidual identity.¹⁶ Iosipos is the first thinker in modern Greek literature for whom we have so much evidence for a psychological approach to his biography, precisely because his entire work is dominated by his attempts at self-definition. Essentially he is the first conscious individual in the history of Balkan thought to skirmish with the superego of tradition in search of his identity.

From the vantage of intellectual history, this public self-disclosure may be understood in connection with the emergence of the romantic strain in modern Greek literature. It is notable that this romantic vein first appears in the work of a true believer in the spirit of the Enlightenment. With respect to the emergence of the romantic sensibility, as in many other points, a parallel may be drawn between the case of Moisiodax and that of Jean Jacques Rousseau. As with the author of the *Confessions*, self-discovery and self-disclosure reveal the individual striving to build his personality through intense conflict with all the factors—social, ideological, political—that diminish and confine his individuality.¹⁷ This feature, the basis of Moisiodax's uniqueness in Greek letters, explains the undoubted capacity of his emotionally loaded discourse to captivate the reader of any period. There is therefore no better way to become acquainted with him than through the texts themselves. To disclose his identity and reveal various aspects of his adventure in self-discovery, no other Modern Greek writer has striven to establish the sort of personal literary genre that Iosipos did when he composed the *Apology* and thereby produced the first Modern Greek essay. Does not testimony of this nature to some extent confound the work of the cruel fate that eradicated the external traces of his presence? And given possession of such testimony, can we still look upon Iosipos Moisiodax as the great enigma he at first seems to be?

¹⁶ Ibid., pp. 210–211.
¹⁷ Cf. Jean Starobinski, *Jean Jacques Rousseau. La transparence et l'obstacle* (Paris, 1971), pp. 216–239.

BIBLIOGRAPHY

PRIMARY SOURCES

Archival and Manuscript Sources

Istituto Ellenico di Studi Bizantini e Postbizantini di Venezia
  Old Archive, Busta 34 (1759–1760).
  Old Archive, Registro 26: *Giornale della Chiesa e Scola, 1752–1773.*
  Old Archive, Registro 209: *Libro Casse de'Guardiani, 1755–1763.*
Mount Athos
  St. Panteleimon Monastery, *Codex 6256 (Old No. 749): Theoria tis geographias suggrapheisa par' Iosipou tou Moisiodakos en etei 1767 Septemvriou 15 en to Voukourestio tis Ouggrovlachias.*
  Vatopedi Monastery, Old Correspondence Archive, *Codex A' (1645–1799).*

Published Works by Iosipos Moisiodax (Chronological)

Ithiki Philosophia metaphrastheisa ek tou italikou idiomatos, Vol. 1. Venice, 1761; Vol. 2. Venice, 1762. Proemium reprinted in P. M. Kitromilides, *Iosipos Moisiodax,* Athens, 1985. 323–344.
Parallagi tou pros Nicoclea logou peri Vasileias tou Isokratous i Kephalaia Politika (Transformation de l'oraison d'Isocrate sur l'art de régner pour Nicoclès faite par Joseph Myssiodax, ou chapitres politiques). Venice, 1779. Greek text reprinted in P. M. Kitromilides, *Iosipos Moisiodax,* 345–355.
Pragmateia peri paidon agogis i Paidagogia. Venice, 1779. Romanian edition: *Tratat despre educatia capiilor sau pedagogia.* Translated by Alexe Horhoianu. Introduction by Joan N. Vlad. Bucharest, 1974.
Apologia. Meros Proton. Vienna: Johann Thomas Trattner, 1780; 2d ed., introduction by A. Aggelou. Athens, 1976.
Theoria tis Geographias. Vienna, 1781. Proemium reprinted in P. M. Kitromilides, *Iosipos Moisiodax,* 357–368.
Simeioseis Physiologikai, logo aplos dokimion. Bucharest, 1784. Reprinted in P. M. Kitromilides, *Iosipos Moisiodax,* 281–321.

Other Published Primary Sources

Alter, Franz Karl. *Philosophisch-Kritische Miscellaneen.* Vienna, 1799.
Asanis, Spyridon. *Ton konikon tomon analytiki pragmateia syggrapheisa men gallisti para tou avva Caille, ek de tis gallikis eis tin ton Latinon phonin proteron metenechtheisa, methirminefthi idi para tou iatrophilosophou Spyridonos Asanous Kephalinos eis tin aploellinikin.* Vienna, 1803.
Carra, Jean Louis. *Histoire de la Moldavie et de la Valachie.* New ed. Neuchâtel, 1781.
Dapontes, Caisarios, *Epistolai dia stichon aplon kata tis yperiphaneias kai peri tis mataiotitos kosmou,* Venice, 1776.

Encyclopédie ou Dictionnaire raisonné des sciences, des arts et des métiers. Vol. 5, Paris, 1755.

Ermis o Logios. Vols. 1–11. Vienna, 1811–1821.

Hauterive, Alexandre-Maurice Blanc de Lanautte, Comte d'. *Mémoire sur l'état ancien et actuel de la Moldavie, présenté à S.A.S. Prince Alexandre Ypsilandy, Hospodar Régnant 1787.* Bucharest, 1902.

Hurmuzaki, Eudoxiu de. *Documente privitoare la Istoria Românilor.* Vol. 13, *Texte Grecești.* Edited by A. Papadopoulos-Kerameus. Bucharest, 1909.

———. *Documente privitoare la Istoria Românilor.* Vol. 14, Part 2: *Documente Grecești (1716–1777).* Edited by N. Iorga, Bucharest, 1917.

Kallonas, Gabriel. *Paidagogia periechousa pany ophelimous nouthesias te kai oion di kanonas peri tou pos dei anatrephesthai ta paidia.* Vienna, 1800.

Katartzis, Dimitrios. *Ta Evriskomena.* Edited by C. Th. Dimaras, Athens, 1970.

Kodrikas, Panayiotis. *Omiliai peri plithyos kosmon tou kyriou Fontenelle.* Vienna, 1794.

———. *Meleti tis koinis ellinikis dialektou.* Paris, 1818.

———. *Ephimerides.* Edited by A. Aggelou. Athens, 1963.

Komninos-Ypsilandis, Athanasios. *Ta meta tin Alosin (1453–1787).* Constantinople, 1870.

Komninos, Ioannis. *Proskynitarion tou Agiou Orous tou Athonos.* Edited by Hieromonk Ioustinos Simonopetritis. Karyes, 1984.

Korais, Adamantios. *Mémoire sur l'état actuel de la civilisation dans la Grèce.* Paris, 1803.

———. *Lykourgou Logos kata Leokratous.* Paris, 1826.

———. *Allilographia.* Vol. 2, *1799–1809.* Edited by C. Th. Dimaras et al. Athens, 1966.

———. *Allilographia.* Vol. 3, *1810–1816.* Edited by C. Th. Dimaras et al. Athens, 1979.

Koumas, Constantinos. *Istoriai ton anthropinon praxeon.* Vol. 12. Vienna, 1832.

Leake, William Martin. *Researches in Greece.* London, 1814.

Logadis, Nikolaos. *Parallilon Philosophias kai Christianismou.* Constantinople, 1830.

Mavrokordatos, Nikolaos. *Philotheou Parerga.* Edited by G. Constantas. Vienna, 1800.

Moschopolitis, Daniel. *Eisagogiki Didaskalia.* Constantinople, 1802.

Notaras, Dositheos. "Istoria peri tis episkopis tou orous Sina," *Symvolai eis tin istorian tis archiepiskopis tou orous Sina.* Edited by A. Papadopoulos-Kerameus. Petrograd, 1908.

Obradović, Dositej. *The Life and Adventures of Dimitrije Obradović.* Translated by George Rappall Noyes. Berkeley, 1953.

Pamblekis, Christodoulos, trans. *I Alithis Politiki.* Venice, 1781.

———. *Peri Philosophou, Philosophias, Physikon, Metaphysikon, Pnevmatikon kai Theion Archon.* Vienna, 1786.

———. *Apandisis Anonymou pros tous aftou aphronas katigorous, eponomastheisa peri theokratias.* Leipzig, 1793.

Papadopoulos, Spyridon. *Istoria tou parondos polemou anametaxy tis Rousias kai tis Othomanikis Portas.* Vols. 1–6. Venice, 1770–1774.
Perdikaris, Michael. *Ermilos.* Vienna, 1817.
Philippidis, Daniel. *Epitomi Astronomias syggrapheisa ypo Ieronymou Lalande [. . .] metaphrastheisa eis tin kathomiloumenin ypo D. D. tou Philippidou.* Vols. 1–2. Vienna, 1803.
———. *Istoria tis Roumounias.* Leipzig, 1816.
———. *Geographikon tis Roumounias.* Leipzig, 1816.
Philippidis, Daniel, and Grigorios Constantas. *Geographia Neoteriki.* Vienna, 1791.
Philippidis, Daniel, Barbié du Bocage, and Anthimos Gazis. *Allilographia (1794–1819).* Edited by Aik. Coumarianou. Athens, 1966.
Photeinos, Dionysios. *Istoria tis palai Dakias, ta nyn Transilvanias, Vlachias kai Moldavias.* Vols. 1–3. Vienna, 1818–1819.
Prokopiou, Dimitrios. "Epitetmimeni eparithmisis ton kata ton parelthonta aiona logion Graikon kai peri tinon en to nyn aioni anthounton," in *Bibliotheca Graeca.* ed. Johannes Fabricius, Vol. 11, 769–808. Hamburg, 1722.
Psalidas, Athanasios. *Alithis evdaimonia iti vasis pasis thriskeias.* Vienna, 1791.
———. *Kalokinimata.* Vienna, 1795.
Réal de Curban, Gaspard de. *La science du gouvernement. Vol. 2, Contenant le gouvernement de France, la Constitution relativement aux Traités jusqu'au dernier d'Aix-la-Chapelle inclusivement, l'Entendue, les Moeurs, les Forces, le Nombre des Habitants, les Revenues, les Loix de chaque Etat de l'Europe, consideré en particulier.* Aix-la-Chapelle, 1761.
Siatisteus, Michael Georgiou. *Alphavitarion Germanikon.* Vienna, 1768.
Skalioras, Ignatios. *Epistoli tis neas philosophias stiliteftiki.* Leipzig, 1817.
Sulzer, Franz Josef. *Geschichte des transalpinischen Daciens.* Vols. 1–3. Vienna, 1782.
Theotokis, Nikiphoros. *Stoicheia Physikis.* Vols. 1–2. Leipzig, 1766.
Velestinlis, Rhigas. *Physikis apanthisma dia tous agchinous kai philomatheis Ellinas.* Vienna, 1790.
Villoison, Jean Baptiste d'Ansse de, ed. *Homeri Ilias ad veteris codicis Veneti fidem recensita.* Venice, 1788.
Voulgaris, Evgenios. *I Logiki ek palaion te kai neoteron syneranistheisa.* Leipzig, 1766.
———. *Epistoli tou sophotatou kyriou Evgeniou archiepiskopou proin Slaviniou kai Chersonos.* Trieste, 1797.
———. *Peri systimatos tou Pantos epitomos ekthesis.* Vienna, 1805.
———. *A. Takouetiou, Stoicheia Geometrias meta simeioseon tou Ouistonos exellinisthenta ek tis latinidos phonis ypo tou Panierotatou Archiepiskopou kyriou Evgeniou tou Voulgareos.* Vienna, 1805.
———. trans. *Genouisiou Stoicheia tis Metaphysikis.* Vienna, 1806.
———. *Syllogi anekdoton syggramaton.* Edited by A. Ainian. Vol. 1. Athens, 1838.
Zaviras, Georgios. *Nea Ellas i ellinikon theatron.* Edited by G. P. Kremos. Athens, 1872. Reprinted with introduction by T. A. Gritsopoulos. Athens 1972.

Select Secondary Sources

This short list includes only works that make an essential contribution to the study of Moisiodax's life and thought and a few items of special importance to the overall argument of the book.

Benakis, Linos G. "Apo tin istoria tou metavyzantinou aristotelismou ston ellinko choro. Amphisvitisi kai yperaspisi tou philosophou ston 18o aiona, Nikolaos Zerzoulis-Dorotheos Lesvios." *Philosophia* 7 (1977): 416–451.

Camariano, Nestor. "L'organisation et l'activité culturelle de la compagnie des marchands grecs de Sibiu." *Balcania* 6 (1943): 201–241.

Camariano-Cioran, Ariadna. "Un directeur eclairé à l'Académie de Jassy il y a deux siècles: Josip Moisiodax." *Balkan Studies* 7 (1966): 297–332.

———. *Les académies princières de Bucarest et de Jassy et leurs professeurs.* Thessaloniki, 1974.

Cicanci, Olga. *Companile grecești din Transilvania și comertul european în anii 1636–1746.* Bucharest, 1981.

———. "Une lettre inédite de Joseph Moisiodax." *Revue des études Sud-Est européennes* 27 (1989): 65–71.

Demos, Raphael. "The Neohellenic Enlightenment (1750–1821)." *Journal of the History of Ideas* 19 (1958): 523–541.

Dimaras, C. Th. *Istoria tis neoellinikis logotechnias.* Athens, 1948; 8th ed. 1987.

———. *Neoellinikos Diaphotismos.* Athens, 1977.

Dimitrakopoulos, Andronikos. *Prosthikai kai diorthoseis eis tin Neoellinikin Philologian Constantinou Satha.* Leipzig, 1871.

Duțu, Alexandru. "Le miroir des princes dans la culture roumaine." *Revue des études Sud-Est européennes* 6 (1968): 439–479.

———. *Les livres de sagesse dans la culture roumaine. Introduction à l'histoire des mentalités Sud-Est européennes.* Bucharest, 1971.

———. *Romanian Humanists and European Culture.* Bucharest, 1977.

———. "La Roumanie." In *L'absolutisme éclairé,* edited by B. Kopeczi, A. Soboul et al., 331–337. Paris-Budapest, 1985.

Florescu, Radu. "The Fanariot Regime in the Danubian Principalities." *Balkan Studies* 9 (1968): 301–318.

Gedeon, Manouel. *I pnevmatiki kinisis tou Genous kata ton XVIII kai XIX aiona,* edited by A. Aggelou-Ph. Iliou. Athens, 1976.

Henderson, G. P. *The Revival of Greek Thought, 1620–1830.* Albany, N.Y., 1970.

Iorga, N. *Byzance après Byzance.* Bucharest, 1935.

Kinini, Katerina. "Le discours à Nicoclès par Misiodax." *Ellinika* 29 (1976): 61–115.

Kitromilides, Paschalis M. *Tradition, Enlightenment, and Revolution: Ideological Change in Eighteenth and Nineteenth Century Greece.* Ph.D. diss., Harvard University, Cambridge, Mass., 1978.

———. *Iosipos Moisiodax. Oi syndetagmenes tis valkanikis skepsis ton 18o aiona.* Athens, 1985.

———. "The Last Battle of Ancients and Moderns. Ancient Greece and Modern Europe in the Neohellenic Revival." *Modern Greek Studies Yearbook* 1 (1985): 79–91.

———. "Cultural Change and Social Criticism: The Case of Iosipos Moisiodax." *History of European Ideas* 10 (1989): 667–676.

———. "The Idea of Science in the Modern Greek Enlightenment." In *Greek Studies in the Philosophy and History of Science*, edited by P. Nicolacopoulos, 187–200. Dordrecht, 1990.

Kondylis, Panayiotis. *O Neoellinikos Diaphotismos. Oi philosophikes idees.* Athens, 1988.

Kordatos, Yiannis. *Dimotikismos kai logiotatismos.* Athens, 1927.

Koumanoudis, Stephanos. *Synagogi neon lexeon.* 1900. Reprint: Athens, 1980.

Kriaras, Emmanuel. "I Paidagogia tou Moisiodakos kai i schesi tis me to paidagogiko syggramma tou Locke." *Byzantinisch-Neugrichische Jahrbücher* 17 (1943): 135–153.

———. "Gavriil Kallonas, metaphrastis ergon tou Locke kai tou Graciàn." *Ellinika* 13 (1954): 294–314.

Mackridge, Peter. "The Greek Intelligentsia 1780–1830. A Balkan Perspective." In *Balkan Society in the Age of Greek Independence*, edited by Richard Clogg, 63–84. London, 1981.

Mourouti-Genakou, Zoi. *O Nikiphoros Theotokis (1731–1800) kai i symboli aftou eis tin paideian tou genous.* Athens, 1979.

Noutsos, P. Chr. "Iosipos Moisiodax: Orismos kai diairesi tis metaphysikis." *Dodoni* 11 (1982): 185–192.

Papacostea-Danielopolu, Cornelia. *Literatura în limba greacă din principatele române (1774–1830).* Bucharest, 1982.

———. "L'organisation de la compagnie grecque de Braşov (1777–1850)." *Balkan Studies* 14 (1973): 313–323.

Papanoutsos, E. P. *Neoelliniki Philosophia.* Vol. 1. Athens, 1953.

Psimmenos, Nikos, ed. *I elliniki philosophia apo to 1453 os to 1821.* Vols. 1–2. Athens, 1989.

Rogel, Carol. "The Wandering Monk and the Balkan National Awakening." *Etudes Balkaniques* (1976) 1: 114–127.

Sathas, Constantinos. *Neoelliniki Philologia.* Athens, 1868.

Stoianovich, Traian. "The Conquering Balkan Orthodox Merchant." *The Journal of Economic History* 20 (June 1960): 234–313.

———. *A Study in Balkan Civilization.* New York, 1967.

Svoronos, Nicos G. "O Dionysios Photeinos kai to istorikon ergon aftou." *Ellinika* 10 (1937–1938): 133–178.

Symposium: L'époque phanariote. Thessaloniki, 1974.

Tsourkas, Cléobule. *Les débuts de l'enseignment philosophique et de la libre pensée dans les Balkans. La vie et l'oeuvre de Theophile Corydalée (1570–1646).* Thessaloniki, 1967.

Tzogas, Charilaos. "O ierodiakonos Iosipos Moisiodax." *Epistimoniki Epetiris Theologikis Scholis*, Vol. 19, 253–281. Thessaloniki, 1974.

Vranousis, Leandros. *Rhigas*, Athens, 1953.

INDEX

Abdulhamit I, Sultan, 173n.15
Aesop, 161
Agapetus Diaconus, 170
Alter, Franz Karl, 100, 123
Althusser, Louis, 8
Ancients and Moderns, 12, 43, 64–65, 118, 133–142, 147–148, 164, 167, 181, 185
Anthimos Iviritis, metropolitan of Hungary-Wallachia, 170
Anthrakitis, Methodios, 21, 49n.56, 55, 72, 107, 139
Apostolos, teacher at Siphnos, 35
Aristotle, Aristotelianism, 21, 29, 30–32, 41–42, 55, 59, 63–65, 72, 137–138, 139, 149, 155, 157
Aron, Raymond, 3
Arrian, 161
Asanis, Spyridon, 116
Astruc, Jean, 79–80
Athens, 36–37
Athonite Academy, 29–35, 55, 61, 100, 122, 153n.1
Aufklärung, 99
Austria, 102, 176
Ayiotaphitis, Agapios, 29

Balanos, Kosmas, 145
Balkans, Balkan society, 10, 12–13, 18, 20, 24, 37–39, 43, 49, 96, 168, 183–185, 187–189
Barbié du Bocage, 116
Baumeister, Christian Friedrich, 138
Baumeister press, 100
Bayle, Pierre, 119
Beccaria, Cesare, 45
Bessarion (Roufos), teacher at Athens, 36
biography, 3–13; as an art, 4–5; as method of historical analysis, 11–12; as method of intellectual history, 187–188; "scientific," 9–10
Blondel, François, 105
Boerhaave, Hermann, 79–80
Bortoli, Antonio, press, 46
Brahe, Tycho, 147, 168–169; Tychonic system, 145

Brancoveanu, Constantine, prince of Wallachia, 83, 85, 170
Braşov, 19, 76–77, 79, 86, 95
Braudel, Fernand, 184
Bucharest, 52, 66, 67, 69, 71, 79, 83, 85, 86, 111–114, 117, 118, 121, 177; Academy of, 126, 170
Budapest, 48, 96, 153n.1

calendar, 104–105, 107–108
Camariano Cioran, Ariadna, 35
Cantacuzeno, Şerban, prince of Wallachia, 169
Cantemir, D., prince of Moldavia, 85
Carlyle, Thomas, 3
Carra, Jean Louis, 76, 79–80, 92
Catherine II, empress of Russia, 53, 107n.39
Central Europe, 12, 19, 49, 51, 77n.21, 95, 99, 120, 138
Cernavoda, 17–19, 51, 77, 127
Charles le Téméraire, duke of Burgundy, 176
Chicago School, 7
Chilandar, monastery at, 23
Christodoulos of Kastoria, 70
Christopoulos, Athanasios, 182n.40
Chrysoloras, Manuel, 161
civic humanism, 173, 177, 179–180
Collingwood, R. G., 5
Colombo, Giovanni Alberto, 42
Comenius (Komensky, J. Amos), 154
Constantas, Grigorios, 39, 116, 182n.40
Constantinople, 22, 48, 53, 83, 93–94, 175; Patriarchate of, 21, 83
Contarini, A., 41
Cook, Captain James, 104, 149–150
Copernicus, Copernicans, 140, 145n.10
Corydaleus, Theophilos, 21, 30, 41, 72, 172
Coste, Pierre, 31, 154
Counter Enlightenment, 81
Crouçaz, Jean Pierre de, 154
Cyprus, 38, 171
Cyril (Kyrillos) V, patriarch of Constantinople, 29, 35n.14

INDEX

Dadanis, Naum, 110
D'Alembert, J., 100, 137
Daniel of Moschopolis, 26–27, 49, 183
Danube, 17–18
Danubian principalities (Wallachia and Moldavia), 18, 51, 58, 62, 75, 79, 82–88, 91, 93–94, 96, 98, 109, 111–112, 120, 138, 149, 157, 163–164, 168–170, 173, 174, 179, 184–186, 188; occupied by Russia, 65, 86
Dapontes, Caisarios, 88n.51, 124n.46
Darvaris, Dimitrios, 20
Dekas, Ioannis (school of), 36–37
Dendrinos, Ierotheos, 22–25, 29, 46, 54
Descartes, Cartesian philosophy, 21, 43, 137–138, 143, 144, 145, 147, 154
Diderot, 53, 151, 155, 163, 167
Dimaras, C. Th., 121–123
Duhamel, Jean Baptiste, 30–31
Durkheim, Emile, 3

Earth, movement of, 105, 118–119, 140, 146–148
Eastern Europe, 84, 185–186
Encyclopédie, 100–101, 137, 155, 163
encyclopedism, 43, 138, 167
English political system, 174–175
enlightened absolutism, 52, 91–92, 167–174, 177, 187
enlightened Catholicism, 31, 44
Enlightenment, 3, 12–13, 17, 20, 30–32, 39, 43, 45, 52, 57, 58–59, 64–65, 71, 97, 102, 103, 104, 108–110, 111, 118–119, 120, 133–134, 136–137, 143, 148, 151–152, 154–155, 158–159, 161, 164, 167, 171, 173, 175, 183, 184, 185, 186, 188–189, 191; American, 188; Balkan, 12–13, 39, 81, 85, 110, 181, 188–190; French, 188; German, 137, 188; Greek, 39, 50, 53, 54, 74, 101, 104, 112, 114, 127, 141–142, 151, 153n.1, 180, 181–182, 186, 188, 190; political thought, 174; Romanian, 186, 188; Scottish, 188; Serbian, 25, 49, 188
Ephraim II, patriarch of Jerusalem, 66–67, 147
Epidauros, 122–123
Ermis o Logios, 113n.10, 127, 182n.40
ethnobiography, 7, 10, 12, 188
Euclid, 33, 56
Europe, 39–40, 65, 70, 78, 89–90, 134–136, 152, 176
Evangelical School (Smyrna), 22

Fénélon, 134
feudalism, 84, 88, 90, 164, 180, 186
Fontenelle, Bernard, 145, 147
Frederick the Great, 91
freedom, 164, 174, 175–178, 180
French Revolution, 67, 81, 127, 175n.19, 177, 181
Freud, Sigmund, 4, 10

Gabriel Kallimachis, metropolitan of Moldavia, 70, 92
Galileo, G., 118, 137, 144
Gazis, Theodoros, 161
Gemistos-Pletho, G., 169
Genovesi, Antonio, 30–31, 61
Germanos, prior of Vatopedi, 124
Ghikas, Grigorios Alexandros III, prince of Moldavia, 52–53, 55–56, 69, 76, 77, 85–86, 91–92, 168–169
Ghikas, Theodoros, 96
Glizounis, 73
Glykys, Nikolaos, press, 98, 101
Golia, monastery at, 123–125
Gouldner, Alvin, 6
Graavesand, G. I., 30
Gracián, Balthazar, 153n.1
Greek East, 13, 19, 32, 37, 38–39, 41, 56, 121, 125, 141
Gregory XIII, pope, 105
Grigorios, teacher at Mykonos, 35

Hadji Michalis, Pavlos, 102
Halley's comet, 118
Hapsburg Empire, 47, 95–96, 101, 168
Hatziathanasiou, Georgios, 109
Hellenic Nomarchy, 181
Herder, J. G., 185–186
Herodian, 161
historiography, 3–6, 8, 10; Italian, 44
Holland, 176, 180n.34. *See also* Netherlands; United Provinces
Holy Sepulchre, 35, 48
Hopovo, monastery at, 23
Hume, David, 3
Hungary, Greek Orthodox merchants in, 47–48, 49, 51, 95–96, 109–110, 117
Huygens, Christian, 149

Iannakos (Ioannis Ioannou), teacher at Thessaloniki, 21–22, 29, 54
Iliadis, Manasis, 139
International Encyclopedia of the Social Sciences, 8–9
Ioannina, 29–30, 61
Iorga, Nicolae, 83
Isocrates, 97–98, 169–171
Italy, 12, 44–45, 53

Jassy, 52, 65, 66, 67, 76, 77, 79, 85, 86, 121, 123; Academy of, 53, 55–63, 69–76, 80, 85, 86, 144, 168
Joseph II, emperor of Austria, 99, 112; Josephinism, 99–100, 101, 177
Joseph the Peloponnesian, monk and teacher of Vatopedi, 121–126
Josephus, 38

Kafsokalyvitis, Neophytos, 67, 121, 123, 125, 161, 170
Kallergis, Ephraim, 96
Kallonas, Gabriel, 88n.51, 153n.1, 154n.3
Kallousios, Ioannis, 70
Kalogeras, Makarios, 21n.17
Karaioannis, Constantinos, 53
Karatzas, Nikolaos, prince of Wallachia, 113
Karlowitz, archdiocese, 23, 47–49
Kastoria, 95
Katartzis, Dimitrios, 58, 73, 78, 112–113, 119, 151, 153, 167, 177, 178, 179, 182n.40, 186
Kepler, Johannes, 168
Kerameus, Daniel, teacher at Siphnos, 36
Kodrikas, Panayiotis, 74, 93–94, 113, 115, 117
Korais Adamantios, 22–23, 25–26, 44, 93, 98, 115–116n.17, 145n.10, 175n.19, 182
Kosmas the Aetolian, 34
Kostikas, Nikolaos, 102
Koumanoudis, Stephanos, 27
Koumas, Constantinos, 27, 154n.3
Kouskouroulis, Constantinos, 102
Koutsovlachs, 18
Kozani, 29–30, 61
Kritias, Nikolaos, 172
Kutchuk, Kainardji, treaty, 65
Kyminitis, Sevastos, 170

La Caille, Jean Andre Nicolas Louis de, 70–71
Lalande, Joseph Jerome de, 105, 116
Laskaris, Constantinos, 160, 161n.20
Lazarou, Nikolaos and Ioannis, press, 117
Leibniz, G. W., 59, 137–138
Leipzig, 100, 149
Lesvios, Veniamin, 190
Levant, 39
Leyden, University of, 40
liberalism, 90, 164, 178, 180
Locke, John, 31–32, 43, 44, 58, 99, 153–155, 158–159, 164n.30
Lucian, 161
Lupu, Dimitrios and Georgios, 124
Luther, 11n.27

Mably, G. B., Abbé de, 134, 176n.21
Machiavelli, N., 180
Makraios, Sergios, 34, 145n.10
Malebranche, N., 21
Maria Theresa, empress of Austria, 99, 168
Markidis-Pouliou brothers, 181
Marx, Marxism, 4, 8, 10
Maupertuis, Pierre-Louis Moreau de, 149–150
Mavrokordatos, Alexandros, 170
Mavrokordatos, Constantinos, prince of Wallachia and Moldavia, 85; reforms of, 91–92
Mavrokordatos, Nikolaos, prince of Moldavia and Wallachia, 85, 134, 170, 173
Mills, C. Wright, 6, 8
Moesia, 18, 118
Moesiodacians, 18–20, 26–27, 37, 47, 49, 82, 96
Moisiodax, Iosipos
biography: ethnic origins, 18–19, 54, 74–75; early education, 19–20; higher education, 21–23, 29–35; university studies, 40–43; ordination, 37–39, 125; preaches in Venice, 37, 40; teaching career, 35–37, 53–57, 62–63, 69–76, 100, 111–112, 126; travels, 21, 48–49, 76–77, 95–97, 99–100, 111, 121; as client, 85–86, 109, 111–112, 114; ideological conflicts, 63–65, 72–74, 75–76, 78–82; influence of, 114–116, 181–182, 184, 186–188; as social critic, 86–91, 139–140, 162–165, 190–191; significance of biography, 10–13, 183–188

Moisiodax, Iosipos (cont.)
  ideas: pedagogical views, 33–34, 98–99, 153–165; philosophical views, 43–44, 57–61, 136–138; political thought, 91–93, 97–98, 167–182; religious views, 100, 107–108, 123, 138, 148, 159; views on language, 73–75, 119–120, 160–163
  works: *Apology*, 17, 24–25, 36–37, 42, 51, 54, 63, 65–66, 72, 74, 76, 88–89, 92, 101–103, 105–108, 111, 115, 120, 127, 136–139, 144, 168, 176, 179; *In Nicoclem*, 97–99, 126, 162, 169–170; *Moral Philosophy*, 43, 46, 48–49, 51–53, 63, 65, 109n.43, 123, 135–137, 168, 181; *Pedagogy*, 98–99, 108, 111, 153, 160, 162; *Simeioseis Physiologikai*, 113, 117–121; *Theory of Geography*, 66–67, 70, 103–109, 111, 113, 115–120, 135, 140–141, 144, 147, 149, 151
Moldavia, 18, 38, 52–53, 56, 62, 69–70, 81, 83, 85, 93, 97, 98n.11, 108, 118, 125, 149, 157, 168
Molinos, Miguel de, 21
Montaigne, Michel de, 154
Montesquieu, 3, 44, 52, 134, 174, 179
Morosini, F., 41
Moschas, Naum, 96, 110
Moschopolis, 26, 49, 95–96, 102
Mount Athos, 23, 29, 34, 35, 38, 69; Chilandar Monastery, 23; Saint Panteleimon Monastery, 66, 145n.10; Vatopedi Monastery, 121–126
Mourouzis, Constantinos, prince of Moldavia, 108
Muratori, Ludovico Antonio, 44–47, 48, 62, 137, 181
Mustafa III, Sultan, 172, 173n.15
Mykonos, 35–36

Nani, B., 41
national identity, nationalism, 20, 25, 185, 188–189
Nenadović, Paul, archbishop of Karlowitz, 47–49
Neophytos, metropolitan of Smyrna, 22, 46–47
Netherlands, 180n.34. *See also* Holland; United Provinces
Newton, Sir Isaac, 59, 118, 137–138, 144–147, 149–150, 152
Nicocles, king of Salamis, 171
Notaras, Chrysanthos, 145, 170, 172

Obradović, Dositej, 23–26, 38, 49
Orthodox Church, 38, 48–49, 83, 107, 141, 184, 189
Orthodox monasteries, listed, 38; Kykkos, 125n.51; Soumela, 170n.9
Ottoman Empire, 38–39, 52, 79, 83, 91, 97, 171–173

Pachomios, teacher at Thessaloniki, 21–22
Padua, University of, 22, 37, 39–43, 46, 51, 151, 179, 180; Greek college at Cottunian, 40, 42; Greek college at Palaiokapa, 40
Pamblekis, Christodoulos, 34, 100–101, 146n.11
Panaretos, prior of Vatopedi, 124
Parios, Ananias, 161
Parios, Athanasios, 34
Parsons, Talcott, 8
Patmos, 21n.17, 23, 38
Peter the Great, emperor of Russia, 168
Phanariots, Phanariotism, 52, 58, 62, 67, 82–85, 86–91, 93–94, 95–96, 97, 111–112, 157, 163–164, 167, 168, 170, 173–174, 177, 178, 179
Philippidis, Daniel, 88n.51, 116, 119, 182n.40, 188
Photeinos, Dionysios, 93, 188
Photiadis, Lambros, 88n.51, 126
Piccolos, Nikolaos, 20
Pindus mountains, 18
Plato, 59; *Politicus*, 97, 169
Plutarch, 3
Poleni, Giovanni, 42, 151
Polyeidis, Theoklitos, 34
Pourchot, Edme, 30
Prokopios the Peloponnesian, 75–76
Prokopiou, Dimitrios, 134
Ptolemy, Ptolemaists, 140, 145, 147–148
Pyrrhonism, 3
Pythagoras, Pythagoreans, 105, 145n.10, 148

Quintilian, 154

Rajić, Jovan, 49
Ramniceanu, Naum, 186
Ranke, Leopold von, 3
Raynal, Abbé de, 176n.21
Réal de Curban, Gaspard de, 177–178
Renaissance, 133–134, 177, 180; Paleologan, 169
republicanism, 175–179, 180–181, 184, 188

Rhigas Velestinlis, 17–18, 20–21, 114–115, 119, 127, 173, 180–183; *Great Chart*, 17, 114, 127
Roman, diocese, 98n.11
Romanian Academy of Sciences, 56, 120n.36
romanticism, 191
Rome, 180
Rousseau, Jean-Jacques, 101, 176, 179, 181, 191
Rudolph, emperor of Austria, 168
Russia, 97, 171

Segner, 55
Selim III, Sultan, 173n.15
Serbia, 23
Siatista, 95, 102
Sibiu, 19
Siphnos, 35–36
Smyrna, 22–24, 29, 48, 50, 175
social sciences, 3–10
Southeastern Europe, 12, 25, 67, 76, 81, 85, 103, 110, 127, 138, 171, 173, 177, 183, 187–189, 190
Soutsos, Michael, prince of Wallachia, 113, 117, 178
Sparta, 180
Spinoza, B., 101
Stephanos, sacristan of Vatopedi, 123
Stephanos of Cyprus (teacher at Siphnos), 35
Stratigos, Simon, 42–43
Sublime Porte, 83, 86
Swift, Jonathan, 133
Switzerland, 175–178, 180
Synesius of Cyrene, 170

Tacquet, André, 55–56, 62, 70
Theodorakis, Doctor, 78–80, 81–82, 103
Theodosiou, Dimitrios, press, 97
Theophilos, bishop of Campania, 34, 119
Theophylact, archbishop of Bulgaria, 170
Theotokis, Nikiphoros, 54–55, 69, 71–72, 80, 81, 107, 145
Thessaloniki, 21–22, 29, 30, 50, 175
Thompson, E. P., 8
Thrace, 19
Thucydides, 161
Tirnovo, 109
Transylvania, 19, 48, 77, 112–113, 118
Transylvanian Alps, 76

Trattner, Johann von, press, 102
Triestse, 48, 96
Tsoukalas, Nikolaos, 37
Tyrnavos, 102

United Provinces, Dutch, 175, 180–181n.34
utilitarianism, 33–34, 43, 58–59, 138, 151–152, 163, 165, 167

Vamvas, Neophytos, 39
Velestino, 18
Venice, 36–37, 39, 43, 46, 48, 49, 96–97, 99, 119, 126, 149, 175–176, 179, 180; Greek Confraternity, 37; Saint George of the Greeks, 37, 40
Vienna, 48–49, 96, 99–101, 102, 111–112, 117, 121, 149, 181; Imperial Library, 101, 103, 150
Vilaras, Ioannis, 182
Villoison, Jean Baptiste Gaspar d'Ansse de, 98, 121–126, 161n.22
Vlachs, 18–19, 27
Vladimerescu, Tudor, 93
Vogoridis, Athanasios, 20
Voltaire, 53, 85, 167, 174, 189; criticized by Rhigas, 119
Voulgaris, Evgenios, 29–34, 35n.14, 39, 53, 54–55, 61, 69, 73, 81, 106–107, 119, 121, 123, 125, 127, 134, 139, 144, 145, 153n.1, 190

Wallachia, 19, 66–67, 69, 77, 81, 83, 85, 93, 97, 108, 111–112, 115, 120, 125, 127, 149, 157, 167, 170, 178
Weber, Max, 4
Wolff, Christian, 30, 137–138
Woolf, Virginia, 4–5
Wückerer, J. F., 30

Xenophon, 161

Ypsilandis, Alexandros, prince of Wallachia, 108, 111–113, 126
Ypsilandis, Constantinos and Dimitrios, 112

Zaviras, Georgios, 100, 126–127
Zerzoulis, Nikolaos, 20, 139, 146
Zographos, Apostolis, 96

GPSR Authorized Representative: Easy Access System Europe - Mustamäe tee
50, 10621 Tallinn, Estonia, gpsr.requests@easproject.com

www.ingramcontent.com/pod-product-compliance
Lightning Source LLC
Chambersburg PA
CBHW052038300426
44117CB00012B/1876